LONDON TRANSPORT RECORDS

AT THE PUBLIC RECORD OFFICE

Part One

compiled by Peter Bancroft

Published by: NEBULOUS BOOKS
Cromwell House, 11 Oliver Rise, Alton, Hampshire, GU34 2BN
Tel: 01420 89264

FROM: PRO file MT74/144.

THE TIMES 1st JANUARY 1948:

RAILWAY HISTORICAL RECORDS
TO THE EDITOR OF THE TIMES

Sir, - The letter which appears in your issue to-day over the signature of Lord Greene and other gentlemen refers to a matter which has already been the subject of much thought by the British Transport Commission. With the assistance of the boards of the four main line railway companies and of the London Passenger Transport Board, steps have already been taken to compile schedules of the documents and relics in their possession. Consideration is now being given to the form in which appropriate collections of the material which merits preservation by reason of its historical or technical interest and importance may be made in convenient centres, where it is hoped they will become available for public inspection. Similar care will be taken for the preservation of written records of permanent interest.

The commission is concerned with other forms of transport besides the railways, and action has also been taken already to ensure that documents in the possession of the canal companies, many of which go back to the eighteenth century, should not be dispersed, lost, or destroyed. The commission welcomes the wide-spread interest which has been manifested in this subject and particularly the appeal made through your columns to those outside the undertakings vested in the commission to take similar action, and will be glad at all times to consult with other bodies interested in the matter.

> Yours faithfully,
> **CYRIL HURCOMB, Chairman, British Transport Commission.**
> 55, Broadway, Westminster, S.W.1, Dec, 31.

ACKNOWLEDGEMENTS:

The publishers would like to thank the following people for their help with Part One: Paul Hadley; John McCrickard; Mr A G Newman; Dave Taylor; Paul Sturm, Nicholas Coney and Miss Beech at the Public Record Office; Derek Holder at Companies House in Cardiff; Richard Samways at the Greater London Record Office.

ISBN 0 9507416 3 9
Copyright © NEBULOUS BOOKS 1996.
Cover artwork by West Farthing Grange, London, SW10.
Typesetting/page layouts by Nebulous Books, Alton.
Printed by Multiplex Medway Limited, Walderslade.

CONTENTS

Some abbreviations used in this book (see also abbreviations used in Part A on page 8):

BRB = British Railways Board
BTC = British Transport Commission
BTHR = British Transport Historical Records
GLC = Greater London Council
GLRO = Greater London Record Office
GWR = Great Western Railway
LBSC = London Brighton & South Coast Railway Company
LCC = London County Council
LCD = London Chatham & Dover Railway Company
LETFC = London Electric Transport Finance Corporation
LMSR = London Midland & Scottish Railway
LNER = London & North Eastern Railway
LPTAT = London Passenger Transport Arbitration Tribunal
LPTB = London Passenger Transport Board
LT = London Transport
LTE = London Transport Executive
PRO = Public Record Office
RFCL = Railway Finance Corporation Limited
SER = South Eastern Railway
SR = Southern Railway
TGWU = Transport & General Workers Union

THE RECORDS OF LONDON TRANSPORT AND ITS PREDECESSORS.

Introduction.

THE BRITISH TRANSPORT COMMISSION.

The story of transport records and relics goes back a long way, but the formation of the British Transport Commission in 1948 meant that for the first time, a unified approach could be applied in the preservation and display of both relics and records. In 1951 the BTC published the report of a Committee under the Chairmanship of Mr S B Taylor, then Deputy Secretary to the BTC, which focused on steps to be taken to preserve the relics and records throughout the undertaking of the BTC.[1] Mr J H Scholes was appointed as the BTC's Curator of Historical Relics as from 2 July 1951, being based at Euston. His task was to implement the recommendations set out in the report with regard to relics.

Various temporary exhibitions were staged in the early days, in the historic Shareholders' Meeting Room at Euston Station. An exhibition there entitled 'London on Wheels' opened in 1953, and showed London travel in the nineteenth century. In November 1956 a semi-permanent exhibition was staged there, entitled 'Transport Treasures'. Its object was to show material illustrating all types of transport and every aspect of the subject. Several of the exhibitions were accompanied by short illustrated booklets, some written by well known transport authors. There was already an existing railway museum at York. Subsequently a museum for further relics was established at Clapham in a former LT bus garage. The small exhibits section was opened there on 29 March 1961. The main area at Clapham, for larger exhibits, opened in 1963. A further museum, devoted to the Great Western Railway, was opened at Swindon in 1962, although this was a joint effort by the BTC and the Borough of Swindon.

July 1951 also saw Mr L C Johnson taking up the position of Archivist, in charge of the Historical Records Office, based at 66 Porchester Road in London. This building (formerly the Great Western Railway's Stationery Store/Deeds Office) already housed the archives of the GWR. It was easier to leave these in place and add everything else to this collection. Muniments rooms were eventually opened in Edinburgh (for Scottish records) and York (for LNER records) in 1955. The muniments rooms at York and Edinburgh also acquired library material, and were eventually provided with reading rooms which had late evening and Saturday morning opening hours. The same enlightened provision was made at Porchester Road which collection became known as the **British Transport Historical Records** collection (BTHR). This held the records of some 800 railway companies, 42 London Transport companies, 93 canal, dock and harbour companies, plus the records of the railway hotels and the Railway Clearing House. A growing collection of periodicals and library material was also included. From the start there was a clear commitment to make all the material available to research workers and students.

FROM BTHR TO PRO.

When the BTC was dissolved in 1962, the transport museum at Clapham and its contents, together with any other relics and records elsewhere, were vested in British Railways. A joint funding arrangement between the BR and LT Boards secured the future of their respective relics and records, but by the late 1960s BR no longer wished to continue to look after relics and records of any kind. Provision was therefore made in the Transport Act of 1968 (Section 144) for these to be offered without charge to the Secretary of State for Education and Science. Any relics and records not claimed by him within six months, could be disposed of in any way BR saw fit. However, before disposing of any record or relic having special associations with the undertaking of the London Transport Board, BR were to offer them to LT. All the former BR relics eventually went to the National Railway Museum at York and Clapham was closed down. BR's records might have gone to York as well, but public pressure about the inconvenience of York as a base for the records caused them to stay at Porchester Road. The entire record collection there was subsequently taken over by the Public Record Office on 1 April 1972 and was eventually transferred to the PRO's then new building at Kew during 1977. The collection was accompanied by an extensive card index, but this has not been added to since its transfer to Kew. These BR records were the subject of an Order in Council in 1984, which means that they have since

---

[1] ***The Preservation of Relics and Records, Report to the British Transport Commission***, published by the BTC in 1951, 40pp, card covers, with illustrations (PRO copy at ZLIB15/41/13).

been treated as though they were public records for the purposes of the Public Records Act 1958 (All items are open to public view, except Staff records less than 75 years old, which may be examined subject to signing an undertaking regarding the confidentiality of the information). Further material is still added to this collection from time to time by BR, *including documents which date back over many years.* Porchester Road is still BR's Records Centre, where all their records go to be appraised and sorted with some eventually going to the PRO at Kew, the National Railway Museum at York, or one of the designated County Record Offices (some also go to Collector's Corner at Euston to be sold off!).

The class lists for most of these BTHR records have been typed and conform with those for other classes of documents at the PRO. The exception is some of the MPS classes, where the old BTHR Registers must still be consulted, as there is no 'typed' class list at present. The remaining MPS classes are soon to be re-listed into the RAIL classes which were allocated to them when the BTHR Collection was first moved to Kew (RAIL1032-1037 inclusive). Typed class lists will be produced at the same time, clearly showing the old MPS references. At the time of writing, class MPS(Y), which will eventually become RAIL1037, has not yet been put on to the PRO's computer and these documents must still be requisitioned using manual tickets for the present. Again there is no 'typed' class list and the BTHR Registers must be consulted as the **only** listing for these maps!

THE GREATER LONDON RECORD OFFICE.

Soon after the passing of the 1968 Transport Act, which had included the provision for LT to reclaim its relics and records, a firm statement was made by LT to the effect that they believed that the proper place for their relics and records was in London. They therefore gave BR notice that they would reclaim their respective records and relics when the move of BR items was being made to York. An agreement had already been reached with the Greater London Council that LT's records, whilst remaining LT property, would be housed in the Middlesex section of the Council's Record Office, then at 1 Queen Anne's Gate Buildings, Dartmouth Street, London, SW1. The relics were actually reclaimed even before Clapham closed and formed the basis of the collection displayed at Syon Park, which opened on 23 May 1973. These items, mostly railway rolling stock/trams/buses moved into the new LT Museum in Covent Garden in 1981. The LT records which had been at Porchester Road were transferred to the GLC's Record Office at Dartmouth Street in November 1975. The records moved from Dartmouth Street in 1979 and that building was sold. The Middlesex and London sections of the Greater London Record Office were then combined, with a public search room at County Hall. However, the London Transport records were actually moved from Dartmouth Street to an outstore at 107 Back Church Lane, London, E1 and those records required for consultation by readers were brought over to County Hall by a van service. In 1982, the Greater London Record Office moved into its present premises at 40 Northampton Road, London, EC1. The Back Church Lane outstore was vacated and all the records held there, including the London Transport records, were moved to Northampton Road.

LT's records there are mostly catalogued under 'Accession 1297' followed by the old BTHR class letters. Some additional material was transferred from the PRO to the GLRO in 1981 (GLRO 'Accession 1687'). Further material has since been added to this collection directly from LT's headquarters at 55 Broadway (GLRO 'Accession Numbers: 1435; 2398; 2414'). There are a number of other Accessions at the GLRO which include material relevant to London Transport. Sadly a number of these have no class lists at present, although the material can be made available for inspection with sufficient notice. The GLRO have also purchased some relevant material themselves ('Accession 2324') and have accepted a donation of TOT staff magazines from elsewhere ('Accession 2575'). LT have also reclaimed at least one item (an album of photographs) from their own records at the GLRO, which has been transferred to the London Transport Museum. A few years ago, a survey showed that these London Transport records were one of the most used classes of deposited records at the GLRO. There was usually at least one person there every day using these LT records. They comprise the complete series of Metropolitan Railway General Manager's Office files, together with other statutory records including many Board Minutes plus some other miscellaneous records. In 1986, following the abolition of the GLC, responsibility for the GLRO was passed to the Corporation of London who now own and run it under the same management as the Corporation of London Record Office and the Guildhall Library.

But the exercise which was carried out when LT reclaimed its records appears to have been dealt with on a very arbitrary basis. In many cases only whole classes of documents were transferred. Single items in other classes were usually ignored and there were instances of LT material being only on some pages of guard books etc. However, it might be said that, from a professional archivist's point of view, records are classified not by subject but by origin. This would lead to some classes of documents containing material of relevance to LT,

Introduction....

being kept together. Nevertheless, as will be seen from the listing which follows, a huge quantity of LT related records remained in the BTHR collection, now at the Public Record Office at Kew.

OTHER PROBLEMS AND OTHER LOCATIONS OF RECORDS.

Further problems are of course created when such things as the recent change of ownership of the Waterloo & City line are made. The Waterloo & City line was originally under the influence of the London & South Western Railway, and was amalgamted with the LSWR from 1 January 1907. The line was absorbed into the Southern Region of British Railways upon nationalisation in 1948. Its older records are correctly with the BTHR collection at Kew (see *for example*: RAIL981/290; RAIL1057/3045; RAIL1075/214; RAIL1110/483 & 484; RAIL1134/512; RAIL1135/527). However, LT researchers may well be interested in the line's history before its transfer to LT. A visit to the PRO at Kew would be essential and justified. It would be wrong to suggest moving some specific items about the Waterloo & City line from Kew to the GLRO! There are also instances of Joint Committees involving both BR and LT predecessor companies. These Joint Committee records should remain with those of whichever Company was providing the Secretariat at any given time.

Another aspect which tends to complicate matters further is that several LT tube lines were eventually extended over the suburban lines of the main line railway companies. Once again material on the early history of these lines is with the records of BR and its predecessors at Kew. Later material would be among LT records. This also applies to the much earlier projection of Bakerloo services over London & North Western Railway tracks to Watford. Similarly, District services were run over London & South Western Railway tracks to Richmond and Wimbledon. In contrast, the Great Northern & City tube railway, which was built to main line running standards, was eventually taken over by British Railways in 1975 as part of the scheme to electrify the suburban lines of the former Great Northern Railway. This originally independent tube railway was taken over by the Metropolitan Railway in July 1913 and passed to the LPTB in July 1933.

London Transport has operated railways, tramways, trolleybuses, omnibuses and services on the River Thames, including all aspects of day to day running and maintenance. Its predecessors and their pre-1933 subsidiaries have also manufactured or modernised vehicles at some time, although the LPTB was prevented from manufacturing vehicles itself after 1933. The LPTB also acted as agents of the Home Office in constructing the eight deep level tube shelters, beneath existing tube stations, during 1940-1942. These were later used as air-raid shelters, or for storage purposes during and after the war. LT's tube stations were also given over to shelterers during the war. All these activities give rise to records in one form or another. The Public Carriage Office of the Metropolitan Police was in control of design and use of buses, through its function of certifying vehicles for licensing, until the Ministry of Transport took over these responsibilities under the 1933 Act. Once again there is much of interest about predecessors of London Transport in these Metropolitan Police records.

There are also records created by other Government Departments, which are rightly at Kew, but will contain material of interest to the London Transport researcher. The London Passenger Transport Arbitration Tribunal Proceedings (Class MT1) should also be mentioned. These remain at Kew, because the LPTAT was a Court of Common Record, with a seal and not actually an LT company. With regard to the pre-LPTB company structure, two useful genealogical tables showing the separate railway organisations merged into the LPTB in 1933, are given on pages 4 and 5 of *Improving London's Transport, a supplement to The Railway Gazette*, published in 1946.[2] Further useful details, including those of bus and tram undertakings absorbed into the LPTB, are given on pages 43-68 of *London Transport - A Record and a Survey*, by Vernon Sommerfield, published by London Transport in 1934 (a second updated edition appeared in 1935). The relevant section in both editions is entitled 'HISTORICAL AND STATISTICAL PARTICULARS of the Principal Traffic Concerns vested in the London Passenger Transport Board'. There is a genealogical table on the inside of the back cover (which is folded back on itself) for companies absorbed by the LPTB, in both the 1934 and 1935 editions.[3] The LPTB's first few annual reports and accounts also contain much information about companies taken over or absorbed in whole or in part. These sources have been used to help compile an extensive listing of Limited Companies (see BT31) absorbed in whole or in part by, or otherwise associated with the London Passenger Transport Board and its predecessors. Some other London area road transport operators have also been included in this list. This particular section is followed by details of more recent limited companies, whose registered office is still at '55 Broadway', or which were at one time wholly owned subsidiaries of LRT. Some of these companies have been privatised in recent years, and some details in this respect have been given

---

[2] There is a copy at the PRO at ZSPC11/256.
[3] There are copies of both editions at the PRO at ZLIB11/25 - 1934 edition, and ZLIB8/85 - 1935 edition.

where possible. Other aspects of LRT operations have also been recently sold or leased to outside companies. Where this includes staff and or operating assets, details have been included.

The two volume *History of London Transport* by T C Barker and Michael Robbins remains the standard published work on the whole subject of LT, although both volumes are now out of print. Volume Two - *The Twentieth Century to 1970*, contains an appendix (Appendix Three on pages 419-499) giving a listing of London Area Omnibus Proprietors from 1920-1933. This will be found useful for an understanding of which operators (including many limited companies) were absorbed by, or taken over in whole or in part by, London Transport and its predecessors.

With regard to tramways taken over by the LPTB in 1933, several of these were owned by Local Authorities. It is likely therefore, that minutes were kept regarding the operation of these tramways, and that these would be with the records of the relevant local authority. It must not be assumed therefore that all LT related records are either at the PRO or the GLRO (for example the minutes of the Erith tramways, owned and operated by Erith Urban District Council from opening until 1933, are held at the Bexley Local Studies Library, Hall Place, Bourne Road, Bexley, Kent). Also, County Record Offices in the home counties may well contain material relevant to the history of LT and its predecessors.

THE LISTS.

So, with all these complications, what is perhaps more important as a first stage, is to try and catalogue what former BTHR records relating to LT remain at the PRO at Kew, thus emphasising the quantity and importance of the material there and to make it easier to locate material on any particular subject. The second part of the listing comprises known files among the records of some Government Departments etc, which also relate to LT. In some instances there are difficulties with the class lists/documents and notes have been included to help in these areas.

The lists which follow cannot be other than a transcription of the descriptions in the existing class lists. These might contain spelling errors or date errors. Pages might be missing from the class lists. Some records in the lists are presently 'closed', but will be released in the future. Some class list pages show only that items are closed, not giving a description of them. Further records are therefore continually being released. These could of course contain material of interest to the London Transport researcher. The descriptions are only as accurate as the original compiler of the class lists made them. But the result will, it is hoped, add to existing knowledge and save considerable time for LT researchers in the future.

References to some other isolated London railway lines have also been included, such as the Post Office Underground Railway (see for example: RAIL1057/699; RAIL1124/173; OS7/13), the Waterloo and Whitehall Railway - a partly built pneumatic tube line (see for example: RAIL1075/215; RAIL1075/361; RAIL1076/1 folio 45; CRES35/4180 & 4181), the proposed Kearney Tube railway (see for example: HO205/124; MT115/93) and the Pneumatic Dispatch Company's small diameter tube railway (see for example: RAIL1007/482; RAIL1075/270). Emett's miniature railway at Battersea Park (originally part of the Festival of Britain) has also been included (see MEPO 2/8942). The Festival of Britain was a significant traffic objective and some new works were undertaken on the tramways and the tube station at Waterloo as a consequence (see WORK25). Similarly, some general London area traffic surveys have been mentioned since these might well include information of interest to the researcher of London's public transport generally. Where does one draw the line in a work of this scope?

It is hoped to publish a Part Two within a year or so, which will contain further material at the PRO, including a formative listing of information in MT29, plus details of material in AN2, and CRIM and CRES classes. If readers know of the whereabouts of any other relevant records, wherever these may be, a note sent to the publishers would be greatly appreciated and acknowledged in any future published lists.

IMPORTANT NOTE: The format of the PRO's class lists has not been followed firstly to save space, but secondly, to encourage users of this listing to always be mindful of the document class headings. In this way, it is hoped to promote the idea that there may be other material in these classes of relevance to research on particular aspects. It will also stress to PRO newcomers what is meant by a 'piece number'. A second date, or range of dates at the end of the descriptions gives the date(s) of the item or correspondence referred to. This has not been shown in a separate column in order to save space.

British Transport Historical Records:

PART A - LIST OF FORMER 'BRITISH TRANSPORT HISTORICAL RECORDS' DOCUMENT CLASSES AND DOCUMENTS RELATED TO LONDON TRANSPORT, WHICH HAVE BEEN TRANSFERRED TO THE GREATER LONDON RECORD OFFICE AND HISTORY LIBRARY, now at 40 NORTHAMPTON ROAD, LONDON, EC1R 0HB (Telephone: 0171 332 3820), catalogued under Accession 1297 except where stated:

A&B = Aylesbury & Buckingham Railway Company

BKW = Baker Street & Waterloo Railway Company

BUS = Miscellaneous 'Bus Companies merged into London General Omnibus Company and London Passenger Transport Board (73 companies)

CLR = Central London Railway Company

CSL = City & South London Railway Company (originally City of London and Southwark Subway Company)

CXEH = Charing Cross, Euston and Hampstead Railway Company

ECGL = Earls Court Grounds Limited

EH = Edgware and Hampstead Railway Company

GNCY = Great Northern and City Railway Company

GNPB = Great Northern Piccadilly and Brompton Railway Company

H&C = Hammersmith and City Railway Company

H&M = Hounslow and Metropolitan Railway Company

H&U = Harrow & Uxbridge Railway Company

HCJ = Hammersmith and City Railway Joint Committee

KL = Kingston and London Railway Joint Committee (London & South Western and District Railways)

LER = London Electric Railway Company

LGCS = London General Country Services Ltd (formerly East Surrey Traction Company Ltd)

LGOC = London General Omnibus Company Limited

LOT = Lots Road Powerhouse Joint Committee

LPT = London Passenger Transport Board

LST = London & Suburban Traction Company Limited

LTB = London Transport Board

LTE = London Transport Executive

LUT = London United Tramways Limited

M&DJ = Metropolitan & District Railways Joint Committee

MDET = Metropolitan District Electric Traction Company Limited

MDR = Metropolitan District Railway Company (Note: One piece from this class - MDR4/15 was withdrawn by LT and passed to the London Transport Museum in June 1994. This is a guard book containing a collection of photographs of MDR; GNP&BR; BS&WR; CCE&HR).

MELT = Metropolitan Electric Tramways Limited

MET = Metropolitan Railway Company

MGCJ = Metropolitan and Great Central Railways Joint Committee

MSGA = Morden Station Garage Limited

MSTJ = Metropolitan and St. Johns Wood Railway Company

MTCC = Metropolitan Tower Construction Co. Ltd (originally International Tower Construction Co. Ltd)

NMT = North Metropolitan Tramways Company

RB = Rule Books - only the following pieces were transferred *and these are catalogued under Accession 1687*:

RB1/425 = London Transport Executive - Rules for Observance by Employees (Railway) 1949.

RB3/96-104 inclusive = London Transport Executive, Working Timetable Appendices - various.

RQC = Railway Equipment & Construction Company Ltd

SMET = South Metropolitan Electric Tramways and Lighting Company Limited

TMO = Tramways (M.E.T.) Omnibus Company Ltd

UER = Underground Electric Railways Company of London Limited

UNC = Union Construction Company Limited

USL = Union Surplus Lands Company Limited

W&B = Whitechapel & Bow Railway Company & Joint Committees

WAT = Watford Joint Railway Committee (Metropolitan and London & North Eastern Railways)

WED = Watford and Edgware Railway Company

WPE = Wembley Park Estate Co. Ltd (formerly The Tower Company Ltd)

British Transport Historical Records:

PART B - LIST OF FORMER 'BRITISH TRANSPORT HISTORICAL RECORDS' DOCUMENT CLASSES AND DOCUMENTS RELATED TO LONDON TRANSPORT, WHICH HAVE BEEN TRANSFERRED TO THE NATIONAL RAILWAY MUSEUM, LEEMAN ROAD, YORK:

RAIL1057/3442 = Collection of Railway Uniform Buttons, including Great Central and Metropolitan Joint Committee (1 button).

RAIL1057/3444 = Collection of Railway Uniform Buttons, including: Underground Railways (4 buttons); Central London Railway (1 button); London Electric Railway (2 buttons); District Railway (6 buttons); City and South London Railway (2 buttons); London Passenger Transport Board (5 buttons); Metropolitan District Railway (2 buttons); East London Railway (1 button); Metropolitan and District Railways (1 button); Metropolitan and Great Western Joint (1 button); Metropolitan and Great Central Joint Railways (3 buttons); Metropolitan and London and North Eastern Joint Railways (2 buttons).

PART C - LIST OF FORMER 'BRITISH TRANSPORT HISTORICAL RECORDS' RELATED TO LONDON TRANSPORT, WHICH ARE STILL AT THE PUBLIC RECORD OFFICE (this list has been compiled simply by looking through the relevant class lists and abstracting any appropriate entries):

Note: The following class lists have been checked as at 5 January 1996:
RAIL1-1176 only.
All MPS classes (see also RAIL1029-1036).
MPS(Y) (will become RAIL1037).
ALL ZPER classes.
All ZSPC classes.

RAIL178 = East London Railway Company:
Piece number 1 = Meetings of Proprietors, with Reports and Accounts, 1865-1883.
Piece number 2 = Meetings of Proprietors, with Reports and Accounts, 1883-1913.
Piece number 3 = Meetings of Proprietors, with Reports and Accounts, 1914-1925.
Piece number 4 = Meetings of Board of Directors, with Index (This volume, numbered 5, is the earliest volume of Board Minutes received), 1883-1884.
Piece number 5 = Meetings of Board of Directors (with Index), 1884-1887.
Piece number 6 = Meetings of Board of Directors (with Index), 1887-1893.
Piece number 7 = Meetings of Board of Directors (with Index), 1893-1903.
Piece number 8 = Meetings of Board of Directors (with Index), 1904-1916.
Piece number 9 = Meetings of Board of Directors (with Index), 1916-1925.
Piece number 10 = Stockholders' address book, 1.12.1884.
Piece number 11 = Stockholders' address book, 1.12.1886.
Piece number 12 = Diagram of railway and connections, 1924.
Piece number 13 = Ledger, 1865-1925.
Piece number 14 = Journal, 1865-1905.
Piece number 15 = Journal No.2, 1906-1925.
Piece number 16 = Cash book, 1865-1872.
Piece number 17 = Cash book No.3, 1883-1915.
Piece number 18 = Cash book No. 4, 1916-1923.
Piece number 19 = Cash book (With Index), 1865-1871.
Piece number 20 = Accounts submitted for payment, 1913-1925.
Piece number 21 = Property purchased register, showing vendor, purchase price and area conveyed, (Indexed) with alphabetical abstract, 1865-1874.
Piece number 22 = Property purchased accounts register, showing property acquired in each parish, (undated).
Piece number 23 = Warning Notice detailing convictions obtained for fraudulent travelling, Nov. 1916.

RAIL179 = East London Railway Joint Committee:
Piece number 1 = Joint Committee minutes (with print of Act of 10.8.1882), 1884.
Piece number 2 = Joint Committee minutes, 1885-1886.
Piece number 3 = Joint Committee minutes (with print of Arbitration Proceedings of 1886), 1886-1888.
Piece number 4 = Joint Committee minutes, 1886-1890.
Piece number 5 = Joint Committee minutes, 1891-1899.
Piece number 6 = Joint Committee minutes (with index), 1900-1908.

RAIL179 = East London Railway Joint Committee: *continued....*

Piece number 7 = Joint Committee minutes, 1884-1885.

Piece number 8 = Joint Committee minutes, 1884-1885.

Piece number 9 = Joint Committee minutes, 1892-1897.

Piece number 10 = Joint Committee minutes, 1919-1923.

Piece number 11 = Signed, minutes Committee (with index), 1884-1886.

Piece number 12 = Signed, minutes Committee, 1887-1891.

Piece number 13 = Signed, minutes Committee, 1891-1897.

Piece number 14 = Signed, minutes Committee (with index), 1897-1903.

Piece number 15 = Signed, minutes Committee, 1903-1910.

Piece number 16 = Signed, minutes Committee, 1910-1920.

Piece number 17 = Signed, minutes Committee (with index), 1920-1927.

Piece number 18 = Signed, minutes Committee, 1928-1948.

Piece number 19 = Joint Committee copy minutes, 1884-1886.

Piece number 20 = Joint Committee copy minutes (with print of Arbitration Proceedings 1886-1889 attached relating to division of responsibility under East London Lease with Mr. Henry Oakley's Award), 1886-1891.

Piece number 21 = Joint Committee copy minutes (with print of further Arbitration proceedings 1892-1899 attached, including reference to New Cross Station), 1892-1901.

Piece number 22 = Index of Joint Committee copy minutes, 1884-1898.

Piece number 23 = Joint Committee copy minutes (with index), 1902-1925.

Piece number 24 = Joint Committee copy minutes (with index), 1885-1893.

Piece number 25 = Joint Committee copy minutes (with index), 1893-1912.

Piece number 26 = Joint Committee copy minutes (with various Arbitration Proceedings and copy of East London Railway Act, 1882), 1884-1886.

Piece number 27 = Joint Committee copy minutes, 1907-1915.

Piece number 28 = Index to above, 1907-1915.

Piece number 29 = Minutes of lessee Companies and Joint Committee (copies and prints) (Indexed), 1884-1885.

Piece number 30 = Minutes of lessee Companies and Joint Committee (copies and prints) (Indexed), 1884-1891.

Piece number 31 = Minutes of lessee Companies and Joint Committee (copies and prints) (Indexed), 1892-1901.

Piece number 32 = Minutes of lessee Companies and Joint Committee (copies and prints) (Indexed), 1902-1925.

Piece number 33 = Minutes of lessee Companies and Joint Committee (printed), 1905-1933.

Piece number 34 = Committee Reports, 1921-1932.

Piece number 35 = Minutes of Sub Committee for Finance, 1912-1918.

Piece number 36 = Arbitration, Awards, Acts and relevant papers regarding division of responsibility under leases, etc. by lessee companies, 1885-1897.

Piece number 37 = Return of Traffic Staff (Comparison with 1890), Nov. 1884.

RAIL223 = Great Central and Metropolitan Railways Joint Committee:

Piece number 1 = Great Central and Metropolitan Railways Joint Committee Minute book, 1899.

RAIL236 = Great Northern Railway Company:

Piece number 518 = King's Cross. Subway to connect with Metropolitan Railway Station, Contract, Specification etc., (with drawing), 1891.

Piece number 538 = King's Cross. Drawings showing proposed new buildings in front of station, c.1890-1905.

Piece number 1018 = Tender for electric lighting on line between Moorgate and Barnet from Railway Electrical Contractors Ltd, 1884.

RAIL250 = Great Western Railway Company, Minutes and Reports:

Piece number 731 = Minutes of Committee of West London Electrification Scheme, 1935-1946.

Piece number 732 = Minutes of Committee of West London Electrification Scheme, 1947.

Piece number 733 = Minutes of Committee of West London Electrification Scheme, 1948.

RAIL252 = Great Western Railway Company: Deeds, Agreements, Contracts, Specifications, Estimates and Plans:

Piece number 178 = Plans - North Acton to Ruislip electric lines: Denham Station; plan of proposed layout, 1937.

RAIL253 = Great Western Railway Company, Miscellaneous Books and Records:
Piece number 286 = Proposed electrification of Hammersmith & City Railway and other lines, 1903.
Piece number 815 = London Passenger Pooling Scheme, 1936.

RAIL258 = Great Western Railway Company: Secretarial Papers:
Piece number 312 = London Traffic: co-ordination London Passenger Transport Board: formation, 1930-1934.

RAIL274 = Great Western Railway Company, Estate and Rating Department:
Piece number 160 = Map of Railways in County of London (undated). Showing freehold and leasehold properties, easements and Receiving Offices for GWR, LNER, LMSR, LPTB, SR and jointly owned railways; filed in Railway Executive Outline of Regions and list of penetrating lines, 1950, 9 feet x 8 feet, folded in 18 inch x 12 inch sections.
Piece number 205 = GWR Estates and Rating Department Survey 1920 (Volume 169) Ealing and Shepherds Bush Railway.

RAIL390 = London and North Eastern Railway, Minutes and Reports:
Piece number 14 = Minutes of meetings of special committee including: London Suburban Traffic, 1923-1947.
Piece number 190 = London Passenger Transport Act 1933: Sub Committee on Accounts and Statistics Minutes 1-183, 1933-1935.
Piece number 542 = Locomotive Committee: electrification of widened lines between King's Cross and Moorgate Street; fitting of trip cocks to 100 engines, 1925-1927.
Piece number 831 = Suburban & Road Traffic Committee - negotiations with London General Omnibus Co., 1931.
Piece number 968 = Parcels business of ex - Metropolitan Rly. Co. - transfer to Main Line Rly. Cos., 1934-1935.
Piece number 982 = London Electric Finance Corporation Ltd., (includes LNER Act 1936, articles of association for LETF Corp. Ltd, and map of proposed electrified railways), 1934-1947.
Piece number 983 = London Passenger Transport Board: main line companies' guarantee on Metropolitan assented stock (See Section 89 of LPT Act 1933) - papers, extracts from minutes etc., relating to payment of LNER Co's proportion, 1934-1947.
Piece number 1079 = Supply and installation of cables between Woodside Park and High Barnet sub-stations, 1937-1942.
Piece number 1080 = Working of freight train traffic over Metropolitan & Gt. Central and Watford joint lines and over Metropolitan lines between Baker Street & Uxbridge etc., 1937.
Piece number 1101 = Doubling of Edgware branch - north London electrification scheme (govt. assistance works), 1937-1938.
Piece number 1108 = Rates and charges - increase in, also increase in fares in London Transport area, 1937-1939.
Piece number 1120 = North London electrification - widening and alterations from Drayton Park to Finsbury Park station Contract No.7, 1938.
Piece number 1133 = North London Electrification scheme - widening at East Finchley and Church End stations, 1938.
Piece number 1137 = North London electrification scheme - new carriage shed, Bounds Green, Contract No.6, 1939.
Piece number 2043 = London Passenger Transport Board Standing Joint Committee Minutes. LNER copy. Indexed. Meeting No.1, 20 July 1933 to meeting No.49, 18 February 1947 and subsequent note and minutes regarding the Committee's dissolution, dated 2 Jan 1948.

RAIL392 = London and North Eastern Railway Company:
Piece number 265 = Kings Cross Station: Proposed treatment of approach and shops: elevations to Euston Road; longitudinal and cross sections through concourse; elevations in portland stone and brick; alternative sketch showing brick and stone treatments; suggested kiosk entrance for Piccadilly Railway signed by Alfred B Yeats Architect, 5 parts, 1931 (See also RAIL392/264 and 266).
Piece number 271 = Kings Cross Terminal and proposed new Metropolitan Line Railway Station: plans showing existing and proposed stations, 12 parts, 1933-1936.

RAIL393 = London and North Eastern Railway, Miscellaneous Books and Records:
Piece number 9 = Passenger fare rates from London (Metropolitan Railway Widened line stations), including route instructions Vol., (c.1922-1923).
Piece number 167 = Proposed tube railway, Liverpool Street to Ilford: report by Messrs. Mott, Hay and Anderson, 1930.

RAIL410 = London and North Western Railway Company:

Piece number 852 = Omnibuses between Euston and Waterloo: London General Omnibus Co. Ltd, 1864.

Piece number 935 = Euston station interchange station and footway with City & South London Railway, 1905.

Piece number 1010 = Euston: Proposed interchange subways, etc, with Underground Electric Company's City and South London Line, 1905.

Piece number 1460 = LNWR and LER joint stock - electric stock of Watford-Bakerloo service: diagrams, 1922.

RAIL411 = London and South Western Railway Company:

Piece number 298 = Agreement with Waterloo & City Railway Co, 1894.

Piece number 299 = Agreement with Waterloo & City Railway Co as to works at Waterloo Stn, 1899.

Piece number 313 = Agreement with Metropolitan District Railway Co, as to abandonment of Surbiton section of Kingston & London Railway, and other matters, 1886.

Piece number 314 = Agreement with Metropolitan District Railway Co, for abandonment of AC Curve at West Brompton, 1892.

Piece number 315 = Agreement with Metropolitan District Railway Co, as to electrification between Hammersmith and Turnham Green, 1901.

Piece number 316 = Agreement with Metropolitan District Railway Co, for electrification between:
    a Hammersmith & Turnham Green.
    b Turnham Green & Richmond.
    c Putney Bridge & Wimbledon.
and erection of electrical sub-stations at Studland Road, Putney Bridge and Wimbledon Park Station, 1903.

Piece number 317 = Supply of electrical current for Wimbledon-Fulham line: Correspondence with the Metropolitan District Railway Co, 1913.

Piece number 318 = Agreement with Metropolitan District Railway Co, and London Electric Railway Co, as to cables for supply of electricity to Richmond (Surrey) Electrical Light & Power Co Ltd, 1916.

Piece number 319 = Agreement with Metropolitan District Railway Co, and London Electric Railway Co, as to cables for supply of electricity to Richmond (Surrey) Electrical Light & Power Co Ltd, 1928.

Piece number 320 = Agreement with Metropolitan District Railway Co, the London Electric Railway Co, and the LNW Railway Co for power supply for working North Western trains between Gunnersbury and Richmond, 1916.

RAIL414 = London Brighton & South Coast Railway Company:

Piece number 309 = Memorandum of Agreement with the SER Co giving them option of becoming equal partners with the Brighton Co in working East London Railway, 1870.

Piece number 320 = Deed of guarantee with the SER Co to pay interest on East London Railway debenture stock, 1881.

Piece number 364 = Through rates via the East London Railway, and other matters: agreement with the GER Co, 1898.

Piece number 400 = Electrification works at New Cross: agreement with East London Railway Joint Committee, 1913.

Piece number 410 = Temporary transfer of men for any work or duty: agreement with East London Railway Joint Committee, 1914.

Piece number 412 = Supply of electricity to East London railway: copy agreement between Metropolitan District Railway Co and London Electric Railway Co, and East London Railway Joint Committee, 1913.

Piece number 413 = Service of trains on East London railway: copy agreement between the Metropolitan Railway Co and the East London Railway Joint Committee, 1914.

Piece number 442 = Junction near Brick Lane and user of line: copy agreement between East London and GER companies, 1869.

Piece number 443 = Running through Wapping Tunnel: Copy undertaking given by East London Railway Co and London Brighton & South Coast Railway Co to Board of Trade, undated.

RAIL420 = London Midland and Scottish Railway Company: Deeds, Agreements, Contracts, Specifications, Estimates, Plans:

Piece number 14 = Euston Station Diagrams: Basements and tubes, 1939.

Piece number 125 = Agreement between Metropolitan District Railway Company & London Electric Railway Company, LMS and Southern Railway Company: laying of tracks and use by LMS between South Acton and West Kensington, with plans (2 parts), July 1926.

RAIL421 = London Midland and Scottish Railway Company, Miscellaneous Books and Records:

Piece number 145 = Removal of anomalies in fares between LMS and London Passenger Transport Board stations, 1947.

British Transport Historical Records:

RAIL422 = London Midland and Scottish Railway Company, Locomotive and Rolling Stock Records:

Piece number 37 = London-Watford electric services - minutes, memoranda, correspondence etc., relating to additional rolling stock and power and sub-station equipment, 1929-1932.

RAIL431 = London Midland and Scottish Railway Company, Solicitor's Records:

Piece number 17 = London General Omnibus Co Ltd, 1928-1930.

Piece number 21 = National Omnibus & Transport Co. Ltd, Eastern National Omnibus Co Ltd, co-ordination agreements etc, 1929-1930.

RAIL647 = Southern Railway Company: Deeds Agreements, Contracts, Specifications, Estimates, Plans:

Piece number 28 = Agreement between East London Railway Joint Committee and SR concerning gas main at New Cross Gate and Rotherhithe Road, Aug 1928.

Piece number 55 = Supplemental agreement between Lords Commissioners of the Admiralty, Minister of Aircraft Production & Minister of Supply, London, Midland & Scottish Railway Company, London & North Eastern Railway Company, Great Western Railway Company, SR & London Passenger Transport Board and Minister of War Transport to agreement dated 11 Dec 1942 concerning financial terms for shipbuilding and ship repair work undertaken by railway companies, Aug 1944.

RAIL650 = Southern Railway Company: Associated Motor Omnibus Companies Records:

Piece number 24 = Standing Joint Committee Minutes and Reports (copies): London Passenger Transport Board, Southern Vectis, Thames Valley, Wilts & Dorset, 1933.

Piece number 28 = Standing Joint Committee Minutes and Reports (copies): Aldershot and Dist., Hants and Dorset, London Passenger Transport Board, 1934.

Piece number 29 = Standing Joint Committee Minutes and Reports (copies): Aldershot and Dist., Hants and Dorset, London Passenger Transport Board, 1935.

Piece number 38 = Standing Joint Committee Minutes and Reports (copies): Aldershot and Dist., Devon General, Hants and Dorset, London Passenger Transport Board, Southern National, Southern Vectis, Thames Valley, Wilts and Dorset, 1936.

Piece number 43 = Standing Joint Committee Minutes and Reports (copies): Aldershot and Dist., Devon General, Hants and Dorset, London Passenger Transport Board, 1937.

Piece number 49 = Standing Joint Committee Minutes and Reports (copies): Aldershot and Dist., Devon General, Hants and Dorset, London Passenger Transport Board, 1938.

Piece number 55 = Standing Joint Committee Minutes and Reports (copies): Aldershot and Dist., Hants and Dorset, London Passenger Transport Board, Southern National, Southern Vectis, Thames Valley, Wilts and Dorset, 1939.

Piece number 60 = Standing Joint Committee Minutes and Reports (copies): Aldershot and Dist., Devon General, Hants and Dorset, London Passenger Transport Board, Southern Vectis, Thames Valley, Wilts and Dorset, 1940.

Piece number 88 = Standing Joint Committee Minutes and Reports (copies): Aldershot and Dist., Devon General, Hants and Dorset, London Passenger Transport Board, 1946.

Piece number 94 = Standing Joint Committee Minutes and Reports (copies): Aldershot and Dist., Devon General, Hants and Dorset, London Passenger Transport Board, 1947.

RAIL713 = Waterloo & City Railway Company:

Piece number 1 = Proprietors' minutes, with Reports and Accounts, 1894-1907.

Piece number 2 = Proprietors' minutes (rough), 1894-1902.

Piece number 3 = Proprietors' minutes (rough), 1903-1907.

Piece number 4 = Board minutes, 1894-1898.

Piece number 5 = Board minutes, 1899-1907.

Piece number 6 = Finance Committee minutes, 1894-1897.

Piece number 7 = Finance Committee minutes, 1897-1900.

Piece number 8 = Finance Committee minutes, 1900-1907.

Piece number 9 = List showing details of maintenance expenses (second half-year), 1899.

RAIL783 = Great Northern Railway Company: Correspondence Files:

Piece number 177 = Metropolitan Widened Lines: special trains, Feb 1883-Jan 1917.

Piece number 197 = Moorgate Street Station: agreement with Metropolitan Railway concerning water for GNR locomotives, Oct 1900-Jan 1907.

Piece number 207 = Moorgate Street Station: working, Oct 1908-Mar 1911.

Piece number 208 = Moorgate Street Station: electric lighting, Feb 1912-Oct 1914.

Piece number 596 = Great Northern and City Railway Company (GNC): Drayton Park: disposal of spoil, Dec 1900-Mar 1901.

RAIL783 = Great Northern Railway Company: Correspondence Files: *continued....*

Piece number 597 = Great Northern and City Railway Company (GNC): Booking agreement: including leaflet published in 1904 by GNC giving information about fares, environs of each station and a diagram of GN &C superimposed onto plan of north west London showing its connections to GNR, Nov 1903-Apr 1905.

Piece number 598 = Great Northern and City Railway Company (GNC): Season ticket traffic in which GNR, NLR, Met and GNC have interests, Aug 1904-Jan 1907.

Piece number 599 = Great Northern and City Railway Company (GNC): Finance, Mar 1905-Jul 1906.

Piece number 600 = Great Northern and City Railway Company (GNC): Three route season tickets, Apr 1907-Jan 1909.

Piece number 601 = Great Northern and City Railway Company (GNC): Power House, Jun 1909-Oct 1909.

Piece number 602 = Great Northern and City Railway Company (GNC): Use by GNR season ticket holders, Apr 1920-Feb 1921.

Piece number 603 = Great Northern and City Railway Company (GNC): Agreement between GNC and GNR to working of GNR trains along GNC and facilities to be provided by GNC for GNR: with later alterations, Jan 1894.

Piece number 604 = Great Northern and City Railway Company (GNC): Agreement to rescind above agreement, May 1901.

Piece number 605 = Great Northern and City Railway Company (GNC): Counts of through season tickets, 1904-1914.

Piece number 621 = Tables of GNR Season ticket holders using Met stations, Apr 1904.

RAIL791 = London & North Western Railway Company: Agreements, Conveyances, Contracts and Deeds:

Piece number 166 = Memorandum of agreement between LNWR and Pneumatic Despatch Co. Ltd for stairs and shoot under new parcels office at Euston Station with plan, 1873.

Piece number 343 = Agreement between LNWR and A&B to wages of staff at Verney Junction, mileage for each company to be measured from actual junction, rent paid by A&B for land occupied by station and charges for terminating traffic by both companies, Sept 1870.

Piece number 344 = Minute of meeting between John Bell (Chairman, Metropolitan Railway Company (MetR)) & Mr. Richards (of MetR) and Frederick Harrison (General Manager, LNWR) & Francis Stevenson (Civil Engineer, LNWR) concerning alterations at Verney Junction Station caused by widening of MetR's Aylesbury Extension; includes correspondence with plan, Nov 1895-Mar 1896.

Piece number 345 = Agreement between LNWR and MetR for mutual easements at Verney Junction with plan, June 1905.

Piece number 486 = Agreement between LNWR and London Electric Railway Company (LER) concerning through electric working on LNWR and LER to Watford with plans, June 1912.

Piece number 487 = Supplemental agreement between LNWR and LER concerning reconstruction of Queens Park Station with plan, August 1914.

Piece number 488 = Agreement between LNWR and LER to erection of dust destructor with plan, June 1919.

Piece number 493 = Agreement between LER and LNWR for inspection and repair of LNWR rolling stock at Lillie Bridge Depot, May 1914.

RAIL793 = Midland Railway Company: Agreements, Conveyances, Contracts and Deeds:

Piece number 62 = Agreement between MR and Metropolitan District Railway Company (MDR) for MR's running powers over Hammersmith Junction Railway, Apr 1876.

Piece number 158 = Agreement between Charing Cross, Euston & Hampstead Railway Company and South Eastern Railway Company & MR for through bookings, June 1899.

RAIL797 = London, Brighton and South Coast Railway Company: Agreements, Conveyances, Contracts and Deeds:

Piece number 5 = Agreement between East London Railway Company (ELR) and LBSC for working of ELR by LBSC, Nov 1869.

Piece number 19 = Whitechapel Agreement between LBSC, South Eastern Railway Company (SER), London, Chatham & Dover Railway Company (LCD), Metropolitan Railway Company (MET), Metropolitan District Railway Company (MDR) and ELR for joint leasing of ELR by LBSC, SER, LCD, Met and MDR, July 1881.

Piece number 31 = Rotherhithe Pumping Station: correspondence concerning manning and maintenance, Aug-Sep 1885.

RAIL927 = Timetables and Relevant Notices, East London Railway:

Piece number 1 = Oct 1884 - Dec 1885.
Piece number 2 = 1886-1890.
Piece number 3 = 1891-1895.
Piece number 4 = 1901-1905.
Piece number 5 = 1906-1910.

RAIL959 = Timetables and Relevant Notices, Metropolitan Railway:

Piece number 1 = Metropolitan Railway - Public, Jan 1897.
Piece number 2 = Metropolitan Railway - Public, July 1897.
Piece number 3 = Metropolitan Railway - Public, 1900.
Piece number 4 = Metropolitan Railway - Public, 1901.
Piece number 5 = Metropolitan Railway - Public, 1902.
Piece number 6 = Metropolitan Railway - Public, 1903.
Piece number 7 = Metropolitan Railway - Public, 1904.
Piece number 8 = Metropolitan Railway - Public, 1912.
Piece number 9 = Metropolitan Railway - Public, 1914.
Piece number 10 = Metropolitan Railway - Public and Service, 1916.
Piece number 11 = Metropolitan Railway - Public, 1916 and 1917.
Piece number 12 = Metropolitan Railway - Public and Service, 1918.
Piece number 13 = Metropolitan Railway - Public and Service, 1920.
Piece number 14 = Metropolitan Railway - Public and Service, 1921.
Piece number 15 = Metropolitan Railway - Public, Nov 1925.
Piece number 16 = Metropolitan Railway - Public, Sept 1926.
Piece number 17 = Metropolitan Railway - Public, May 1931.
Piece number 18 = Metropolitan Railway - Service, 1871-1880.
Piece number 19 = Metropolitan Railway - Metropolitan Widened Lines, 1881-1890.
Piece number 20 = Metropolitan Railway - Metropolitan Widened Lines, 1891-1900.
Piece number 21 = Metropolitan Railway - Service, Nov 1884.
Piece number 22 = Metropolitan Railway - Service, May 1886.
Piece number 23 = Metropolitan Railway - Service (Extension to Aylesbury and Verney Junction), Sep 1892.
Piece number 24 = Metropolitan Railway - Service, Oct 1893.
Piece number 25 = Metropolitan Railway - Service, Nov 1903.
Piece number 26 = Metropolitan Railway - Service, 1919.
Piece number 27 = Metropolitan Railway - Service (1 and 2 Sections), 1 May 1928.
Piece number 28 = Metropolitan Railway - Service (4 Section), 18 June 1928.
Piece number 29 = Metropolitan Railway - Service (1 and 2 Sections), 1 Oct 1929.
Piece number 30 = Metropolitan Railway - Service (1 and 2 Sections), 1 May 1930.
Piece number 31 = Metropolitan Railway - Service (4 Section), 7 Jul 1930.
Piece number 32 = Metropolitan Railway - Service (1 Section), 6 Oct 1930.
Piece number 33 = Metropolitan Railway - Service (3 Section), 6 Oct 1930.
Piece number 34 = Metropolitan Railway - F.A. Cup Final, Wembley, 25 Apr 1931.
Piece number 35 = Metropolitan Railway - Service (1 and 2 Sections), 1 May 1931.
Piece number 36 = Metropolitan Railway - Service (4 Section), 20 July 1931.
Piece number 37 = Metropolitan Railway - Service (1 and 2 Sections), 4 Apr 1932.
Piece number 38 = Metropolitan Railway - Service (1 and 2 Sections) (Sundays), 1 May 1932.
Piece number 39 = Metropolitan Railway - Service (4 Section) (Sundays), 18 July 1932.
Piece number 40 = Metropolitan Railway - Service (3 Section) (Sunday), 7 Nov 1932.
Piece number 41 = Metropolitan Railway - Service (1 and 2 Sections) (Sundays), 12 Dec 1932.
Piece number 42 = Metropolitan Railway - Service (2 Section) (Sundays), 13 Mar 1933.

RAIL960 = Timetables and Relevant Notices, Metropolitan District Railway:

Piece number 1 = Metropolitan District Railway - Working, Dec 1876-Oct 1878.
Piece number 2 = Metropolitan District Railway - Working, Oct 1878-Oct 1879.
Piece number 3 = Metropolitan District Railway - Working, Nov 1879-Nov 1882.
Piece number 4 = Metropolitan District Railway - Working, Dec 1883-Dec 1884.
Piece number 5 = Metropolitan District Railway - Working, Jan 1886-Dec 1886.
Piece number 6 = Metropolitan District Railway - Working, Dec 1886-Nov 1887.
Piece number 7 = Metropolitan District Railway - Working, Nov 1887-Nov 1888.
Piece number 8 = Metropolitan District Railway - Working, Nov 1888-Nov 1889.
Piece number 9 = Metropolitan District Railway - Working, Nov 1889-Nov 1890.
Piece number 10 = Metropolitan District Railway - Working, Nov 1890-Nov 1891.
Piece number 11 = Metropolitan District Railway - Working, Jan 1892-Nov 1892.
Piece number 12 = Metropolitan District Railway - Working, Nov 1892-Nov 1893.
Piece number 13 = Metropolitan District Railway - Working, Nov 1894-Nov 1895.
Piece number 14 = Metropolitan District Railway - Working, Nov 1895-Nov 1896.
Piece number 15 = Metropolitan District Railway - Working, Nov 1897-Nov 1898.
Piece number 16 = Metropolitan District Railway - Working, Nov 1898-Nov 1899.
Piece number 17 = Metropolitan District Railway - Working, Nov 1899-Oct 1900.
Piece number 18 = Metropolitan District Railway - Working, Oct 1900-Nov 1901.
Piece number 19 = Metropolitan District Railway - Public, Nov 1901-Oct 1902.
Piece number 20 = Metropolitan District Railway - Public, Oct 1902-Nov 1903.

British Transport Historical Records:

RAIL960 = Timetables and Relevant Notices, Metropolitan District Railway: *continued....*
Piece number 21 = Metropolitan District Railway - Public, June 1905.
Piece number 22 = Metropolitan District Railway - Public, Dec 1907.

RAIL981 = Timetables and Relevant Notices, Special and Miscellaneous Timetables:
Piece number 290 = Waterloo & City Railway, Pocket timetable, Dec 1898.
Piece number 329 = Metropolitan & Great Central Railways, Pocket timetable, Nov 1906.
Piece number 330 = Metropolitan & Great Central Railways, Pocket timetable between London and Sandy Lodge, May 1910.
Piece number 331 = Metropolitan & Great Central Railways, Pocket timetable, Oct 1910.
Piece number 332 = Metropolitan & Great Western Railways, Pocket Guide from Westbourne Park, timetables and fares, March 1874.
Piece number 333 = Metropolitan Railway, Pocket sheet timetable of Whitsun trains between Farringdon Street and Paddington. <u>Also</u>: Great Western and Great Northern through trains, timetables and fares, May 1864.
Piece number 334 = Metropolitan Railway, Pocket Timetable. Opening of Harrow to Ruislip and Uxbridge, July 1904.
Piece number 335 = Metropolitan Railway. Fast trains to British Empire Exhibition, May 1925.
Piece number 605 = Timetables of various companies 1893, including the Metropolitan Railway and Metropolitan District Railway.
Piece number 606 = Timetables of various companies 1902, including the Metropolitan Railway.
Piece number 608 = Timetables of various companies 1907, including the Metropolitan District Railway.
Piece number 610 = Timetables of various companies 1907, including the Metropolitan Railway.

RAIL983 = Timetables and Relevant Notices, Underground Electric Railways Company of London:
Piece number 1 = Underground Electric Railways Company of London, Traffic Notices (bound), 1926.
Piece number 2 = Underground Electric Railways Company of London, Traffic Notices (bound), 1927.
Piece number 3 = Underground Electric Railways Company of London, Traffic Notices (bound), 1930.
Piece number 4 = Underground Electric Railways Company of London, Traffic Notices (bound), 1932 (see also RAIL984/1-3 inclusive).
Piece number 5 = Underground Electric Railways Company of London, Working timetables and traffic Notices, May 1929-Dec 1930 including:
Bakerloo Line (L.E.R.) Working Timetables, No.114, Oct 1929.
Bakerloo Line (L.E.R.) Holiday Notice (Whitsun), June 1930.
Bakerloo Line (L.E.R.) Holiday Notice (Bank), Aug 1930.
Bakerloo Line (L.E.R.) Working Timetables, No.116, Oct 1930.
Bakerloo Line (L.E.R.) Holiday Notice (Christmas and New Year), Dec 1930-Jan 1931.
Central London Railway, Working Timetable, No.67, Nov 1929.
Central London Railway, Working Timetable, No.68, Mar 1930.
Central London Railway, Holiday Notice (Whitsun), June 1930.
Central London Railway, Holiday Notice (Bank), Aug 1930.
Central London Railway, Working Timetable, No.70, Oct 1930.
Central London Railway, Holiday Notice (Christmas and New Year), Dec 1930-Jan 1931.
District Line, Working Timetables, No.96 and Supplement, July 1929.
District Line, Working Timetables, No.97, Oct 1929.
District Line, Working Timetables, No.98 and Supplement, Feb 1930.
District Line, Easter Trains Notice, Apr 1930.
District Line, Working Timetables, No.96 and Supplement, May 1930.
District Line, Working Timetables, No.99, May 1930.
District Line, Appendix to Working Timetable, 1930.
District Line, Whitsun Trains Notice, June 1930.
District Line, Working Timetables, No.100 and Supplement, June 1930.
District Line, Bank Holiday Notice, Aug 1930.
District Line, Working Timetables, No.101 and Supplement, Oct 1930.
District Line, Christmas and New Year Trains Notice, Dec 1930-Jan 1931.
Piccadilly Line (L.E.R.), Working Timetables, No.113, Oct 1929.
Piccadilly Line (L.E.R.), Whitsun Trains Notice, June 1930.
Piccadilly Line (L.E.R.), Working Timetables, No.114, June 1930.
Piccadilly Line (L.E.R.), Bank Holiday Trains Notice, Aug 1930.
Piccadilly Line (L.E.R.), Working Timetables, No.114 (Reissue), Oct 1930.
Piccadilly Line (L.E.R.), Christmas and New Year Trains Notice, Dec 1930-Jan 1931.
Piece number 6 = Underground Electric Railways Company of London, Train Services (Passenger) to and from Uxbridge, May 1931.

British Transport Historical Records:

RAIL984 = Timetables and Relevant Notices, London Underground Guides and
      Timetables:

Piece number 1 = Traffic Notices, 1933.
Piece number 2 = Traffic Circulars, 1934.
Piece number 3 = Traffic Circulars, 1935.
Piece number 4 = Underground Guide, May 1936.
Piece number 5 = Underground Guide, Nov 1936.
Piece number 6 = Underground Timetable, Sept 1937.
Piece number 7 = Underground Timetable, Jan 1938.
Piece number 8 = Underground Timetable, May 1938.
Piece number 9 = Underground Timetable, Oct 1938.
Piece number 10 = Underground Timetable, Nov 1938.
Piece number 11 = Underground Guide, Winter 1957-1958.
Piece number 12 = Underground Guide, Summer 1958.
Piece number 13 = Underground Guide, Spring 1959.
Piece number 14 = Underground Guide, Summer 1959.
Piece number 15 = Underground Guide, Autumn 1959.
Piece number 16 = Underground Guide, Winter 1959-1960.
Piece number 17 = Underground Guide, Mar 1960.
Piece number 18 = Underground Guide, June 1960.
Piece number 19 = Underground Guide, Autumn 1960.
Piece number 20 = Underground Guide, Summer 1961.
Piece number 21 = Underground Guide, Winter 1961.
Piece number 22 = Underground Guide, Spring 1962.
Piece number 23 = Bakerloo Line (L.P.T.B.) Working Timetables, No.132, Oct 1936.
Piece number 24 = Bakerloo Line (L.P.T.B.) Working Timetables, No.134, Oct 1937.
Piece number 25 = Bakerloo Line (L.P.T.B.) Working Timetables, No.135, May 1938.
Piece number 26 = Bakerloo Line (L.T.E.) Working Timetables, No.31, Nov 1949.
Piece number 27 = Bakerloo Line (L.T.E.) Working Timetables, No.34, June 1952.
Piece number 28 = Bakerloo Line (L.T.E.) Working Timetables, Easter Trains Notice, Apr 1953.
Piece number 29 = Bakerloo Line (L.T.E.) Working Timetables, No.36, Nov 1953.
Piece number 30 = Bakerloo Line (L.T.E.) Working Timetables, No.37, Sept 1954.
Piece number 31 = Bakerloo Line (L.T.E.) Working Timetables, No.38 (Saturdays), Feb 1955.
Piece number 32 = Bakerloo Line (L.T.E.) Working Timetables, No.39, May 1955.
Piece number 33 = Bakerloo Line (L.T.E.) Working Timetables, No.41, Sept 1957.
Piece number 34 = Bakerloo Line (L.T.E.) Working Timetables, No.42, Mar 1958.
Piece number 35 = Bakerloo Line (L.T.E.) Working Timetables, No.43, June 1958.
Piece number 36 = Bakerloo Line (L.T.E.) Working Timetables, No.43 (Alterations to), Mar 1959.
Piece number 37 = Bakerloo Line (L.T.E.) Working Timetables, No.45, Sept 1960.
Piece number 38 = Bakerloo Line (L.T.E.) Working Timetables, No.46, June 1961.
Piece number 39 = Bakerloo Line (L.T.E.) Working Timetables, No.47, Sept 1961.
Piece number 40 = Bakerloo Line (L.T.E.) Working Timetables, No.48, June 1962.
Piece number 41 = Bakerloo Line (L.T.E.) Working Timetables, No.49 (Saturdays), Sept 1962.
Piece number 42 = Bakerloo Line (L.T.E.) Working Timetables, Christmas Trains Notice, Dec 1962.
Piece number 43 = Bakerloo Line (L.T.E.) Working Timetables, No.50, June 1963.
Piece number 44 = Bakerloo Line (L.T.E.) Working Timetables, No.51, Sept 1963.
Piece number 45 = Central London Line (L.P.T.B.) Working Timetables, No.84, Oct 1936.
Piece number 46 = Central London Line (L.P.T.B.) Working Timetables, No.86, Oct 1937.
Piece number 47 = Central Line (L.T.E.) Working Timetables, No.6 (Epping Extension), Sept 1949.
Piece number 48 = Central Line (L.T.E.) Working Timetables, No.7 (Sundays), Feb 1950.
Piece number 49 = Central Line (L.T.E.) Working Timetables, No.8, June 1950.
Piece number 50 = Central Line (L.T.E.) Working Timetables, No.9, Feb 1951.
Piece number 51 = Central Line (L.T.E.) Working Timetables, No.9 (Alterations to), Aug 1951.
Piece number 52 = Central Line (L.T.E.) Working Timetables, No.12, Apr 1953.
Piece number 53 = Central Line (L.T.E.) Working Timetables, No.13, Nov 1953.
Piece number 54 = Central Line (L.T.E.) Working Timetables, No.14, Oct 1954.
Piece number 55 = Central Line (L.T.E.) Working Timetables, No.15, Feb 1955.
Piece number 56 = Central Line (L.T.E.) Working Timetables, No.16, Nov 1955.
Piece number 57 = Central Line (L.T.E.) Working Timetables, No.17, Oct 1956.
Piece number 58 = Central Line (L.T.E.) Working Timetables, No.18, Nov 1957.
Piece number 59 = Central Line (L.T.E.) Working Timetables, No.19, Apr 1958.
Piece number 60 = Central Line (L.T.E.) Working Timetables, No.21, Mar 1960.
Piece number 61 = Central Line (L.T.E.) Working Timetables, No.22, Sep 1961.
Piece number 62 = Central Line (L.T.E.) Working Timetables, No.23, Mar 1962.
Piece number 63 = Central Line (L.T.E.) Working Timetables, No.24, Oct 1962.

RAIL984 = Timetables and Relevant Notices, London Underground Guides and Timetables: *continued....*

Piece number 64 = Central Line (L.T.E.) Working Timetables (Holiday Trains Notice), Dec 1962.

Piece number 65 = Central Line (L.T.E.) Working Timetables, No.24A (Sundays), May 1963.

Piece number 66 = Central Line (L.T.E.) Working Timetables, No.25, Jul 1963.

Piece number 67 = Central Line (L.T.E.) Working Timetables, No.26, Oct 1963.

Piece number 68 = Passenger Timetables. Piccadilly, Hammersmith, South Harrow and Uxbridge (Piccadilly), Sept 1935.

Piece number 69 = Passenger Timetables. Richmond and the City (District), Sept 1935.

Piece number 70 = District and Piccadilly Lines (L.P.T.B.) Working Timetables, No.8 (W), May 1936.

Piece number 71 = District and Piccadilly Lines (L.P.T.B.) Working Timetables, No.10 (S), Oct 1936.

Piece number 72 = District and Piccadilly Lines (L.P.T.B.) Working Timetables, No.11 (W), May 1937.

Piece number 73 = District and Piccadilly Lines (L.P.T.B.) Working Timetables, No.12 (S), May 1937.

Piece number 74 = District and Piccadilly Lines (L.P.T.B.) Working Timetables, No.13 (S), Oct 1937.

Piece number 75 = District and Piccadilly Lines (L.P.T.B.) Working Timetables, No.14 (W), May 1938.

Piece number 76 = District and Piccadilly Lines (L.P.T.B.) Working Timetables, No.15 (S), May 1938.

Piece number 77 = District and Piccadilly Lines (L.P.T.B.) Working Timetables, No.18 (W), May 1939.

Piece number 78 = District and Piccadilly Lines (L.P.T.B.) Working Timetables, No.19 (S), May 1939.

Piece number 79 = District and Piccadilly Lines (L.P.T.B.) Working Timetables, No.20 (W), July 1939.

Piece number 80 = District and Piccadilly Lines (L.P.T.B.) Working Timetables, No.21 (S), Oct 1939.

Piece number 81 = District and Piccadilly Lines (L.P.T.B.) Working Timetables, No.23 (S), May 1940.

Piece number 82 = District and Piccadilly Lines (L.P.T.B.) Working Timetables, No.25 (S), Sept 1940.

Piece number 83 = District and Piccadilly Lines (L.T.E.) Working Timetables, No.61 (W), Nov 1949.

Piece number 84 = District and Piccadilly Lines (L.T.E.) Working Timetables, No.62 (S), Nov 1949.

Piece number 85 = District and Piccadilly Lines (L.T.E.) Working Timetables, - (Football at Fulham Notice), Jan 1950.

Piece number 86 = District and Piccadilly Lines (L.T.E.) Working Timetables, No.63 (W), June 1950.

Piece number 87 = District and Piccadilly Lines (L.T.E.) Working Timetables, No.64 (S), June 1950.

Piece number 88 = District and Piccadilly Lines (L.T.E.) Working Timetables, No.65 (W), Nov 1951.

Piece number 89 = District and Piccadilly Lines (L.T.E.) Working Timetables, No.66 (S), Nov 1951.

Piece number 90 = District and Piccadilly Lines (L.T.E.) Working Timetables, No.67 (W), May 1952.

Piece number 91 = District and Piccadilly Lines (L.T.E.) Working Timetables, No.68 (S), May 1952.

Piece number 92 = District and Piccadilly Lines (L.T.E.) Working Timetables, - (Easter Trains, District), Apr 1953.

Piece number 93 = District and Piccadilly Lines (L.T.E.) Working Timetables, - (Easter Trains, Piccadilly), Apr 1953.

Piece number 94 = District and Piccadilly Lines (L.T.E.) Working Timetables, No.70 (W), Nov 1953.

Piece number 95 = District and Piccadilly Lines (L.T.E.) Working Timetables, No.71 (S), Nov 1953.

Piece number 96 = District and Piccadilly Lines (L.T.E.) Working Timetables, No.72 (W), Sept 1954.

Piece number 97 = District and Piccadilly Lines (L.T.E.) Working Timetables, No.73 (S), Sept 1954.

Piece number 98 = District and Piccadilly Lines (L.T.E.) Working Timetables, No.74 (W), May 1955.

Piece number 99 = District and Piccadilly Lines (L.T.E.) Working Timetables, No.75, June 1956.

Piece number 100 = District and Piccadilly Lines (L.T.E.) Working Timetables, No.76, Apr 1957.

Piece number 101 = District and Piccadilly Lines (L.T.E.) Working Timetables, No.77, July 1957.

Piece number 102 = District and Piccadilly Lines (L.T.E.) Working Timetables, No.78, June 1958.

Piece number 103 = District and Piccadilly Lines (L.T.E.) Working Timetables, No.79, Dec 1958.

Piece number 104 = District and Piccadilly Lines (L.T.E.) Working Timetables, No.80, Mar 1959.

Piece number 105 = District and Piccadilly Lines (L.T.E.) Working Timetables, No.81, Sept 1959.

Piece number 106 = District and Piccadilly Lines (L.T.E.) Working Timetables, No.82, Mar 1960.

Piece number 107 = District and Piccadilly Lines (L.T.E.) Working Timetables, No.83, Oct 1960.

Piece number 108 = District and Piccadilly Lines (L.T.E.) Working Timetables, No.84, June 1961.

Piece number 109 = District and Piccadilly Lines (L.T.E.) Working Timetables, No.85, June 1962.

Piece number 110 = District and Piccadilly Lines (L.T.E.) Working Timetables, No.86, Sept 1962.

Piece number 111 = District and Piccadilly Lines (L.T.E.) Working Timetables, - (Christmas Trains, Piccadilly), Dec 1962.

Piece number 112 = District and Piccadilly Lines (L.T.E.) Working Timetables, - (Christmas Trains, District), Dec 1962.

Piece number 113 = District and Piccadilly Lines (L.T.E.) Working Timetables, No.87, June 1963.

Piece number 114 = District and Piccadilly Lines (L.T.E.) Working Timetables, No.88, Sept 1963.

Piece number 115 = Metropolitan Line (L.P.T.B.) Passenger Services, Alterations to Passenger Timetable for April, July 1935.

Piece number 116 = Metropolitan Line (L.P.T.B.) Passenger Services, Cheap evening fares to Town, 1936.

Piece number 117 = Metropolitan Line (L.P.T.B.) Working Timetables, No.4 Section (City Widened Lines) No.34, July 1933.

RAIL984 = Timetables and Relevant Notices, London Underground Guides and
Timetables: *continued....*

Piece number 118 = Metropolitan Line (L.P.T.B.) Working Timetables, No.1 Section (and Supplement), Nov 1933.

Piece number 119 = Metropolitan Line (L.P.T.B.) Working Timetables, No.3 Section (Gt.N. and City), Jan 1934.

Piece number 120 = Metropolitan Line (L.P.T.B.) Working Timetables, No.1 Section (and Supplement), Jan 1934-Apr 1934.

Piece number 121 = Metropolitan Line (L.P.T.B.) Working Timetables, No.1 Section (and Supplement), Apr 1934.

Piece number 122 = Metropolitan Line (L.P.T.B.) Working Timetables, No.3 Section (Gt.N. and City) (revised), Apr 1934.

Piece number 123 = Metropolitan Line (L.P.T.B.) Working Timetables, - (Wembley Fixtures Notice), Apr 1934 - May 1934.

Piece number 124 = Metropolitan Line (L.P.T.B.) Working Timetables, No.4 Section (City Widened Lines) No.41, July 1934.

Piece number 125 = Metropolitan Line (L.P.T.B.) Working Timetables, No.1 Section No.42, Oct 1934.

Piece number 126 = Metropolitan Line (L.P.T.B.) Working Timetables, No.43 (Supplement only), Oct 1934.

Piece number 127 = Metropolitan Line (L.P.T.B.) Working Timetables, No.1 Section No.44, Jan 1935.

Piece number 128 = Metropolitan Line (L.P.T.B.) Working Timetables, No.45 (Supplement only), Jan 1935.

Piece number 129 = Metropolitan Line (L.P.T.B.) Working Timetables, No.4 Section No.46 (City Widened Lines), Jan 1935.

Piece number 130 = Metropolitan Line (L.P.T.B.) Working Timetables, No.1 Section No.49, Apr 1935.

Piece number 131 = Metropolitan Line (L.P.T.B.) Working Timetables, No.50 (Supplement only), Apr 1935.

Piece number 132 = Metropolitan Line (L.P.T.B.) Working Timetables, No.3 Section No.51 (City Widened Lines), July 1935.

Piece number 133 = Metropolitan Line (L.P.T.B.) Working Timetables, No.1 Section No.52, Sept 1935.

Piece number 134 = Metropolitan Line (L.P.T.B.) Working Timetables, No.1 Section No.54 (with Supplement), May 1936-Nov 1936.

Piece number 135 = Metropolitan Line (L.P.T.B.) Working Timetables, No.55 (Supplement only), May 1936.

Piece number 136 = Metropolitan Line (L.P.T.B.) Working Timetables, No.2 Section No.56, July 1936.

Piece number 137 = Metropolitan Line (L.P.T.B.) Working Timetables, No.3 Section No.57 (City Widened Lines), July 1936.

Piece number 138 = Metropolitan Line (L.P.T.B.) Working Timetables, No.1 Section No.58, May 1937.

Piece number 139 = Metropolitan Line (L.P.T.B.) Working Timetables, No.59 (Supplement only), May 1937.

Piece number 140 = Metropolitan Line (L.P.T.B.) Working Timetables, No.3 Section No.60 (City Widened Lines), July 1937.

Piece number 141 = Metropolitan Line (L.P.T.B.) Working Timetables, - (Notice of LNER take-over of Freight working and new services), Nov 1937.

Piece number 142 = Metropolitan Line (L.P.T.B.) Working Timetables, No.1 Section No.61, May 1938.

Piece number 143 = Metropolitan Line (L.P.T.B.) Working Timetables, No.3 Section No.62, July 1938.

Piece number 144 = Metropolitan Line (L.P.T.B.) Working Timetables, No.2 Section No.64, Oct 1938.

Piece number 145 = Metropolitan Line (L.P.T.B.) Working Timetables, No.1 Section No.65, Nov 1938.

Piece number 146 = Metropolitan Line (L.P.T.B.) Working Timetables, No.3 Section No.67, July 1939.

Piece number 147 = Metropolitan Line (L.P.T.B.) Working Timetables, No.1 Section No.68, July 1939.

Piece number 148 = Metropolitan Line (L.P.T.B.) Working Timetables, No.2 Section No.74, Dec 1940.

Piece number 149 = Metropolitan Line (L.P.T.B.) Working Timetables, No.2 Section No.75 (Sundays), Dec 1940.

Piece number 150 = Metropolitan Line (L.P.T.B.) Working Timetables, No.1 Section No.85, Oct 1941.

Piece number 151 = Metropolitan Line (L.P.T.B.) Working Timetables, No.1 Section No.90, May 1942.

Piece number 152 = Metropolitan Line (L.P.T.B.) Working Timetables, No.1 Section No.115, June 1947.

Piece number 153 = Metropolitan Line (L.T.E.) Working Timetables, No.1 Section No.125, Nov 1949.

Piece number 154 = Metropolitan Line (L.T.E.) Working Timetables, - No.125a (East London Section), Nov 1949.

Piece number 155 = Metropolitan Line (L.T.E.) Working Timetables, - No.125b (City Widened Lines), Sept 1949.

Piece number 156 = Metropolitan Line (L.T.E.) Working Timetables, No.1 Section No.127 (with Alterations), Jun 1950.

Piece number 157 = Metropolitan Line (L.T.E.) Working Timetables, No.1 Section (Bank Holiday Notice), Aug 1950.

Piece number 158 = Metropolitan Line (L.T.E.) Working Timetables, No.2 Section (Bank Holiday Notice), Aug 1950.

Piece number 159 = Metropolitan Line (L.T.E.) Working Timetables, No.2 Section No.130 (with Alterations), Sept 1950.

Piece number 160 = Metropolitan Line (L.T.E.) Working Timetables, No.1 Section No.132, Sept 1951.

Piece number 161 = Metropolitan Line (L.T.E.) Working Timetables, No.1 Section No.136, June 1952.

RAIL984 = Timetables and Relevant Notices, London Underground Guides and Timetables: *continued....*

Piece number 162 = Metropolitan Line (L.T.E.) Working Timetables, No.1 Section No.141 (with Alterations), Nov 1952.

Piece number 163 = Metropolitan Line (L.T.E.) Working Timetables, No.1 Section (Easter Trains Notice), Apr 1953.

Piece number 164 = Metropolitan Line (L.T.E.) Working Timetables, No.2 (Easter Trains Notice), Apr 1953.

Piece number 165 = Metropolitan Line (L.T.E.) Working Timetables, No.2 Section No.145, June 1953.

Piece number 166 = Metropolitan Line (L.T.E.) Working Timetables, No.1 Section No.147, Nov 1953.

Piece number 167 = Metropolitan Line (L.T.E.) Working Timetables, No.2 Section No.151, June 1954.

Piece number 168 = Metropolitan Line (L.T.E.) Working Timetables, No.1 Section No.156, May 1955.

Piece number 169 = Metropolitan Line (L.T.E.) Working Timetables, No.1 Section No.160, June 1956.

Piece number 170 = Metropolitan Line (L.T.E.) Working Timetables, No.2 Section No.161, June 1956.

Piece number 171 = Metropolitan Line (L.T.E.) Working Timetables, - No.162 (City Widened Lines), June 1956.

Piece number 172 = Metropolitan Line (L.T.E.) Working Timetables, No.1 Section No.168, July 1957.

Piece number 173 = Metropolitan Line (L.T.E.) Working Timetables, No.1 Section No.170, June 1958.

Piece number 174 = Metropolitan Line (L.T.E.) Working Timetables, No.172 (Alterations only), Sept 1958.

Piece number 175 = Metropolitan Line (L.T.E.) Working Timetables, No.1 Section No.174 (Sundays), Mar 1959.

Piece number 176 = Metropolitan Line (L.T.E.) Working Timetables, No.1 Section No.181 (with Alterations), Jan 1960.

Piece number 177 = Metropolitan Line (L.T.E.) Working Timetables, No.2 Section No.185, Sept 1960.

Piece number 178 = Metropolitan Line (L.T.E.) Working Timetables, No.1 Section No.188, June 1962.

Piece number 179 = Metropolitan Line (L.T.E.) Working Timetables, No.1 Section No.194, June 1962.

Piece number 180 = Metropolitan Line (L.T.E.) Working Timetables, No.1 Section (Christmas Trains Notice), Dec 1962.

Piece number 181 = Metropolitan Line (L.T.E.) Working Timetables, No.2 Section (Christmas Trains Notice), Dec 1962.

Piece number 182 = Metropolitan Line (L.T.E.) Working Timetables, No.1 Section No.199, June 1963.

Piece number 183 = Metropolitan Line (L.T.E.) Working Timetables, No.2 Section No.204, Sept 1963.

Piece number 184 = Metropolitan Lines, and Metropolitan & Great Central Joint Committee (L.P.T.B.) Passenger Timetables (bound), Nov 1933-Sept 1935.

Piece number 185 = Metropolitan Lines, and Metropolitan & Great Central Joint Committee (L.P.T.B.) Passenger Timetables, Jan 1935.

Piece number 186 = Metropolitan Lines, and Metropolitan & Great Central Joint Committee (L.P.T.B.) Passenger Timetables, Nov 1939.

Piece number 187 = Metropolitan Lines, and Metropolitan & Great Central Joint Committee (L.P.T.B.) Passenger Timetables No.2, Jan 1940.

Piece number 188 = Metropolitan Lines, and Metropolitan & Great Central Joint Committee (L.P.T.B.) Passenger Timetables No.3, Apr 1940.

Piece number 189 = Metropolitan Lines, and Metropolitan & Great Central Joint Committee (L.P.T.B.) Passenger Timetables No.4, Aug 1940.

Piece number 190 = Metropolitan Lines, and Metropolitan & Great Central Joint Committee (L.P.T.B.) Passenger Timetables No.5, Dec 1940.

Piece number 191 = Metropolitan Lines, and Metropolitan & Great Central Joint Committee (LNER/LT Joint) Passenger Timetables No.1, Mar 1941.

Piece number 192 = Metropolitan Lines, and Metropolitan & Great Central Joint Committee (LNER/LT Joint) Passenger Timetables No.2, May 1942.

Piece number 193 = Metropolitan Lines, and Metropolitan & Great Central Joint Committee (LNER/LT Joint) Passenger Timetables No.2, Oct 1946.

Piece number 194 = Edgware, Highgate and Morden Line, and Northern City Line (L.P.T.B.) Working Timetables, No.147, Nov 1933.

Piece number 195 = Edgware, Highgate and Morden Line, and Northern City Line (L.P.T.B.) Working Timetables, - (Northern City Line), Oct 1934.

Piece number 196 = Edgware, Highgate and Morden Line, and Northern City Line (L.P.T.B.) Working Timetables, - (Northern City Line), Feb 1935.

Piece number 197 = Edgware, Highgate and Morden Line, and Northern City Line (L.P.T.B.) Working Timetables, - (Northern City Line), July 1936.

Piece number 198 = Edgware, Highgate and Morden Line, and Northern City Line (L.P.T.B.) Working Timetables, No.153 (Saturdays excepted), Oct 1936.

Piece number 199 = Edgware, Highgate and Morden Line, and Northern City Line (L.P.T.B.) Working Timetables, No.153 (Saturdays only), Oct 1936.

Piece number 200 = Edgware, Highgate and Morden Line, and Northern City Line (L.P.T.B.) Working Timetables, No.154, Mar 1937...

British Transport Historical Records:

RAIL984 = Timetables and Relevant Notices, London Underground Guides and Timetables: *continued....*

Piece number 201 = Edgware, Highgate and Morden Line, and Northern City Line (L.P.T.B.) Working Timetables, No.155 (Sundays), Mar 1937.

Piece number 202 = Edgware, Highgate and Morden Line, and Northern City Line (L.P.T.B.) Working Timetables, - (Northern City Section), July 1937.

Piece number 203 = Northern Line (L.T.E.) Working Timetables, No.186 (inc. BR Eastern Region High Barnet and Edgware branches freight trains), Oct 1949.

Piece number 204 = Northern Line (L.T.E.) Working Timetables, Alterations to Bank Holiday services, Aug 1950.

Piece number 205 = Northern Line (L.T.E.) Working Timetables, No.1, Nov 1951.

Piece number 206 = Northern Line (L.T.E.) Working Timetables, No.2 (inc. BR Eastern Region High Barnet and Edgware branches freight trains), Oct 1952.

Piece number 207 = Northern Line (L.T.E.) Working Timetables, No.2A Northern City section, Nov 1952.

Piece number 208 = Northern Line (L.T.E.) Working Timetables, No.3 (inc. BR Eastern Region High Barnet and Edgware branches freight trains), Nov 1953.

Piece number 209 = Northern Line (L.T.E.) Working Timetables, No.3A Northern City section, Nov 1953.

Piece number 210 = Northern Line (L.T.E.) Working Timetables, No.4 (inc. BR Eastern Region High Barnet and Edgware branches freight trains), June 1954.

Piece number 211 = Northern Line (L.T.E.) Working Timetables, No.5 (inc. BR Eastern Region High Barnet and Edgware branches freight trains), Oct 1954.

Piece number 212 = Northern Line (L.T.E.) Working Timetables, No.6 (inc. BR Eastern Region High Barnet and Edgware branches freight trains), Apr 1955.

Piece number 213 = Northern Line (L.T.E.) Working Timetables, No.8 (inc. BR Eastern Region High Barnet and Edgware branches freight trains), Aug 1956.

Piece number 214 = Northern Line (L.T.E.) Working Timetables, No.9 (inc. BR Eastern Region High Barnet and Edgware branches freight trains), Nov 1957.

Piece number 215 = Northern Line (L.T.E.) Working Timetables, No.9A Northern City section, Nov 1957.

Piece number 216 = Northern Line (L.T.E.) Working Timetables, No.11 (inc. BR Eastern Region High Barnet and Edgware branches freight trains), Mar 1959.

Piece number 217 = Northern Line (L.T.E.) Working Timetables, No.12 (inc. BR Eastern Region High Barnet and Edgware branches freight trains), Sept 1959.

Piece number 218 = Northern Line (L.T.E.) Working Timetables, No.14 (inc. BR Eastern Region High Barnet and Edgware branches freight trains), June 1961.

Piece number 219 = Northern Line (L.T.E.) Working Timetables, No.15 (Saturdays) (inc. BR Eastern Region High Barnet and Edgware branches freight trains), Mar 1962.

Piece number 220 = Northern Line (L.T.E.) Working Timetables, No.15A Northern City section, Mar 1962.

Piece number 221 = Northern Line (L.T.E.) Working Timetables, No.16 (inc. BR Eastern Region High Barnet and Edgware branches freight trains), June 1962.

Piece number 222 = Northern Line (L.T.E.) Working Timetables, Christmas period trains, Dec 1962.

Piece number 223 = Northern Line (L.T.E.) Working Timetables, No.17 (inc. BR Eastern Region High Barnet and Edgware branches freight trains), July 1963.

RAIL1001 = Bye Laws and Regulations, Railways:

Piece number 40 = East London Railway Bye Laws and Regulations, 1875.

Piece number 41 = East London Railway Bye Laws and Regulations 1906 - in poster form.

Piece number 65 = Great Western and Metropolitan Railways, Hammersmith & City Railway, Bye Laws and Regulations, 1927.

Piece number 128 = Great Western Railway: Hammersmith & City Railway, Bye Laws and Regulations, 1875.

Piece number 129 = Great Western Railway: Hammersmith & City Railway, Bye Laws and Regulations, 1905.

Piece number 199 = Metropolitan and London & North Eastern Railways, Bye Laws & Regulations, 1927.

Piece number 200 = Metropolitan and London & North Eastern Railways, Bye Laws & Regulations, 1927.

Piece number 201 = Metropolitan Railway, Bye Laws and Regulations, 1863.

Piece number 202 = Metropolitan Railway, Bye Laws and Regulations, 1874.

Piece number 203 = Metropolitan Railway, Bye Laws and Regulations, 1906.

Piece number 204 = Metropolitan Railway, Bye Laws and Regulations, 1926.

Piece number 276 = Waterloo & City Railway, Bye Laws and Regulations, 1905.

RAIL1005 = Archivist's Historical Miscellanea:

Piece number 36 = Metropolitan and Metropolitan District Railways, including original correspondence.

Piece number 37 = London Underground Centenary Celebrations, 1963.

Piece number 57 = London Underground Railways.

Piece number 134 = Photographs: Stations (includes photograph of Kensington (Addison Road)).

Piece number 220 = Closure of Wotton Tramway.

RAIL1005 = Archivist's Historical Miscellanea: *continued....*

Piece number 259 = Trams and Tramways, including LTE circulars and posters re running of last London tram, 1952.

Piece number 277 = Metropolitan Railway: diagram showing opening and other dates.

Piece number 278 = London Transport railway chronology, issued by London University Extension Courses, 1956.

Piece number 369 = London Transport Victoria Line: press releases, 1951 and 1961-1964.

Piece number 408 = Decimal Currency introduction training material. British Railways Board, British Transport Films and London Transport. Leaflets, course instructor's notes, colour slides etc.

RAIL1006 = Archivist's Historical Miscellanea (York Collection):

Piece number 65 = Centenary of the London Underground, 1863-1963. "Times" Supplement.

RAIL1007 = Record Office Files and Historical Miscellanea:

Piece number 14 = Proposed goods and coal depots alongside Metropolitan District Railway, Hounslow and Harrow Lines. Report by Messrs. Bullough and Richardson.

Piece number 15 = Coal depots in London district, list of, showing tenants.

Piece number 27 = West London Railway. User by Hammersmith & City joint trains.

Piece number 124 = London Underground Railways.

Piece number 210 = London Passenger Transport Board stocks (1933).

Piece number 215 = Whitechapel & Bow Railway.

Piece number 289 = London Passenger Transport Act, 1933. Pooling scheme.

Piece number 482 = Pneumatic Despatch Co. Tube railway for conveyance of mails and parcels.

Piece number 538 = Hammersmith Junction Railway (Metropolitan District Richmond Extension).

RAIL1008 = Various Transport Undertakings, Correspondence and Papers:

Piece number 75 = Letters from W Gravett to I K Brunel about his position as an engineer of the Thames tunnel works (1828).

Piece number 76 = Correspondence with Maudslay Sonsand Field regarding supply of materials for Thames Tunnel (1827).

Piece number 77 = Thames Tunnel progress reports, Check of Staff employed, Accounts for unloading barges (1826-1827).

Piece number 78 = Thames Tunnel - celebrations on completion of a further 20 feet after the inundation etc (1827).

Piece number 79 = Letter from Captain Codrington to I K Brunel referring to Thames Tunnel and to political matters affecting the entrance of the Allied Fleets into the Bay of Navarino (1828).

Piece number 80 = Thames Tunnel: resolutions of the Court of Directors of the tunnel Company; letters from G H Wollaston to the engineers in regard to progress of work; other correspondence, including letters from Francis Giles CE, Joshua Field, Thomas Maudslay, John Rennie (afterwards Sir John); papers of W Smith, Chairman (1826-1830).

RAIL1014 = General Classes, Historical Records and Papers, Great Western Railway Collection:

Piece number 2 (Folio 22) = Hammersmith and City Railway. Prospectus of a proposed railway from Hammersmith to Paddington, thence to Farringdon Street and Finsbury Circus Stations of the Metropolitan Railway (April 1862).

Piece number 37 = Photograph Album. Section 8. Places:
No.49 Underground, Baker Street, booking hall - photograph.
No.50 Underground, Piccadilly Circus, exterior - photograph.

RAIL1017 = Papers Etc - Southern Group:

Piece number 1 = Miscellanea:
Folio 128. London and South Western Railway - Poster as to opening of Waterloo and City Railway, 8 Aug 1898.

Piece number 19 = St James Park Underground Station. Description of train service recording clocks at - Photograph (undated).

RAIL1018 = Historical Records, Papers Etc - London Transport Group:

Piece number 1 = London Transport Group, Certificates:
Folio 1. Associated Acceptances, Ltd - Incorporation, 23 Nov 1928.
Folio 2. Associated Omnibus Co, Ltd - Incorporation, 27 Nov 1900.
Folio 3. Associated Omnibus Co, Ltd - Incorporation, 28 Apr 1922.
Folio 4. Blue Line Coaches, Ltd - Incorporation, 30 July 1930.
Folio 5. Earls Court Grounds, Ltd - Incorporation, 18 Dec 1914.
Folio 6. East Surrey Traction Co, Ltd - Incorporation, 28 Jan 1932.

RAIL1018 = Historical Records, Papers Etc - London Transport Group: *continued....*
Piece number 1 = London Transport Group, Certificates: *continued....*
Folio 7. Eastern General Omnibus Co, Ltd - Incorporation, 24 Feb 1930.
Folio 8. Gearless Motor Omnibus Co, Ltd - Incorporation, 28 Apr 1922.
Folio 9. General Southern Services, Ltd - Incorporation, 19 Mar 1930.
Folio 10. London and Suburban Traction Co, Ltd - Incorporation, 20 Nov 1912.
Folio 11. London and Suburban Traction Co, Ltd - Entitled to commence business, 23 Nov 1912.
Folio 12. London General Omnibus Co, Ltd - Incorporation, 25 July 1912.
Folio 13. London General Omnibus Co, Ltd - Entitled to commence business, 26 July 1912.
Folio 14. Metropolitan District Electric Traction Co, Ltd - Incorporation, 15 July 1901.
Folio 15. Morden Station Garage Limited - Incorporation, 16 Sept 1926.
Folio 16. Northern General Omnibus Co, Ltd - Incorporation, 24 Feb 1930.
Folio 17. Northern General Omnibus Co, Ltd - Change of name to General Northern Services Ltd, 11 July 1930.
Folio 18. Overground Ltd - Incorporation, 10 May 1926.
Folio 19. Railway Equipment and Construction Co, Ltd - Incorporation, 1 Dec 1900.
Folio 20. Red Line Coaches Ltd - Incorporation, 30 July 1930.
Folio 21. Tramways (M.E.T.) Omnibus Co. Ltd - Incorporation, 13 Jan 1912.
Folio 22. Tramways (M.E.T.) Omnibus Co. Ltd - entitled to commence business, 13 Jan 1912.
Folio 23. Tramways (M.E.T.) Omnibus Co. Ltd - registration of Trust Deed and particulars of Debenture Stock, 24 Dec 1913.
Folio 24. Underground Electric Railways Company of London, Ltd - Incorporation, 9 Apr 1902.
Folio 25. Union Construction Co. Ltd - Incorporation, 16 Oct 1901.
Folio 26. Union Construction Co. Ltd - Change of name to Union Construction and Finance Co. Ltd - 15 Feb 1929.
Folio 27. Union Construction Co. Ltd - Registration of Order of Court confirming alteration of objects, 13 Feb 1929.
Folio 28. Union Surplus Lands Co, Ltd - Incorporation, 26 June 1914.
Folio 29. Vanguard Motorbus Co, Ltd - Incorporation, 4 May 1910.
Folio 30. Western General Omnibus Co, Ltd - Incorporation, 24 Feb 1930.
Folio 31. Yellow Line Coaches, Ltd - Incorporation, 30 July 1930.
Piece number 2 = London Transport Group, Miscellanea:
Folio 1. London Transport Christmas Card and New Year Card, 1937 and 1940.
Folio 2. District Railway - details of train services to the Health Exhibition (with map of railway on reverse side), c. 1884.
Folio 3. District Railway - Time Table of trains to and from Mansion House, May 1875.
Folio 4. City and South London Railway - Descriptive booklet of Inauguration by H.R.H. The Prince of Wales, Time Table and Instructions for Locomotives, with copy of letter of later date from G.A.F. Grindle, Nov 1890 and 12 May 1966.
Piece number 3 = London Transport Group, Miscellanea: Ten posters for the coronation of Queen Elizabeth II, 1953.
Piece number 4 = London Transport Group: Sir John Elliot Papers. Private and personal correspondence arising mainly from Sir John's appointment and activities as Chairman of the London Transport Executive of the British Transport Commission, 1953-1959.
   Note: See also AN6/1-6 and 58-63 for various other Sir John Elliot correspondence and papers.
Piece number 5 = London Transport Group: Sir John Elliot Papers. Copies of articles, speeches, etc by Sir John on transport affairs, 1953-1965.
Piece number 6 = London Transport Group: Sir John Elliot Papers. London General Omnibus Company: centenary celebrations, 1956.
Piece number 7 = London Transport Group: Sir John Elliot Papers. Reviews, drawings, etc concerning Sir John's book about Paris during the Revolution, 'The Way of the Tumbrils', 1957-1958.
Piece number 8 = London Transport Group: Sir John Elliot Papers. London Transport bus strike: press cuttings, 1958.
Piece number 9 = London Transport Group: Sir John Elliot Papers. Memorial volume of prints of London Transport posters presented to Sir John on his retirement by the staff of the Publicity Office, 1959.
Piece number 10 = London Transport Group: Sir John Elliot Papers. Miscellaneous correspondence and papers arising from Sir John's membership of the British Airports Authority and the campaign against the proposed Third London Airport at Stanstead, 1967-1968.
Piece number 11 = London Transport Group: Sir John Elliot Papers. Material for memoirs, and obituaries written by Sir John, mostly for 'The Times', c.1949-1983 (2 parts), undated.
Piece number 12 = London Transport Group: Sir John Elliot Papers. Photographs (public and social occasions), c.1951-1967.

British Transport Historical Records:

RAIL1020 = Historical Records Etc - Miscellanea:
Piece number 1 = Volume of miscellaneous notices, circulars, etc:

Folio 64. Passes, Permits and Free Tickets - General instructions to Staff of Metropolitan District, London Electric, City and South London and Central London Railways. - descriptive circular (1 Aug 1929).

Folio 66. Passes on London Transport and Underground Railways - circulars, photographs, lists etc. (1928-1944 and undated). **Note:** Four photographs have been removed from this item and can now be found under CN18/1.

Piece number 8 = Articles of Partnership between Mr George Shillibeer and Mr William Morton, Omnibus and Cabriolet Proprietors, 2 Jan 1832.

Piece number 11 = Volume, includes Picture Postcards issued by various railways including: City and South London Railway.

RAIL1021 = Historical Records, Papers Etc - Miscellanea, North Eastern:
Piece number 11 = Volume of Miscellanea:

Folio 10. Central London Railway - arrangements for trains on opening, 27 July 1900.

Folio 11. Central London Railway - instructions to staff on opening, 25 June 1900.

RAIL1025 = Labour and Staff Matters:
Piece number 141 = London Underground railways: proceedings of inaugural meeting of Staff Council, 1922.

Piece number 142 = L.P.T.B.: scheme for establishment of local staff committees, 1938.

Piece number 143 = L.T.E.: scheme for establishment of staff councils, negotiating committees and wages board, 1957.

Piece number 144 = Negotiating machinery: including London Transport Executive, 1948.

Piece number 168 = Stoppage of London Central Omnibus Service - report by a Court of Enquiry, 1937.

Piece number 198 = The Health of London Central Busmen - Report of Inquiry, 1939.

RAIL1027 = Law Cases and Arbitration:
Piece number 45 = East London Railway Company versus London Brighton and South Coast Railway Company, 1876-1877 (See also RAIL1027/376).

Piece number 52 = Law Cases and Arbitration. Metropolitan Railway Company versus HM Postmaster General, 1878.

Piece number 116 = Law Cases and Arbitration. Great Central Railway Co versus Metropolitan Railway Co, 1898.

Piece number 125 = Metropolitan Railway Co and Corporation of the City of London, 1900-1901.

Piece number 132 = Metropolitan Railway Co and Metropolitan District Railway Co, Arbitration, 1901.

Piece number 133 = Metropolitan Railway Co versus Great Western Railway Co and Corporation of City of London. Volume 1. Petition, Cases and Appendix, 1901.

Piece number 134 = Metropolitan Railway Co versus Great Western Railway Co and Corporation of City of London. Volume 2. Appendix (Plans), 1901.

Piece number 151 = Metropolitan Railway Co versus Great Western and Gt Central Railway Cos, 1904.

Piece number 152 = London Deptford & Greenwich Tramways Co versus London County Council, 1904.

Piece number 210 = London United Tramways Ltd versus London County Council, 1911.

Piece number 229 = Metropolitan Railway Company versus Assessment Committees of Borough of Kensington, Holborn Union (Parish of Finsbury) and Borough of Paddington, 1916.

Piece number 284 = Metropolitan Railway Co versus Delaney, 1921.

Piece number 353 = London Passenger Transport Board versus London County Council. Volume 1. First to Tenth days, 1941.

Piece number 354 = London Passenger Transport Board versus London County Council. Volume 2. 11th to 22nd days and Judgement, 1941.

Piece number 376 = London Brighton and South Coast Railway Co versus East London Railway Company. Court of the Railway Commissioners, 1877.

RAIL1030 = Maps, Plans & Surveys, Railways - Individual Companies (formerly MPS2):
Piece number 151 = Lower Thames Tunnel Railways - Parliamentary deposited plan of proposed railway, Session 1907 (1906).

Piece number 218 = Charing Cross, Euston & Hampstead and Great Northern, Piccadilly & Brompton Railways: Map of Lines and Stations (c.1906).

RAIL1033 = Maps, Plans, Surveys: Towns, Ports and Local Areas:
See section under the heading of Maps.

RAIL1034 = Maps, Plans, Surveys: London and London Transport:
See Section under the heading of Maps.

RAIL1037 = Maps, Plans, Surveys - York Collection:
See Section under the heading of Maps.

RAIL1038 = Board of Trade Railway Department and Ministry of Transport, Proceedings Under Railway and Canal Traffic Acts 1854-1894:

Piece number 34 = Railway Companies proposed classification of merchandise traffic and schedule of maximum rates and charges - Metropolitan Railway Company, (undated).

RAIL1053 = Board of Trade and Ministry of Transport Reports and Returns:

Piece number 209 = Copy of the map defining the metropolitan urban districts under the provisions of the Cheap Train Act 1883 together with copy of certificate as to various railway stations within the said districts, 1883.

Piece number 211 = Workmen's trains and fares, metropolitan lines: Board of Trade reports, 1884-1905.

Piece number 229 = Ventilation of tunnels on Metropolitan Railway: report, 1897.

Piece number 261 = Board of Trade, London Traffic Branch, reports, 1907.

Piece number 262 = Board of Trade, London Traffic Branch, reports, 1908.

Piece number 263 = Board of Trade, London Traffic Branch, reports, 1909.

Piece number 264 = Board of Trade, London Traffic Branch, reports, 1910.

Piece number 265 = Board of Trade, London Traffic Branch, reports, 1911.

Piece number 266 = Board of Trade, London Traffic Branch, reports, 1912.

Piece number 267 = Board of Trade, London Traffic Branch, reports, 1913.

Piece number 268 = Board of Trade, London Traffic Branch, reports, 1914-1915.

Piece number 358 = Railway (London Plan) Committee: final report to Minister of Transport, 1948.

Piece number 359 = London Plan Working Party: British Transport Commission report to Minister of Transport, 1949.

Piece number 364 = Report of Committee of Enquiry into London Transport, 1955.

Piece number 366 = Parking survey of Inner London; interim report, 1956.

Piece number 370 = "Crush-Hour" Travel in Central London: report of the first year's work of the Committee for Staggering of Working Hours in Central London, 1958.

RAIL1057 = Miscellaneous Papers and Records:

Piece number 699 = Post Office Tube Railway (London) - Article from the Railway Gazette, 3 March 1939/ Post Office Green Paper Number 36 - published 1937/Booklet M.12/Map of Route.

Piece number 712 = London Underground Railways - Article from Railway Gazette, 13 December 1940, as to Jubilee of City & South London Railway (For a map showing dates of electrification - see DVL/20 - *but can find no new reference for DVL/20?*).

Piece number 2710 = This Taff Vale Railway file contains a booklet entitled: St John's Church, Cardiff. Divine Service in memory of those Railwaymen who laid down their lives for their Country in the Great War, 1914-1918, Wednesday, May 14th, 1919. This lists the dead of many railway companies, including: East London Railway Joint Committee, page 21 = 4 names.
Metropolitan Railway Company, page 105 = 129 names.
Underground Electric Railways of London, pages 149-152 = 356 names.

Piece number 2809 = Fulham Railway and Fulham and Walham Green Railway. Miscellaneous letters, Act 1865, map 15 Feb 1862, etc (1862-1879).

Piece number 2883 = Railway Centenary 1925. List of possible exhibits: Section 4 is entitled 'Metropolitan Railway'.

Piece number 2909 = Metropolitan Outer Circle Railway. Correspondence, plans, etc. concerning proposed railway, 1881-1889.

Piece number 2920 = Metropolitan District Railway. Extracts from Great Western Railway minutes as to relations, etc. with Metropolitan District Railway, 1899-1905.

Piece number 2972 = Hounslow and Metropolitan Railway. Miscellaneous papers relating to above railway, leading up to licence to cross the Brentford Branch. Plans enclosed, 1881.

Piece number 2974 = Baker Street and Waterloo Railway. Proposed extension to Paddington, 1910.

Piece number 2987 = Uxbridge and Rickmansworth Railway. Miscellaneous papers including arrangements as to abandonment of portion between Uxbridge and Denham, 1861-1898.

Piece number 2993 = Aylesbury and Buckingham Railway. Papers relating to above railway, the construction and use of a joint station at Aylesbury and the train service on the Wycombe line; also settlement with Metropolitan Railway for stock of that Company for outstanding debt, 1866-1893.

Piece number 3007 = Royal Agricultural Society of England. Miscellaneous papers, including meeting and show at Park Royal, 1905.

Piece number 3034 = Malicious Explosions at London Stations. Explosion at Victoria Station, etc. 1884, and attempted explosions at Charing Cross, Paddington and Ludgate Hill Railway Stations. Report by HM Inspectors of Explosives (Command 3972), 1884.

Piece number 3045 = Waterloo and City Railway. Historical file containing prospectus, maps, newspaper accounts of opening, and traffic notice 166 (1898) as to operation, 1882-1901.

RAIL1057 = Miscellaneous Papers and Records: *continued....*

Piece number 3074 = Railway Finance Corporation Limited (RFCL); London Electric Transport Finance Corporation Ltd. (LETFCL). Copy letters between Great Western Company and Ministry of Transport concerning financial arrangements; copy of Railways (Agreement) Act 1935 and Agreement made thereunder; memo and articles of Association of RFCL; copy of London Passenger Transport (Agreement) Act 1935 and Agreement made thereunder; trust deed, etc; and similar papers for LETFCL, 1935.

Piece number 3448 = London County Council Tramways Development. Joint Report of Officers to the Highways Committee, March 10, 1914, copy no.78; includes estimates of cost with large folding map showing existing and proposed routes. Loosely inserted is a further report by the Chief Officer of Tramways, dated March 19, 1914.

Piece number 3450 = The London Tramways Company. Weekly returns of passenger traffic 1870-1887, showing miles run, number of passengers carried, total receipts, average daily receipts. Volume in manuscript (This copy is thought to have been acquired by LCC in 1898), 1870-1877.

Piece number 3451 = London Underground Railways. General strike 1926. A file of instructions to staff May 1926, inc circulars of thanks to volunteers signed by Ashfield; also Hampstead & City Line timetable, 1926.

Piece number 3475 = Construction and Loading Gauge Diagrams. Bound Volume of dimensioned diagrams dated variously 1896-1918, including:

Folio 12 = Metropolitan Railway (New Works).
Folio 15 = Metropolitan Railway (three loading gauges).
Folio 20 = District Railway (undated).

Piece number 3520 = East London Railway. Memorandum prepared by Great Eastern Railway Co. detailing history of ELR and arrangements for its working, dated February 21, 1916; with large scale plan of line and connections, 1916.

Piece number 3534 = The London ABC Railway Rates Book, 1935.

Piece number 3590 = Metropolitan Railway. Permanent Way and Components, engineer's drawings:

1. Conductor rail 100 lb/yd, 1917.
2. Tender form with specification of silicone steel rails, 1910.
3. Cutting & Embankment, 1914.
4. Standard bullhead rail 86 lb/yd (undated).
5. Common Chair, plan & section, 1908.
6. Solid oak treenail, 1899.
7. Coach screw for permanent way (undated).
8. Section of track showing chairs and fastenings, 1911.
9. Tie bolt (Great Northern & City Railway), 1912.
10. 85 lb running rail section (Great Northern & City Railway), 1908.
11. Permanent way (in tunnel) (Great Northern & City Railway), 1900.
12. Teak key (undated).
13. Fishplates for 86 lb rail, 1911.
14. Anti-creep iron at heel of switches, 1914.
15. Illuminated speed-restriction lamp, 1914.
16. Arrangement of warning board, 1914.

Piece number 3738 = Metropolitan Railway, Christmas Card, 1918, among others.

Piece number 3750* = Letters, Railway and Canal companies - specimens of letter heads and some envelopes of English railway companies (includes for example: Aylesbury & Buckingham Railway - 1 item of correspondence showing example of letterhead; Brompton & Piccadilly Circus Railway Company - 1 item of correspondence showing example of letterhead).

Piece number 3751* = Letters, Railway and Canal companies - specimens of letter heads and some envelopes of English railway companies (includes for example: Central London Railway - 5 items of correspondence showing examples of letterheads; City & South London Railway - 2 items of correspondence showing examples of letterheads).

Piece number 3753* = Letters, Railway and Canal companies - specimens of letter heads and some envelopes of English railway companies (includes for example: Great Northern & City Railway - 2 items of correspondence as examples of letterheads).

Piece number 3756* = Letters, Railway and Canal companies - specimens of letter heads and some envelopes of English railway companies (includes for example: London Passenger Transport Board - 7 items of correspondence as examples of letterheads; London Underground Electric Railways - 1 item of correspondence as example of letterhead).

Piece number 3757* = Letters, Railway and Canal companies - specimens of letter heads and some envelopes of English railway companies (includes for example: Metropolitan District Railway - 4 items of correspondence as examples of letterheads; Metropolitan Railway - 6 items of correspondence as examples of letterheads).

* NOTE: Piece numbers 3750-3762 inclusive - in this class - are substantial files containing examples of letterheads in alphabetical order of company name. Only the above five files were sampled to ascertain that there is material of relevance to LT and predecessors. In most instances, the examples are actual items of correspondence, rather than blank letterheads.

RAIL1059 = Miscellaneous Returns and Statistics:

Piece number 44 = London County Council, statistics of the administrative county of London and of the public services carried on therein, together with certain statistics of the adjacent districts, 1906-1907.

Piece number 45 = London County Council, statistics of the administrative county of London and of the public services carried on therein, together with certain statistics of the adjacent districts, 1910-1911.

Piece number 46 = London County Council, statistics of the administrative county of London and of the public services carried on therein, together with certain statistics of the adjacent districts, 1914-1915.

Piece number 47 = London County Council, statistics of the administrative county of London and of the public services carried on therein, together with certain statistics of the adjacent districts, 1920-1921.

Piece number 48 = London County Council, statistics of the administrative county of London and of the public services carried on therein, together with certain statistics of the adjacent districts, 1925-1926.

Piece number 49 = London County Council, statistics of the administrative county of London and of the public services carried on therein, together with certain statistics of the adjacent districts, 1931-1932.

Piece number 50 = London County Council, statistics of the administrative county of London and of the public services carried on therein, together with certain statistics of the adjacent districts, 1935-1937.

RAIL1062 = General Classes, Parliamentary: Railway and Canal Acts (indexed) which **may** contain LT related Acts. Piece numbers 1-4 (inclusive) are the index volumes covering c.1720-1940. Piece numbers 5-137 (inclusive) are the bound acts themselves. Not all acts are bound in however.

RAIL1063 = General Classes, Parliamentary: Special Acts, including some special Railway and Canal Acts (indexed alphabetically) and contains LT related material, for example:

Piece number 386 = London Passenger Transport Board Act, 1933.

Piece number 418 = London Passenger Transport Board Act, 1933.

Piece number 457 = East London Railway Act, 1877.

Piece number 459 = East London Railway Act, 1879.

Piece number 462 = Charing Cross & Waterloo Electric Railway Act 1882 **and** Metropolitan Railway (Kingston & London Railway) Act, 1882 **and** East London Railway Act, 1882.

Piece number 466 = East London Railway Act, 1885.

Piece number 514 = Ealing & South Harrow Railway Act, 1894.

Piece number 547 = London Passenger Transport Board Act, 1947.

Piece number 665 = London Electric Railway Companies Facilities Act, 1915.
and so on....

RAIL1064 = General Classes, Parliamentary: Supplementary Acts (indexed) and contains LT related material, for example:

Piece number 341 = London Passenger Transport - various miscellaneous acts.

RAIL1066 = General Classes, Parliamentary Bills and Minutes of Evidence, etc, Railways and Canals, etc. Contains material relevant to London Transport (including tramway acts), for example:

Piece number 62 = Charing Cross, Euston & Hampstead Railway Act, 1899.

Piece number 74 = Baker Street and Waterloo Railway Act, 1892.

Piece number 75 = Baker Street & Waterloo Railway Act, 1892; Central London Railway Act, 1892.

Piece number 76 = Baker Street & Waterloo Railway Act, 1899.

Piece number 77 = Baker Street & Waterloo Railway Act, 1900.

Piece number 78 = Baker Street & Waterloo Railway Act, 1902; Charing Cross, Euston & Hampstead Railway (No.1 and No.2), 1902.

Piece number 384 = Brompton & Piccadilly Circus Railway, 1897.

Piece number 385 = Brompton & Piccadilly Circus Railway (New Lines etc.), 1902.

Piece number 386 = Brompton & Piccadilly Circus Railway (New Lines), 1902; Central London Railway (New Lines), 1902; Charing Cross, Hammersmith & District Railway (Nos.1 & 2), 1902.

Piece number 623 = Central London Railway Act, 1890.

Piece number 624 = Central London Railway Act, 1890.

Piece number 625 = Central London Railway Act, 1891.

Piece number 626 = Central London Railway Act, 1892

Piece number 627 = Central London Railway - including report of Committee appointed by Board of Trade relating to vibration produced by working of C.L. Railway, 1901-1903 (see also RAIL1124/150).

Piece number 628 = Central London Railway (New Lines), 1902.

Piece number 629 = Central London Railway Act, 1909.

Piece number 630 = Central London Railway Act, 1911.

British Transport Historical Records:

RAIL1066 = General Classes, Parliamentary Bills and Minutes of Evidence, etc, Railways and Canals, etc. Contains material relevant to London Transport (including tramway acts), for example: *continued....*

Piece number 631 = Central London Railway (Fares etc), 1920.
Piece number 632 = Central London Railway Act, 1930.
Piece number 649 = Charing Cross, Euston & Hampstead Railway, 1910.
Piece number 650 = Charing Cross, Hammersmith & District Electric Railway (No.1 and No.2), 1902.
Piece number 690 = City & Brixton Railway, 1898.
   and so on....

RAIL1068 = General Classes, Parliamentary Bills, other than Railways and canals: minutes of evidence etc:

Piece number 48 = Cabs and omnibuses (Metropolis) bill, 1906.
Piece number 70 = Croydon and district electric tramway, 1902.
Piece number 136 = Tramways orders confirmation (No.3), City of London and Metropolitan tramways, 1881.
Piece number 149 = London County Council, Tramways, 1892.
Piece number 150 = London County Council, Tramways and street widening, 1901.
Piece number 151 = London County Council, Tramways and street improvements, 1904.
Piece number 152 = London Passenger Transport Board Bills. Proceedings in Lords and Commons, 1934.
Piece number 158 = South London tramways, 1879.
Piece number 160 = London United tramways, 1898.
Piece number 161 = London United tramways, 1900.
Piece number 162 = London United tramways (light railways extensions), 1901-1903.
Piece number 163 = London United tramways, 1902.
Piece number 165 = West Metropolitan tramways, 1882.
Piece number 166 = West Metropolitan tramways, 1882.
Piece number 199 = Metropolitan electric tramways bill. Proceedings in House of Lords, 1908.

RAIL1071 = Parliamentary Deposited Plans:

Piece number 59 = Central London Railway, 1891.
Piece number 60 = Oxford Street and City Railway, 1863-1864.
Piece number 61 = Charing Cross and Euston Railway, 1885.
Piece number 62 = London Central electric railway, 1883.
Piece number 63 = London Central subway railway, 1888.
Piece number 64 = Central Metropolitan railway, 1882.
Piece number 65 = Marble Arch, Regents Circus and City subway, 1885.
Piece number 66 = Mid London electric railway, 1884.
Piece number 67 = London Central subway, 1884.
Piece number 68 = King's Cross, Charing Cross and Waterloo subway, 1885.
Piece number 69 = City and West End railway, 1872-1873.
Piece number 70 = Metropolitan and Regents Circus railway, 1877-1878.

RAIL1075 = General Classes, Prospectuses etc. of Railway and Other Undertakings:

Piece number 57 = Metropolitan Railway (Paddington to the Post Office) with sundry letters, 1854-1855.
Piece number 58 = Metropolitan Railways Junction Railway - plan of proposed (1845?).
Piece number 105 = Central London Railway, 21 June 1895.
Piece number 115 = East London Railway - Prospectus and application form for part of £400,000 Preference Stock, 31 October 1873-1874.
Piece number 127 = Great Northern and City Railway to open 8 Feb 1904 - with map, 6 Feb 1904.
Piece number 134 = Harrow and Uxbridge Railway, 29 November 1899.
Piece number 138 = Joint Railways and City Terminus Railway - with map (1856).
Piece number 142 = Latimer Road and Acton Railway - extension to Acton of Hammersmith and City (Metropolitan) Railway - two prospectuses dated October and November with enclosures, 1884.
Piece number 161 = Metropolitan District Railway, 3 Mar 1932.
Piece number 162 = Metropolitan General Grand Junction Railways - with map (undated).
Piece number 163 = Metropolitan Railway. Paddington to the Post Office - with map, Feb 1855.
Piece number 164 = Metropolitan Railway - 7 Mar 1932.
Piece number 214 = Waterloo and City Railway - (two copies) 17 Mar 1894.
Piece number 215 = Waterloo and Whitehall Railway from Waterloo to Charing Cross Pneumatic System - with map, Abstract of notes of adjourned second half yearly meeting 1866, and Report and Statement of Accounts for 1867 and 1868 (1865-1868).
Piece number 249 = General Map of London shewing the street improvements and Railway Termini (Thames Embankment Railway) as suggested by J Pennethorne, Esq., Architect to the Commissioners of H.M. Woods and Forests, 1846.

British Transport Historical Records:

RAIL1075 = General Classes, Prospectuses etc. of Railway and Other Undertakings: *continued....*

Piece number 250 = Map of London shewing various railways, c.1859.

Piece number 251 = London Universal Railway plotted on map of London as drawn for the Post Office Directory, 1860.

Piece number 258 = Metropolitan Railway - map, 1860.

Piece number 270 = Pneumatic Despatch Company - Report to the First Ordinary General Meeting, 1 Aug 1861.

Piece number 284 = Watford Rickmansworth and Uxbridge Railway - map, 1860.

Piece number 308 = East London Railway - Two copies of prospectus, one with form of application for shares, 1865.

Piece number 341 = Permanent London Publicity Company - Contract form with list of protected stations, 1866.

Piece number 361 = Waterloo and Whitehall Railway (Pneumatic System) - Prospectus, 23 Feb 1865.

Piece number 369 = Collection of Colonel Sir Gerard Smith K.C.M.G.
Folio 2 = City and Richmond Railway - prospectus with map (c.1835).

Piece number 418 = Metropolitan Railway Suspension Bridge - prospectus (Designed by Captain Samuel Brown R.N., K.H., etc.) undated.

RAIL1076 = General Classes, Prospectuses: Railway and other undertakings (York Collection), contains LT related material as follows:

Piece number 1 = Prospectuses and Associated Papers:
Folio 27 = Metropolitan and St John's Wood Railway, Jan 1865.
Folio 45 = Waterloo and Whitehall Railway (Pneumatic System), 8 June 1865.

Piece number 7 = Central London Railway, 21 June 1895.

RAIL1078 = General Classes, Prospectuses: Omnibus and other companies:

Piece number 2 = Amalgamated Motor Bus Co. Ltd (operating in London).

Piece number 4 = Associated Omnibus Co. Ltd.

Piece number 9 = Gearless Motor Omnibus Co. Ltd.

Piece number 10 = Great Eastern London Motor Omnibus Co. Ltd.

Piece number 11 = London and District Motor Bus Co. Ltd.

Piece number 12 = London and South Coast Motor Service, Ltd.

Piece number 13 = London Central Motor Omnibus Co Ltd.

Piece number 14 = London Electrobus Co. Ltd.

Piece number 15 = London Motor Omnibus Co. Ltd.

Piece number 16 = London Omnibus Co. Ltd (1855).

Piece number 17 = London Power Omnibus Co Ltd.

Piece number 18 = London Power Omnibus Co Ltd.

Piece number 19 = London Standard Motor Omnibus Co. Ltd.

Piece number 20 = London Standard Motor Omnibus Co. Ltd.

Piece number 27 = Premier Omnibus Co. Ltd.

Piece number 30 = Star Omnibus Co. London, Ltd.

Piece number 31 = Thomas Tilling Ltd.

Piece number 32 = Vanguard Motorbus Co. Ltd.

Piece number 33 = General Tramway Co. Ltd (undated).

Piece number 34 = London Omnibus Tramway Co. Ltd, 1857.

Piece number 48 = London General Omnibus Co. Ltd "Return of Types of Motor Stage Carriages Approved", giving date, proprietor or company, address, and descriptive details of vehicles. "Information obtained by Mr Mills", 1921.

RAIL1080 = Railway Clearing House, Minutes and Reports:

Piece number 606 = London Passenger Transport Board and Main Line Railway Companies: Accounts Advisory Committees, 1934-1945.

Piece number 607 = London Passenger Transport Board and Main Line Railway Companies: Fares & Services Advisory Committees, 1934-1939.

Piece number 608 = London Passenger Transport Board and Main Line Railway Companies: Traffic Advisory Committee, 1934-1946.

Piece number 609 = London Passenger Transport Board and Main Line Railway Companies: Technical Committee, 1937-1946.

RAIL1085 = Railway Clearing House, Miscellaneous Books and Records:

Piece number 142 = Railway, London Transport and Docks and Inland Waterways Executives. Code of practice for lighting, heating, and ventilation of Railway and other premises with a memorandum on fluorescent lighting, 1949.

British Transport Historical Records:

RAIL1097 = Railway Clearing House, Membership Covenants:
Piece number 106 = Metropolitan Railway, 1920.
Piece number 116 = Metropolitan District Railway, 1928.

RAIL1101 = Railway Rates Tribunal, Railway Company Papers:
Piece number 8 = London area passenger and freight charges: application by LPTB, GWR, LMSR, LNER and SR for 5% increase - Proceedings and judgement, 1939.
Piece number 9 = Ditto - Briefs, diagrams, correspondence, posters and other papers, Nos. 1-23, and un-numbered.
Piece number 10 = ditto - ditto, Nos. 24-31 and 33, and un-numbered.
Piece number 11 = ditto - ditto, No. 32.
Piece number 12 = ditto - ditto, un-numbered.

RAIL1110 = Reports and Accounts, Railway companies:
Piece number 9 = Aylesbury & Buckingham Railway, 1873-1885.
Piece number 10 = Aylesbury & Buckingham Railway, 1886-1890.
Piece number 11 = Aylesbury Railway, 1836-1846.
Piece number 12 = Baker Street & Waterloo Railway, 1899-1910./Charing Cross Euston & Hampstead Railway, 1897-1910./Great Northern, Piccadilly & Brompton Railway, 1899-1910.
Piece number 64 = Central London Railway, 1895-1932.
Piece number 69 = City & South London Railway, 1886-1933.
Piece number 114 = East London Railway, 1865-1899.
Piece number 115 = East London Railway, 1900-1924.
Piece number 116 = East London Railway Joint Committee (accounts only), 1913-1932.
Piece number 169 = Great Northern & City Railway, 1898-1912.
Piece number 171 = Great Northern, Piccadilly & Brompton Railway, 1903-1910.
Piece number 207 = Collection containing Metropolitan & Great Central Joint Committee, 1908-1911.
Piece number 211 = Hammersmith & City Railway Joint Committee (G.W. & Metropolitan), 1878-1938.
Piece number 221 = Hammersmith & City Railway, 1866-1895.
Piece number 241 = Latimer Road & Acton Railway, 1884-1891.
Piece number 295 = London Electric Railway, 1910-1932.
Piece number 296 = London Passenger Transport Board, 1934-1947.
Piece number 313 = Metropolitan & District Joint Committee (City Lines and Extensions), 1913-1933.
Piece number 314 = Metropolitan & Great Central Joint Committee, 1906-1943.
Piece number 315 = Metropolitan District Railway, 1865-1900.
Piece number 316 = Metropolitan District Railway Co, 1901-1933.
Piece number 317 = Metropolitan Railway, 1853-1893.
Piece number 318 = Metropolitan Railway, 1894-1933.
Piece number 319 = Metropolitan & St John's Wood Railway, 1873-1881./Metropolitan Railway, 1863-1907.
Piece number 465 = Underground Electric Railway Company of London, 1902-1933.
Piece number 483 = Waterloo & City Railway, 1894-1906.
Piece number 484 = Waterloo & City Railway (with prospectus), 1894-1904.
Piece number 513 = Whitechapel & Bow Railway, 1899-1932./Whitechapel & Bow Railway Joint Committee, 1902-1932.
Piece number 524 = Metropolitan and L.&.N.E. Railways (Watford Joint Railway Committee), 1924-1939.

RAIL1114 = Reports and Accounts, Hotel, Road Transport and other companies:
Piece number 15 = London Electric Finance Corporation Ltd, 1935-1938.
Piece number 29 = London & Suburban Traction Co Ltd, 1913-1933.
Piece number 30 = LCC Tramways: tramway accounts (1904-1911) and steamboats accounts (1905-1909).
Piece number 31 = LCC Tramways, 1901-1904 and 1911-1927.
Piece number 32 = LCC Tramways, 1928-1933.
Piece number 33 = London General Omnibus Company Ltd (Compagnie Generale des Omnibus de Londres), written in French - translated from English Reports after 1859. 1857-1911.
Piece number 34 = London General Omnibus Company Ltd, 1859-1875.
Piece number 35 = London General Omnibus Company Ltd, 1876-1891.
Piece number 36 = London General Omnibus Company Ltd, 1892-1912.
Piece number 37 = London General Omnibus Company Ltd, 1912-1933.
Piece number 38 = London Road Car Company Ltd, 1883-1908.
Piece number 39 = London United Tramways Ltd, 1902-1933.
Piece number 40 = Metropolitan Electric Tramways Ltd, 1902-1933.
Piece number 41 = North Metropolitan Tramways Co, 1870-1912.
Piece number 42 = South Metropolitan Electric Tramways and Lighting Co. Ltd, 1907-1933.
Piece number 43 = Tower Co Ltd, 1891-1907.
Piece number 44 = Tramways (MET) Omnibus Co. Ltd, 1912-1933.

RAIL1114 = Reports and Accounts, Hotel, Road Transport and other companies: *continued....*

Piece numbers 45-71 (inclusive) contain Omnibus, traction, and tramway companies of Great Britain: series of annual guard books of reports and accounts, each prefaced with a list of contents. Contains material relating to predecessors of London Transport, *for example:* **Piece number 45** is a guard book for 1913, and contains among others, annual reports for: Associated Omnibus Company, Ltd; British Automobile Traction, Ltd; Gearless Motor Omnibus Company, Ltd; London General Omnibus Company, Ltd; London & Suburban Traction Company, Ltd; London United Tramways, Ltd; Metropolitan Electric Tramways, Ltd; Metropolitan Steam Omnibus Company, Ltd; National Steam Car Company, Ltd; New Central Omnibus Company, Ltd; South Metropolitan Electric Tramways & Lighting Co. Ltd; Thomas Tilling, Ltd; Tramways (M.E.T.) Omnibus Company, Ltd; East Ham County Borough Tramways; Leyton Urban District Council Tramways; West Ham County Borough Tramways.

RAIL1115 = Reports and Accounts, Welfare:
Piece number 48 = Metropolitan Railway Pension Fund, 1915-1932.

RAIL1119 = Reports of Commissions:
Piece number 7 = Metropolitan railways and termini: report with evidence, 1846.
Piece number 8 = Ditto, plans and sections, 1846.
Piece number 51 = London Traffic: appendices and tables, 1904.
Piece number 52 = London Traffic: report, Vol.1, 1905.
Piece number 53 = London Traffic: minutes of evidence, Vol.2, 1905.
Piece number 54 = London Traffic: appendices, Vol.3, 1905.
Piece number 55 = London Traffic: appendices, Vol.4, 1906.
Piece number 56 = London Traffic: maps and diagrams, Vol.5, 1906.
Piece number 57 = London Traffic: maps and diagrams, Vol.6, 1906.
Piece number 58 = London Traffic: report (with maps and diagrams), Vol.7, 1905.
Piece number 59 = London Traffic: appendix and maps, Vol.8, 1905.
Piece number 105 = London Transport, 1919.
Piece number 127 = London cross-river traffic: report, 1926.
Piece number 128 = London cross-river traffic: evidence and appendices, 1926.
Piece number 129 = London squares, 1928.

RAIL1124 = Reports of Committees:
Piece number 55 = Metropolitan communications: report (with evidence), 1855.
Piece number 66 = Metropolitan railways communications: House of Lords Committee's first to third reports, with index; and joint committee report, 1863-1864.
Piece number 67 = Metropolitan railway communication: joint report, Colonel Yolland's reports for 1863 and 1864, and sundry Board of Trade reports, 1863-1864.
Piece number 100 = Tramways: reports (with evidence), 1877-1879.
Piece number 121 = Metropolitan Railway (Park Railway and Parliament Street Improvement Bill): report (with evidence), 1884.
Piece number 133 = Electric and cable railways (metropolis): report and evidence (South Eastern Railway copy) (incomplete), 1892.
Piece number 138 = Metropolitan Railway, ventilation of tunnels: report (with evidence), 1897.
Piece number 147 = London underground railways: report (with evidence), 1901.
Piece number 150 = Central London Railway (Vibration): report, 1902 (see also RAIL1066/627).
Piece number 161 = Cabs and Omnibuses (Metropolis) Bill: report (with evidence), 1906.
Piece number 173 = Post Office (London) Railway Bill: report (with evidence), 1913.
Piece number 178 = Road Locomotives and heavy motor cars: exhibits to evidence submitted to Local Government Board committee by London General Omnibus Co., 1916.
Piece number 188 = Transport (Metropolitan Area): proofs of evidence submitted on behalf of Underground group of companies (three items), 1919.
Piece number 200 = London Traffic: report of advisory committee, 1920.
Piece number 216 = Charing Cross bridge: various reports and papers, 1924-1936.
Piece number 217 = Travelling facilities to and from north and north east London: report (with evidence) of London and Home Counties Traffic Advisory Committee, 1926.
Piece number 218 = Travelling Facilities to and from South-East London: report (with evidence) of London and Home Counties Traffic Advisory Committee, 1926.
Piece number 219 = London and Home Counties Traffic Advisory Committee: first annual report, for the year 1925 (1926).
Piece number 224 = Co-ordination of passenger transport facilities in London Traffic Area: report of London and Home Counties Traffic Advisory Committee, 1927.
Piece number 238 = City airport (King's Cross): scheme proposed by C W Glover and Partners, 1931.
Piece number 240 = London motor coach services: first report of committee of enquiry, 1932.

RAIL1124 = Reports of Committees: *continued....*

Piece number 241 = London motor coach services: final report of committee of enquiry, 1933.

Piece number 250 = Evacuation: report of committee of M.P.'s (Command 5837), 1938.

Piece number 252 = Highway development survey (Greater London): report by Sir Charles Bressey and Sir Edwin Lutyens, 1938.

Piece number 263 = London coal tipping control: interim report by Minister of Fuel and Power, 1945.

Piece number 264 = London regional planning: reports of advisory committee and of technical sub-committee (H.M.S.O.), 1946.

Piece number 267 = Railway (London Plan) Committee and London Plan Working Party: reports, 1946-1948.

Piece number 269 = London Planning Administration Committee: report to Minister of Town and Country Planning (H.M.S.O.), 1949.

RAIL1134 = Rule Books:

Piece number 3 = Baker Street & Waterloo Railway, 1906.

Piece number 45 = District Railway, 1872.

Piece number 83 = Great Northern, Piccadilly & Brompton Railway, 1906.

Piece number 132 = Great Western Railway - Ealing and Shepherds Bush section. Supplement to rules and regulations, 1920.

Piece number 133 = Great Western Railway - Ealing and Shepherds Bush section. Supplement to rules and regulations, 1927.

Piece number 307 = London County Council Tramways. Rules and regulations for motormen, 1911.

Piece number 308 = London County Council Tramways. Rules and regulations for motormen, 1928.

Piece number 309 = London Electric Railway, Central London Railway, City & South London Railway, Ealing & Shepherds Bush Railway, 1919.

Piece number 344 = Metropolitan and Great Central Joint Committee, 1920.

Piece number 345 = Metropolitan and London & North Eastern Railway (Watford Joint Railway Committee), 1932-1936.

Piece number 346 = Metropolitan District Railway, 1881.

Piece number 347 = Metropolitan District Railway, 1904.

Piece number 348 = Metropolitan Railway, General instructions, 1868.

Piece number 349 = Metropolitan Railway, Rules and regulations, 1874.

Piece number 350 = Metropolitan Railway, Rules and regulations, 1877.

Piece number 351 = Metropolitan Railway, Rules and regulations, 1904.

Piece number 352 = Metropolitan Railway, Rules and regulations, 1921.

Piece number 353 = Metropolitan Railway, Rules and regulations, 1933.

Piece number 354 = Great Western, Metropolitan and West London Railways Electric traction. Supplement to Metropolitan Co.'s appendix No.2 to the working timetable dated Apr. 1912.

Piece number 512 = Southern Railway, Waterloo & City Line, 1924.

Piece number 530 = Underground, Metropolitan District, London Electric and Central London Railways. Instructions for protection of employees and movement of vehicles, undated.

RAIL1135 = Rules and Regulations, General Instructions and Appendices to Working Timetables: General Instructions to Staff:

Piece number 9 = District Railway, General, 1896.

Piece number 10 = District Railway, Opening of Whitechapel and Bow Joint Line, 1902.

Piece number 86 = Great Western Railway Co., London and North Eastern Railway Co, London Midland and Scottish Railway Co., Southern Railway Co., London Passenger Transport Board. Air Raid Precautions, 1942.

Piece number 358 = London Passenger Transport Board. Operation of Ticket Offices. Examination, Cancellation and Collection of Tickets. Charging of Excess Fares, 1936.

Piece number 359 = London Passenger Transport Board. Operation of Ticket Offices. Cloakroom Arrangements and Charges. Issue of Weekly and Season Tickets. Examination, Cancellation and Collection of Tickets. Charging of Excess Fares. Disposal of Lost Property, 1939.

Piece number 360 = London Passenger Transport Board. Supplementary Wartime Instructions to Ticket Office and Collecting Staff, 1943.

Piece number 361 = London Passenger Transport Board. Chiswick Works Employees, 1937.

Piece number 362 = London Passenger Transport Board. Garage Inside Staff, 1937.

Piece number 363 = London Passenger Transport Board. Traction Current Supply, 1938.

Piece number 364 = London Passenger Transport Board. London Aircraft Production. Employees (c.1941).

Piece number 371 = Metropolitan Railway, Neasden Power Station, 1905.

Piece number 372 = Metropolitan Railway, Train Signalling by Electric Lock and Block, System between St. Pancras Tunnel Box, Great Northern East and West Boxes, Holborn Low Level and Moorgate Street (Widened Lines) With Special Instruction Modifying the Working between King's Cross and Farringdon Street where Track Circuiting has been provided, 1914.

Piece number 373 = Metropolitan Railway, Naval and Military Special Traffic Arrangements, 1915.

RAIL1135 = Rules and Regulations, General Instructions and Appendices to Working Timetables: General Instructions to Staff: *continued....*

Piece number 527 = Southern Railway, Waterloo and City Line, 1940.

Piece number 538 = Underground Electric Railways of London. Excess Fares, Ticket Availability, Season Tickets, Charges for Accompanied Merchandise. Dogs, Bicycles, Mailcarts etc. Cloakroom Arrangements and Lost Property charges, 1928.

RAIL1136 = Rules and Regulations, General Instructions, and Appendices to Railway Companies' Working Timetables, Etc:

Piece number 28 = Great Western Railway Nos.2 and 17 Sections. Hammersmith and City Line, Kensington (Olympia), Ealing Broadway and Liverpool Street via Wood Lane. Also West London and West London Extension Joint Railway, 1939.

Piece number 73 = London Midland and Scottish Railway. Supplementary Appendix Instructions, Working of Trains over the Electrified Line between Barking and Upminster. Also Multiple Aspect Automatic and Semi-Automatic Colour-Light Signalling, 1932.

Piece number 88 = London Transport, Section 1 of Appendix, 1936.

Piece number 92 = Metropolitan District Railway, 1930.

Piece number 121 = Underground Electric Railways of London, 1928.

Piece number 122 = Underground Electric Railways of London, Supplement, 1930.

RAIL1140 = Shareholders' Guides and Manuals, Bradshaw's 1848-1923 (these guides, published annually from 1848-1923, include much of interest on companies which were later absorbed into the London Passenger Transport Board in 1933, together with joint lines).

RAIL1149 = Special Collections: I. K. Brunel Collection:

Piece number 13 = Item including some information on the Thames Tunnel (undated).

RAIL1158 = Stock and Share Certificates:

Piece number 3 = Miscellaneous, including London and North Eastern, Southern, and subsidiary companies' certificates. BTC Archivist's collection, Indexed. Various dates:

Folio 67. Waterloo and City Railway Company, Debenture Stock - Certificate number 23 - not issued.

Part II. The Metropolitan Saloon Omnibus Company, Limited, Share Certificate No.4217 dated 4 March 1857.

Part III. Compagnie Generale Des Omnibus De Londres - Bearer Share Certificate, First Series issued in Paris.

RAIL1167 = Railway Sidings Agreements:

Piece number 13 = Aylesbury: Metropolitan and Great Central Joint Committee and International Alloys Ltd: terminated 31 Jan 1972 (1942).

Piece number 14 = Aylesbury: Metropolitan and Great Central Joint Committee and International Alloys Ltd: terminated 31 Jan 1972 (1945).

Piece number 16 = Aylesbury: Great Western and Great Central Railways Joint Committee and Metropolitan and Great Central Joint Committee: agreement with Corporation of Aylesbury (1920-1940).

Piece number 17 = Aylesbury: Great Western and Great Central Railways Joint Committee and Metropolitan and Great Central Joint Committee: agreement with Corporation of Aylesbury (1920; 1936).

Piece number 83 = Chelsea Basin: LMS, GWR and London Passenger Transport Board (1936-1945).

Piece number 103 = Earls Court: Midland Railway Company and Gigantic Wheel and Recreation Tower Company Ltd, 1896.

Piece number 253 = Shepherds Bush: LNWR and GWR and Central London Railway Company, 1900.

Piece number 272 = Stonebridge Park: Midland Railway Company and North Metropolitan Electric Power Supply Company, 1905-1910.

Piece number 280 = Upper Holloway: Midland Railway Company and London County Council, 1908.

Piece number 311 = Wendover: Metropolitan and Great Central Joint Committee and President of Air Council, 1923-1961.

Piece number 344 = South Ruislip: British Transport Commission and Express Dairy Co (London) Ltd, 1906-1966.

RAIL1172 = Railway Staff Conference, Correspondence and Papers:

Piece number 88 = Tramcar drivers, Sept 1919 to June 1921.

Piece number 93 = Definition of London termini: Metropolitan Railway's (MetR) enquiry with regard to its stations, April 1920.

Piece number 178 = Railway Shopmen. IC decision no 846, payment of electrical workers engaged on new work, London Electric Railway (LER), Mar 1923 - Oct 1931.

Piece number 179 = Railway Shopmen. IC decision no 844, grading and rating of pipe fitters, LER, Oct 1923.

RAIL1172 = Railway Staff Conference, Correspondence and Papers: *continued....*

Piece number 329 = Railway Shopmen. IC decision no 1143 and 1153, substation attendants in charge of sub-stations, stokers, Waterloo and City Railway power station, July 1924 - Jan 1926.

Piece number 952 = Extension of NWB Scottish Award to England and Wales, Feb 1922 - Oct 1922 (includes memorandum of agreement between Metropolitan District Railway Company, LER, City and South London Railway Company, Central London Railway Company, NUR and RCA, dated 22 Mar 1922).

Piece number 953 = Extension of NWB Scottish Award to England and Wales, Feb 1922 - Oct 1922 (includes memorandum of agreement between Metropolitan District Railway Company, LER, City and South London Railway Company, Central London Railway Company, NUR and RCA, Mar 1923 - Dec 1923).

Piece number 954 = Extension of NWB Scottish Award to England and Wales, Feb 1922 - Oct 1922 (includes memorandum of agreement between Metropolitan District Railway Company, LER, City and South London Railway Company, Central London Railway Company, NUR and RCA, Mar 1924 - Feb 1957).

Piece number 1145 = Railway Electrical Staff. Rates of pay: London Passenger Transport Board (LPTB), includes IC decision no 1617, Nov 1930 - Nov 1939.

Piece number 1153 = Railway Electrical Staff. Claim for increase of 11/- per week, LPTB, includes IC decision no 1574, Oct 1933-Sept 1938.

Piece number 1159 = Railway Electrical Staff. Application for increase of 1d per hour to shift workers, LPTB, Jan 1941 - July 1941.

Piece number 1200 = Railway Police: MetR, Oct 1920 - Feb 1921.

Piece number 1249 = National Union of Railwaymen and Railway Clerks Association Programmes: Rates of pay and conditions of service: professional and technical staff of main line companies and LPTB (later London Transport Executive), Aug 1940 - July 1944.

Piece number 1250 = National Union of Railwaymen and Railway Clerks Association Programmes: Rates of pay and conditions of service: professional and technical staff of main line companies and LPTB (later London Transport Executive), July 1944 - Sept 1948.

Piece number 1251 = National Union of Railwaymen and Railway Clerks Association Programmes: Rates of pay and conditions of service: professional and technical staff of main line companies and LPTB (later London Transport Executive), Feb 1947 - May 1947.

Piece number 1266 = National Union of Railwaymen and Railway Clerks Association Programmes: Rates of pay and conditions of service: London General Omnibus Co, drivers and conductors; includes memoranda of agreements between London General Omnibus Co Ltd, Thomas Tilling Ltd (London Undertaking) & British Automobile Traction Co Ltd and TGWU, dated 21 Nov 1921 and 4 Sept 1925 (draft).

Piece number 1677 = Machinery of Negotiation: Compulsory arbitration during war-time: arbitration tribunal, LPTB; strikes and lock-outs, amendment of defence regulations, June 1940 - June 1959.

Piece number 1688 = Machinery of Negotiation: Rates of pay: agreements between LPTB and TGWU omnibus and coach drivers, conductors and shop staff; agreement for increased pay for railway engineering shop and electrical engineering shop staffs, Nov 1933 - Nov 1938.

Piece number 1690 = Machinery of Negotiation: Transfer of parcels business from LPTB (MetR) to main line companies: includes list dated Mar 1934 of staff with their addresses, Dec 1933 - Sept 1934.

Piece number 1692 = Rates of pay and conditions of service: motor omnibus drivers and conductors in inner London area, Oct 1932 - Jan 1934.

RAIL1174 = Superannuation and Welfare Records, Railway Companies and other transport organisations:

Piece number 9 = Metropolitan Railway (MetR), rules, statement of accounts, reports, correspondence for the following staff associations and clubs (with papers relating to their future administration under the London Passenger Transport Board).

Engineer and Railway Volunteer Staff Corps.
Old Comrades' Association.
Mutual Provident and Approved Society.
Clerks' Levy Fund.
Benevolent Fund.
Employees' Disablement and Levy Fund.
Athletic Association.
Neasden Works, Hospital Saturday Fund.
Neasden Works, Surgical Aid Fund.
Neasden Works, Convalescent Homes Fund.
Superannuation Auxiliary Fund.
Central Charities Fund.
No.89 (MetR) division, St John Ambulance Brigade.
Supplementary Pension Fund.
Ambulance Centre Pension Fund.
various London County Council Tramways Staff Associations.
(This item is shown as 'Wanting')

Piece number 22 = Railway Savings Bank. Copies of Rules: 1868 - 1941 (includes MetR, 1880).

Piece number 251 = Rule Books, 1891-1907 (includes MetR Pension Fund, 1907).

MAPS:

MPS2 = see RAIL1030

MPS5 = Maps, Plans, Surveys: Towns, Ports and Local Areas (to be re-listed as RAIL1033 during 1997/98):

Piece number 59 = Hammersmith Parish, 1853.

Piece number 201 = Maps (6 inches to 1 mile) of areas including the following settlements: - Hounslow, Barnes, Neasden, Harrow, c.1910.

Piece number 379 = O.S. Map (Scale 6 inches to 1 mile) of Inner London, including the city, and the Middlesex, Kent, and Surrey shores of the River Thames from Westminster to the Isle of Dogs, superimposed in colour, 1880.

Piece number 380 = O.S. Map (Scale 5 feet to 1 mile) of parts of Finsbury, Bishopsgate Ward, and the City around Finsbury Circus, 1896.

Piece number 381 = Engraved Map (Scale 5 feet to 1 mile) of part of City of London, c.1908.

MPS6 = Maps, Plans, Surveys: London and London Transport (to be re-listed as RAIL1034 during 1997/98):

Piece number 11 = London Underground Electric Railways - Lines open and in construction, and proposed, 1905.

Piece number 12 = Stanford's Map of Metropolitan Railways, Tramways, etc. 1906.

Piece number 14 = London Depots - Midland Railway, 1906.

Piece number 15 = Stanford's 4 inch Map of West London, 1907.

Piece number 16 = Stanford's Map of Metropolitan Railways, Tramways, etc, 1911.

Piece number 17 = London Passenger Transport Board's area map (three miles to an inch), 1933.

Piece number 18 = London Passenger Transport Board's area map (one mile to an inch), 1933.

Piece number 19 = Sundry L.P.T.B. maps showing Train, Tube, Bus and Tram routes, 1933 & 1934.

Piece number 20 = Sundry L.P.T.B. maps showing Train, Tube, Bus and Tram routes, 1935.

Piece number 21 = Davies New Map of London and environs - Published by Stanford, 1880.

Piece number 24 = Ordnance sheet of central London showing property belonging to railway companies, 1897.

Piece number 28 = Copy of Macaulay's London Railways simplified and explained, showing the various lines and their connections. Published by C. Smith & Son, Charing Cross, c.1875.

Piece number 29 = A new map of the Metropolitan Railways, Tramways, etc. (deposited session 1868), 1868.

Piece number 30 = Kelly's map of London and Suburbs, undated.

Piece number 31 = District Map of Greater London and environs, 2nd edition, 1908.

Piece number 32 = Underground Electric Railways of London Limited, 1904.

Piece number 33 = London Tube Railways, 1907.

Piece number 40 = A collection of loose maps showing roads, railways, tramways, parishes, etc., etc. of London and environs, 1904.

Piece number 41 = Three maps showing the growth of railway route mileage for the years 1845, 1860, 1880 and 1900, and railway schemes for the Metropolis 1855-1885 and 1885-1903 inclusive, 1904.

Piece number 42 = Guard Book containing a collection of Bus and Underground Maps issued by the London General Omnibus Company, Underground Railways of London, London Passenger Transport Board and London Transport executive, from 1910 onwards.

Piece number 43 = District Railway Map of London (5th edition), c.1892-5.

Piece number 44 = Stanford's new 2 inch map of London and its environs, 1932.

Piece number 45 = Map of the City of London (West Area) and the surrounding boroughs (Scale 25" to 1 mile), c.1916.

Piece number 46 = Map showing the area under the control of the London Passenger Transport Board, also the boundaries of the London Traffic Area and Metropolitan Traffic Area (Scale 3 miles to 1 inch), 1933.

Piece number 47 = Map of the Whitechapel, London area (including the Tower of London), Scale: 88 feet to 1 inch, 1875.

Piece number 49 = Stanford's special map of the railways and stations in London and its environs; accompanied by a guide to the metropolitan railways, omnibus and steam-boat routes, 1869.

Piece number 51 = Map of London railways simplified and explained (pub. by C. Smith & Son), 1873.

Piece number 52 = "District" Railway Map of London (with list of stations on the "Inner" "Middle" and "Outer" Circle lines, c.1873.

Piece number 53 = Map of London and Suburbs, showing main line railways, and connecting Underground railways, Mch.1935.

Piece number 54 = London Transport's map of all routes, - road and rail, 1934.

Piece number 58 = Stanford's 6 inch Library Map of London and its Suburbs, showing proposed Metropolitan Railways and Improvements, 1864.

Piece number 59 = Stanford's Map of Railways and Electric Tramways in London and its environs, 1907.

British Transport Historical Records:

MPS6 = Maps, Plans, Surveys: London and London Transport **(to be re-listed as RAIL1034 during 1997/98):** *continued....*

Piece number 61 = Proposed Underground Goods Railways - Map compiled by Messrs Whitley and Carkeet-James, 4/1/1926.

Piece number 63 = 6 inch O.S. Map of East London (including Barking, Shoreditch, Woolwich and New Cross), c.1904.

Piece number 69 = A country map of the environs of London - The District Railway, 1898.

Piece number 71 = Map of the Metropolitan Railway and its connections, c.1890.

Piece number 72 = Map of London Transport Underground System, 1952.

Piece number 73 = Map showing Underground, British Railways and Bus routes in London, 1956.

Piece number 74 = London Transport Underground System, 1960.

Piece number 75 = Map of London and suburbs showing existing lines and those proposed by Northern Junction Railway, Great Northern Railway, Metropolitan and Great Northern Railways and Midland Railway, 1914.

Piece number 77 = Map of London railways: printed by Dangerfield Lith, c.1885

MPS(Y) = Maps, Plans and Surveys - York Collection **(to be re-listed as RAIL1037 during 1997/98):**

Piece number 397 = Railway Clearing House map of London and its Environs, 1902.

Piece number 401 = Railway Clearing House map of London and its Environs, 1910.

Piece number 582 = Railway Clearing House map of London and Environs, 1919.

LIBRARY MATERIAL:

ZLIB8 = Library - Electrification, including London Underground Railways. This contains a number of items of LT interest, including *for example*:

Piece number 9 = Great Northern Railway Company, Scheme for the Electrification of the Suburban Lines submitted by Dick, Kerr, & Co. Ltd, 1903.

Piece number 10 = Electrical Equipment for London's Underground Railway (British Electrical & Allied Manufacturers' Association publication), 1933.

Piece number 16 = Electrification on the Metropolitan District Railway (Extracted from "Tramway and Railway World" (B.T.H. Ltd)), 1905.

Piece number 54 = Automatic signalling on the Underground Railways of London (Signalling Pamphlet No.9) (Westinghouse Brake Co. Ltd), 1906.

Piece number 61 = Electrical equipment of track on the Underground Railways of London (Reprint from Journal of Institution of Electrical Engineers), 1927.

Piece number 67 = Electrification of London Underground Railways, S.B. Fortenbaugh, 1905.

Piece number 104 = The Handling of Urban and Suburban Passenger Traffic by Railway, Electric Traction, Tramways and Motor Omnibuses (Underground Group of Companies print of paper given at World Power Conference Sectional Meeting, Scandinavia, 1933), 1933.

Piece number 127 = Underground Railways in London - A Select Bibliography, by C F Lindsey, 1973.

Note: A full card index to all BTHR library items, by both subject and author, is included as part of the main BTHR card index. (The reference room at the PRO includes a copy of *A Bibliography of British Railway History*, compiled by George Ottley, which will also be found useful in highlighting published material of relevance to LT, but it only covers railways/tramways).

PERIODICALS:

ZPER1 = UNDERGROUND (LONDON UNDERGROUND RAILWAY SOCIETY JOURNAL) Volumes 1-14 (1961 - 1974 as monthly issues) and 'Underground' (occasional booklets) from 1975 to 1981.

ZPER26 = LONDON TRANSPORT MAGAZINE, Volumes 1 - 26, April 1947 to March 1973 (Note: Aug-Sept 1950 is one issue; Nov-Dec 1950 is one issue; March and April 1956, July and August 1959 and December 1970 were not produced due to strikes in the printing industry).

ZPER34 = ILLUSTRATED LONDON NEWS, May 1842 to July 1965, will contain items of interest.

ZPER105 = TILLINGS STAFF MAGAZINE 1928 and 1931-1933.

ZPER115 = LONDON TRANSPORT (LERAA) RAILWAY CLUB NEWS SHEET, 1968/1969 (Vol I Nos 1-12, Vol II Nos 13-14 and miscellaneous papers).

ZPER116 = TOT MAGAZINE Vols 1 - 11 (1923-1933), but not complete.

PERIODICALS: *continued....*

ZPER117 = PENNYFARE MAGAZINE Vols 1 - 5 (1934-1938) but not complete.

ZPER140 = UNDERGROUND NEWS (LONDON UNDERGROUND RAILWAY SOCIETY JOURNAL) 1975 - 1981.

Note: The card index which accompanies the BTHR records, includes a section on London Transport. This includes references to many periodical articles of relevance to LT, which can then be located among the ZPER classes.

SPECIAL COLLECTIONS:

ZSPC11 = W E HAYWARD COLLECTION. This contains books and booklets which relate to London Transport railways as follows:

Piece number 15 = Metropolitan Steam, by E J S Gadsden, 1963.

Piece number 109 = Romance of London's Underground, by W J Passingham, 1932.

Piece number 110 = Handling London's Underground Traffic, by J P Thomas, 1928.

Piece number 111 = Underground Railways (Their Construction and Working), by Vernon Sommerfield, 1934.

Piece number 112 = London's Underground, by F Henry Howson, 1951.

Piece number 242 = The Railways of Tottenham, by G H Lake, 1946.

Piece number 256 = Improving London's Transport (Special Number of the Railway Gazette), The Railway Gazette, 1946.

Piece number 344 = File of Booklets, Magazine Cuttings, Postcards, etc, relating to London, various dates.

Piece number 345 = File of Booklets, Magazine Cuttings, Postcards, etc, relating to London, various dates.

Piece number 353 = File of Booklets, Magazine Cuttings, Postcards, etc, relating to Metropolitan Railway, various dates.

Piece number 354 = File of Booklets, Magazine Cuttings, Postcards, etc, relating to Metropolitan Railway, various dates.

Piece number 355 = File of Booklets, Magazine Cuttings, Postcards, etc, relating to Metropolitan Railway, various dates.

Piece number 356 = File of Booklets, Magazine Cuttings, Postcards, etc, relating to Metropolitan Railway, various dates.

Piece number 357 = File of Booklets, Magazine Cuttings, Postcards, etc, relating to Metropolitan Railway, various dates.

Piece number 358 = File of Booklets, Magazine Cuttings, Postcards, etc, relating to Metropolitan Railway, various dates.

Piece number 359 = File of Booklets, Magazine Cuttings, Postcards, etc, relating to Metropolitan District Railway, various dates.

Piece number 360 = File of Booklets, Magazine Cuttings, Postcards, etc, relating to Metropolitan District Railway, various dates.

Piece number 665 = File of Magazine Cuttings, Booklets, etc: Relating to London Underground Railways, various dates.

Piece number 666 = File of Magazine Cuttings, Booklets, etc: Relating to London Underground Railways, various dates.

Piece number 667 = File of Magazine Cuttings, Booklets, etc: Relating to London Underground Railways, various dates.

Piece number 726 = Railway Clearing House Map, London and its environs, 1899.

Piece number 727 = Railway Clearing House Map, London and its environs, 1935.

Piece number 748 = Railway Clearing House Map, District Railway - London, undated.

LIST OF PHOTOGRAPHS NOTED IN PART C:

RAIL1005/134 - Photograph of Kensington (Addison Road), among others.

RAIL1014/37 - Photograph album including:
    No.49 Underground, Baker Street, booking hall.
    No.50 Underground, Piccadilly Circus, exterior.

RAIL1017/19 - Photograph of train service recording clocks at St James Park Underground Station (undated).

RAIL1018/ 12 - Photographs (public and social occasions) c.1951-1967, London Transport (Sir John Elliot Papers).

RAIL1020/1, Folio 66 - Passes on London Transport and Underground Railways (includes photographs). Four of these photographs have been extracted from RAIL1020/1 and can now be found under CN18/1, an album containing these and various other photographs which required conserving and could not be left in the original files.

PART D - OTHER RECORDS RELATED TO LONDON TRANSPORT, INCLUDING GOVERNMENT DEPARTMENTS:

The following class lists have been checked as at 5 January 1996:
All AN classes; BT31 (up to 1965) for companies listed; BT34 for companies listed.
FH; HO186 - HO212 inclusive.
MEPO 1-4 (Piece numbers which are closed at the time of compiling this list have been included, if a description is given. Those where a description is not given might contain material of interest, when these files are eventually released).
MT1-5; MT6 (Piece numbers 1-3541); MT7-MT135; OS1-OS25.

RAILWAY EXECUTIVE COMMITTEE/BRITISH TRANSPORT COMMISSION/ BRITISH RAILWAYS BOARD:

AN2 = Railway Executive Committee, War of 1939-1945. A full list of files relevant to London Transport is in preparation.

AN3 = Railway Executive Committee (1939-1947), Minutes and Reports:
Piece number 31 = Consultative Committees' Minutes - 6. Civil Engineers, 1938-1947 (The LPTB were represented on the Committee and there is a great deal of interesting information in this file, and no doubt many others in this class. Appendix to Engineering Committee minute number 447 of 29 Jan 1945 gives a list of tank traps etc on LPTB properties).
Piece number 83 = Copy of Ministry of War Transport's "Planning for Post War Reconstruction of Main Line Railways, and London Transport Facilities." 1943.

AN8 = British Transport Commission, Reports:
Piece number 20 = Co-ordination of railway facilities in London area, Mar 1954 (See also AN97/71-91).
Piece number 21 = Co-ordination of railway facilities in London area, London Freight Facilities Committee, Mar 1957 (See also AN97/92-93).
Piece number 70 = Scope and content of accounts: BR and London Transport Railways, March 1956.

AN31 = British Railways, London Midland Region: Station Plans and Drawings:
Piece number 12 = Photographs of stations: A-B, not dated (including photograph of Aylesbury).
Piece number 14 = Photographs of stations: D-L, not dated (including photograph of Edgware).

AN85 = British Transport Commission: Minutes and Papers, 13 August 1947 - 20 December 1962, will contain many items of interest. A full list of minutes relevant to London Transport is in preparation.

AN97 = British Transport Commission, Committees:
Piece numbers 71-91 = Co-ordination of Railway Facilities in London Area - Minutes and Reports, 1948-1953 (See also AN8/20).
Piece numbers 92-93 = London Freight Facilities Committee, 1954-1957 (See also AN8/21).

AN104 = British Transport Historical Records, Administrative Papers:
Piece number 7 = Catalogue and Transfer Lists: British Rail and London Transport, 1948.

AN109 = British Railways and Predecessor Railway Companies: Hotels and Catering Services: Minutes, Reports, Papers and Miscellaneous Records:
Piece number 533 = London - Craven Hotel: Development of hotel site: London Transport Fleet Line development; case of resident tenants, 1965-1971.
Piece number 534 = London - Craven Hotel: Fleet Line and Jubilee line development: compensation claim, 1968-1975 (see also AN109/527).
Piece number 1102 = London Transport: planning notes, economic background reports, 1963-1967.

AN120 = Chief Mechanical and Electrical Engineer's Department, Correspondence and Papers:
Piece number 28 = Transfer of Lines and services from BR to London Transport, September 1967-December 1969.

AN128 = International Railway Congress Association, XVI Session London 1954, Records:
Piece number 35 = Brochure issued by London Transport for Visits and Excursions - Lillie Bridge Depot (2 parts).
Piece number 36 = Brochure issued by London Transport for Visits and Excursions - Acton Works (2 parts).

Government Department Records etc:

BOARD OF TRADE:

BT13 = Board of Trade and Successors: Establishment Department: Correspondence and Papers:

Piece number 42/E20302 = London Traffic Branch - Temporary discontinuance (see E.22527/1911), 1908.

Piece number 44/E21045 = London Traffic Branch - Ordnance Survey Draughtsmen on loan: Payment, etc, 1909.

Piece number 47/E22527 = London Traffic Branch - Continuation for further year (see E.20302/1908), 1911.

Piece number 48/E23446 = London Traffic Branch - Continuation on Modified Basis (see E.22527/1911), 1911.

Piece number 53/E24971 = London Traffic Branch - Private Bill Procedure - Inter-Departmental Committee, 1913.

Piece number 67/E29305 = London Traffic Branch - Duties of, 1916.

Piece number 67/E29397 = London Traffic Branch: Abolition of, 1916.

Piece number 70/E30006 = London Traffic Branch - Transfer of Furniture etc. Local Government Board, 1916.

Piece number 70/E30092 = London Traffic Branch: Closing of, 1916.

BT31 = Companies Registration Office: Files of dissolved Companies (1855-1970):

Companies taken over in whole or in part by, or otherwise associated with London Transport and its predecessors (including some other London area omnibus operators), showing full *PIECE NUMBER* references for ordering purposes, i.e. box number, followed by Company number:

A1 Omnibus Company Limited = 29228/208302

A T Bennett & Company, Limited = 27044/179709

Alberta Omnibus Company, Limited = 28915/203662

Allber Omnibus Company, Limited = 29404/211679

Allen Omnibus Company, Limited = 22227/135369

Amersham & District Motor Bus & Haulage Company, Limited = 32315/158786

Aro Omnibus Company, Limited = 29482/213445

Associated Omnibus Company, Limited = 16522/67942

Associated Omnibus Company, Limited = 27177/181386

Atlas Omnibus Company, Limited = 28640/199588

Auto-Car Services, Limited = 32170/132125

Autocar (Tunbridge Wells) Company, Limited = 13130/108143

Aylesbury Omnibus Company, Limited = 33292/259887

Bayswater Omnibus Company, Limited = 29157/207282

Belgravia Omnibus Company, Limited = 32812/219797

Biss Brothers, Limited = 28783/201611

Brackin & Vandy Limited = 28870/202925

Brailey, Limited = 29368/210893

Britannia Traction Company, Limited = 29450/212706

British Automobile Development Company, Limited - see Tilling and British Automobile Traction, Limited

British Automobile Traction Company, Limited - see Tilling and British Automobile Traction, Limited

British General Omnibus Company, Limited = 20496/120491

British Lion Omnibus Company, Limited = 29208/208006

Brixton Motor Omnibus Company, Limited = 29299/209443

Bromley Autocar Company, Limited = 9612/71435

Burlington Omnibus Company, Limited = 28664/199918

C.W. Batten & Company, Limited = 29213/208082

Cambrian Coaching and Goods Transport Limited = 26391/172461 (formerly London and South Coast Transport, Limited, name changed on 20 July 1921 to Goods Transport Limited and then to Cambrian Coaching and Goods Transport, Limited on 7 February 1922)

Cambrian Landray Coaching, Limited = 27389/183711

Celtic Omnibus Company, Limited = 29505/214009

Central Omnibus Company, Limited = 27782/188372

Charles Randall, Limited = 29216/208145

Chesham and District Bus Company, Limited = 33169/247272

City & Suburban Motor Omnibus Company, Limited = 11180/85315

City Coach Company, Limited = 36451/231703 (formerly New Empress Saloons, Limited, name changed 16 March 1936)

Comfort Omnibus Company, Limited = 28900/203417

Commonwealth Omnibuses, Limited = 29208/208008

Cornwall Motor Omnibus Company, Limited = 28391/196291

Cosgrove Omnibus Company, Limited = 29248/208609

County of Surrey Electrical Power Distribution Company, Limited - see South Metropolitan Electric Tramways and Lighting Company, Limited

Criterion Omnibus Company, Limited = 29480/213378

BT31 = Companies Registration Office: Files of dissolved Companies (1855-1970):
   continued....

Direct Omnibus Company, Limited = 29453/212784
District Omnibus Company, Limited = 2149/9944
District Omnibus Services, Limited (The) = 30588/245196
Dolphin Omnibus Company, Limited = 29384/211257
Dominion Omnibus Company, Limited = 29469/213136
E Gray & Sons (Transport) Limited = 28561/198606 (formerly Edward Gray (Transport) Limited, name changed
      17 November 1924)
East Ham Omnibus Company, Limited = 28861/202739
East Surrey Traction Company, Limited - see London General Country Services, Limited
Edward Gray (Transport) Limited - see E Gray & Sons (Transport) Limited
Edward Paul, Limited = 27566/185637 (there is a later company with the same name, company number
      214194, but this had been dissolved also)
Electric Traction Company, Limited = 5814/40798
Embassy Motors, Limited = 29743/219404
Empress Omnibus Company, Limited = 27746/187874
F S Petrol-Electric Omnibus Company, Limited = 27800/188591
F W Omnibus Company, Limited = 29927/223676
Farwell Omnibus Company, Limited = 29137/206984
Field Marshal Omnibus Company, Limited = 29547/214921
Fleet Omnibus Company, Limited = 27777/188320
Florence Omnibus Company, Limited = 29563/215255
French, Limited = 11114/84683
Gearless Motor Omnibus Company, Limited = 11468/88234
Gearless Motor Omnibus Company, Limited = 17768/88878
Gearless Motor Omnibus Company, Limited = 27178/181393
Gigantic Wheel and Recreation Towers Company, Limited = 5774/40460
Gleaner Omnibus Company, Limited = 28684/200198
Goods Transport Limited - see Cambrian Coaching and Goods Transport Limited
Grafton Omnibus Company, Limited = 29594/215967
Grangewood Omnibus Company, Limited = 28841/202470
Great Eastern London Motor Omnibus Company, Limited = 11448/88044
Great Eastern London Suburban Tramways and Omnibus Company, Limited = 7255/51310
Green Line Coaches, Limited = 33190/249363
Gretna Omnibus Company, Limited = 29499/213832
H F B, Limited = 29527/214528
H H Omnibus Company, Limited = 29807/220964
H L Omnibus Company, Limited = 30040/226101
H M Merry Motor Transport Services, Limited = 29640/216990
Haywood and Nowell, Limited = 29183/207624
Henslowe Bus Company, Limited = 28682/200164
Highgate Hill Tramways Company, Limited = 6871/48333
Hooker & Irvine, Limited = 29454/212792
Horseshoe Traction Company, Limited = 29445/212563
International Tower Construction Company, Limited - see Metropolitan Tower Construction Company, Limited
Invicta Traction Company, Limited = 29462/212984
Jockey Omnibus Company, Limited = 29608/216276
John Hough, Limited = 29468/213100
Kew, Richmond & Kingston Tramways Company, Limited = 1669/5908
Lancastrian Omnibus Company, Limited = 29863/222327
Lea Valley Omnibus Company, Limited = 29385/211276
Legion Omnibus Company, Limited = 29607/216251
Lewis Omnibus Company, Limited = 33138/243886
London & County Tramways Company, Limited = 1664/5856
London & District Motor Bus Company, Limited = 11020/83760
London and District Omnibus Company, Limited - see London Road Car Company 2680/14350
London and South Coast Transport Limited - see Cambrian Coaching and Goods Transport Limited
London and Suburban Traction Company, Limited = 32141/125469
London Central Motor Omnibus Company, Limited = 11458/88139
London Circular Omnibus Company, Limited = 27673/186934
London Electric Omnibus Company, Limited = 6821/47990
London Electrobus Company, Limited = 17731/88381
London Exhibitions, Limited = 15403/41536
London General Country Services Limited = 32091/114728 (formerly East Surrey Traction Company Limited,
      name changed on 20 January 1932)
London General Omnibus Company, Limited = 14304/1376
London General Omnibus Company, Limited = 32131/123410

BT31 = Companies Registration Office: Files of dissolved Companies (1855-1970):
    continued....

London General Street Tramway Company, Limited = 1372/3783
London Motor Omnibus Company, Limited = 10221/76670
London Motor Omnibus Company, Limited = 10950/83158
London Motor Omnibus Syndicate, Limited = 10009/74792
London Omnibus Carriage Company, Limited = 3599/22122
London Omnibus Tramway Company, Limited = 295/1028
London Omnibus Tramway Company, Limited = 506/2010
London Power Omnibus Company, Limited = 11030/83844
London Premier Omnibus Company, Limited = 20422/119769 (formerly Premier Omnibus Company, Limited,
    name changed 13 May 1914)
London Public Omnibus Company, Limited = 29891/222970
London Road Car Company, Limited = 2680/14350 (formerly London and District Omnibus Company, Limited,
    name changed in 1881. Upon dissolution, the company name was immediately re-used to register a new
    company, number 3096 for which a separate file is listed below)
London Road Car Company, Limited = 3096/17734
London Steam Omnibus Company, Limited - see Motor Traction Company, Limited
London Tramways Company, Limited = 1581/5198
London United Tramways, Limited = 5918/41621
London United Tramways, Limited = 31849/71844 (formerly London United Tramways (1901), Limited, name
    changed circa March 1907)
London United Tramways (1901), Limited - see London United Tramways, Limited 31849/71844
Lonsdale Omnibus Company, Limited = 29348/210414
Loveland Omnibus Company, Limited = 29569/215394
McMahon Omnibus Company, Limited = 30009/225417
Majestic Omnibus Company, Limited - see Superways, Limited
Marathon Omnibus Company, Limited = 29475/213265
Mason Omnibus Company, Limited (The) = 29873/222499
Meteor Omnibus Company, Limited = 29223/208234
Metropolitan District Electric Traction Company, Limited = 9535/70843
Metropolitan Electric Tramways, Limited = 31368/42526 (formerly Metropolitan Tramways and Omnibus
    Company, Limited, name changed 13 January 1902)
Metropolitan Railway Surplus Land Company, Limited = 1540/4910
Metropolitan Railway Warehousing Company, Limited = 1147/2393c
Metropolitan Saloon Omnibus Company, Limited = 24B/122
Metropolitan Steam Omnibus Company, Limited = 11794/91540
Metropolitan Steam Omnibus Company, Limited = 22709/139322
Metropolitan Tower Construction Company, Limited = 5130/34612 (formerly International Tower Construction
    Company, Limited, name changed 14 October 1891)
Metropolitan Tramway Company, Limited = 1194/2659c
Metropolitan Tramways and Omnibus Company, Limited - see Metropolitan Electric Tramways, Limited
Motor Bus Company, Limited = 11111/84647
Motor Car Emporium, Limited = 15868/54970
Motor Omnibus Syndicate, Limited = 7912/56718
Motor Traction Company, Limited = 8054/58017 (incorporated 30 June 1898 as London Steam Omnibus
    Company, Limited, name changed on 6 September 1899 to Motor Traction Company, Limited)
N W Land & Transport Company, Limited = 33011/234591
National Omnibus and Transport Company, Limited = 35001/114932 (Vols. 1 & 2); 35002/114932 (Vols. 3 & 4);
    35003/114932 (Vols. 5 & 6); 35004/114932 (Vols. 7 & 8); 35005/114932 (Vol. 9); 35006/114932 (Vols.
    10 & 11); 35007/114932 (Vol. 12); 35008/114932 (Vols. 13 & 14); 35009/114932 (Vols. 1F & 2F),
    (formerly National Steam Car Company Limited, name changed 13 February 1920)
National Steam Car Company, Limited - see National Omnibus and Transport Company, Limited
New Central Omnibus Company, Limited = 20393/119497
New Central Omnibus Company, Limited = 22435/137012
New Empress Saloons, Limited - see City Coach Company, Limited
New Era Omnibus Company, Limited = 27595/185964
Newlands & District Motor Services Limited = 30464/237934
New London & Suburban Omnibus Company, Limited = 6222/44094
New Times Motor Omnibus Company, Limited = 27619/186244
Northern Omnibus Company, Limited = 29486/213525
Nulli Secundus Omnibus Company, Limited = 29509/214106
Olympic Traction Company, Limited = 29442/212512
Omnibus Proprietors, Limited = 5075/34139
Overground, Limited = 14017/125488
Overington, Limited = 28749/201140
P.C. Omnibus Company, Limited = 29683/217886
Passenger Transport, Limited = 27788/188443

Government Department Records etc:

BT31 = Companies Registration Office: Files of dissolved Companies (1855-1970): *continued....*

Paterson Omnibus Company, Limited = 32787/217484
Premier Line, Limited = 33208/251078
Premier Omnibus Company, Limited - see London Premier Omnibus Company, Limited
Priest Brothers, Limited = 29509/214082
Primrose Omnibus Company, Limited = 29438/212418
R.A. Motor Services, Limited = 29311/209668
Railway Equipment and Construction Company, Limited = 9176/68029
Randall & Shepherd, Limited = 29765/219928
Redburn's Motor Services, Limited = 27891/189731
Redcar Services, Limited = 32594/192472
Red Rose Motor Services, Limited = 28287/194888
Samuelson Transport Company, Limited = 26552/174223
Sear Bros, Limited = 30065/226676
Shamrock Traction Company, Limited = 28585/198936
Silver Star Omnibus Company, Limited = 29835/221657
Skylark Motor Coach Company, Limited = 33028/235522
Skylark Omnibus Company, Limited = 29472/213201
Southall Ealing and Shepherds Bush Tram Railway Company, Limited = 1540/4907
South Metropolitan Electric Tramways and Lighting Company, Limited = 31694/61593 (Incorporated 19 April 1899, as County of Surrey Electrical Power Distribution Company, Limited, name changed 7 Aug 1904)
South Western Motor Car Company, Limited = 9244/68631
Star Omnibus Company, Limited = 16158/61088
Superbus, Limited = 28601/199201
Superways, Limited = 29307/209580 (formerly Majestic Omnibus Company, Limited, name changed 16 February 1929)
Swift Omnibus Company, Limited = 29316/209769
T and W Omnibus Company, Limited = 29470/213145
Thomson Motor Services, Limited = 29244/208549
Tilling and British Automobile Traction, Limited = 34778/84013(Vol.1); 34779/84013(Vol.2); 34780/84013(Vol.3); 34781/84013(Vols:4, 5 and 6) (incorporated 24 March 1905 as British Automobile Development Company, Limited. Name changed to British Automobile Traction Company, Limited on 6 February 1912 and again to Tilling and British Automobile Traction, Limited on 16 May 1928)
Timpson's Omnibus Services, Limited = 29449/212643
Tottenham Hotspur Omnibus Company, Limited = 29335/210198
Tower Carriers, Limited = 26225/170672
Tower Company, Limited - see Wembley Park Estate Company, Limited
Tramways (M.E.T.) Omnibus Company, Limited = 32116/119684
Ubique Omnibus Company, Limited = 28160/193259
Underground Electric Railways Company of London, Limited = 31858/73376
Union Construction & Finance Company, Limited = 31849/71610 (formerly Union Construction Company, Limited, name changed 15 February 1929)
Union Construction Company, Limited - see Union Construction & Finance Company, Limited
Union Surplus Lands Company, Limited = 32189/136673
Universal Omnibus Company, Limited = 29335/210188
Vanguard Motor Bus Company, Limited = 11793/91529
Vanguard Motorbus Company, Limited = 19454/109460
Veleta Omnibus Company, Limited = 29927/223687
Victoria Road Car Company, Limited = 29689/218000
Victor Omnibus Company, Limited = 29852/222050
Vivid Omnibus Company, Limited = 29467/213095
W & P Omnibus Company, Limited = 29249/208625
Waltham Motor Services, Limited = 29390/211383
Ward Electrical Car Company, Limited = 4244/27503
Wellington Omnibus Company, Limited = 29659/217360
Wembley Park Estate Company, Limited = 15007B/29551 (formerly Tower Company, Limited, name changed 23 October 1906)
Western Omnibus Company, Limited = 27945/190458
Westminster Coaching Services Limited = 32903/228036
Westminster Omnibus Company, Limited = 32640/199337
White Star Omnibus Company, Limited = 29608/216285

BT31 - Companies taken over in whole or in part by, or otherwise associated with London Transport and its predecessors, for which company numbers were found, but NO FILE WAS FOUND IN BT31:
A & W Omnibus Company, Limited = 223752 (company dissolved/file destroyed)
A E Blane, Limited = 261480
A G Summerskill, Limited = 208301 (file destroyed)

Government Department Records etc:

BT31 - Companies taken over in whole or in part by, or otherwise associated with London Transport and its predecessors, for which company numbers were found, but NO FILE WAS FOUND IN BT31: *continued....*

Acme Pullman Services, Limited = 242710

Aldershot & District Traction Company, Limited = 123372 (name changed to Aldershot Omnibus Company Limited on 1 January 1972, company dissolved on 7 September 1991)

Aldershot Omnibus Company, Limited - see Aldershot & District Traction Company, Limited

Amalgamated Omnibus Services and Supplies, Limited = 237784 (file destroyed)

Ambassador Bus Company, Limited = 225210 (file destroyed)

Associated Acceptances, Limited = 235064 (incorporated on 23 November 1928, later became Aveling-Barford International Limited, company in liquidation on 4 November 1988)

Associated Coaches (Ongar) Limited = 248955 (company dissolved and file destroyed)

Associated Commercial Vehicles, Limited - see Associated Equipment Company, Limited

Associated Equipment Company, Limited = 122573 (incorporated on 13 June 1912, later became Associated Commercial Vehicles Limited, company in liquidation)

Aveling-Barford International, Limited - see Associated Acceptances, Limited

BBP Omnibus Company, Limited = 221938 (file destroyed)

Birch Brothers, Limited = 64031

Blue Belle Motors, Limited = 190304 (company dissolved and file destroyed)

Blue Line Coaches, Limited = 249822

Buck's Expresses (Watford), Limited = 243662

Cardinal Omnibus Company, Limited = 217821 (file destroyed)

Chariot Omnibus Services, Limited = 216372 (file destroyed)

Chocolate Express Omnibus Company, Limited = 184508 (file destroyed)

City Motor Omnibus Company, Limited = 187075

Claremont Omnibus Company, Limited = 211937

Cleveland Omnibus Company, Limited = 213404

Dangerfields, Limited = 264510

Durell Motors, Limited = 217008

E Brickwood, Limited = 115861 (file destroyed)

E Burmingham & Company, Limited = 179504

E Flower & Son, Limited = 217242

E Puttergill, Limited = 211478 (file destroyed)

Eagle Omnibus Company, Limited = 222512 (file destroyed)

Earl Motor Omnibus Company, Limited = 211088 (file destroyed)

Eastern General Omnibus Company, Limited = 246019

Eastern National Omnibus Company, Limited (The) = 237553 (incorporated 28 February 1929, company dissolved on 1 June 1993)

Eastward Coaches, Limited = 244565

Edward Hillman's Saloon Coaches, Limited = 267639

Elms Longman Motor Services, Limited = 207925

Empress Motors, Limited = 211078 (incorporated 13 January 1926, company still trading)

Enterprise Transport Company, Limited = 238484 (file destroyed)

Essex Omnibus Company, Limited = 212709 (file destroyed)

Fairway Coaches, Limited = 219932 (formerly Varsity Omnibus Company, Limited, name changed 3 October 1928)

Fallowfield and Knight, Limited = 227849

Filkins and Ainsworth, Limited = 185000 (file destroyed)

Fleet Transport Services, Limited = 233597

G H Allitt & Sons, Limited = 212607 (name changed later to Wells & Son (Transport), Limited)

General Northern Services, Limited = 246023 (formerly Northern General Omnibus Company, Limited, name changed 11 July 1930)

General Southern Services, Limited = 246618

Glandfield Omnibus Company, Limited = 220978

Glen Omnibus Company (London), Limited = 254913 (file destroyed)

Gordon Omnibus Company, Limited = 212220 (file destroyed)

Gravesend & District Bus Services, Limited = 201762 (file destroyed)

Harold Smith Company, Limited = 217957

Havelock Motors, Limited = 202905

Ingarfield & Bright, Limited = 231816

Liberty Bus Company, Limited = 207467

London Electric Transport Finance Corporation, Limited = 302870

London Road Car Company, Limited = 105595 (file destroyed)

Loumax Omnibus Company, Limited = 246337 (file destroyed January 1964)

Maidstone & District Motor Services, Limited (The) = 114841 (incorporated 22 March 1911, company still trading)

Government Department Records etc:

BT31 - Companies taken over in whole or in part by, or otherwise associated with London Transport and its predecessors, for which company numbers were found, but NO FILE WAS FOUND IN BT31: *continued....*

Metropolitan Railway Country Estates, Limited = 155892 (incorporated 7 June 1919, later became Broseley Estates Limited, named changed again on 1 October 1990 to Ideal Homes North West Limited, company still trading)

Miller Traction Company, Limited = 218757 (file destroyed)

Morden Station Garage, Limited = 216240

Nelson Omnibus Company, Limited = 218957 (file destroyed)

Northern General Omnibus Company, Limited - see General Northern Services, Limited

North Star Omnibus and Coach Services, Limited = 257143 (name later changed to Whismar, Limited, company dissolved on 28 September 1993)

Penn Bus Company, Limited = 255506 (file destroyed March 1964)

Peraeque Transport Company, Limited = 220047 (file destroyed)

Perkin's Omnibus Company, Limited = 224763 (file destroyed)

Phoenix Omnibus Company, Limited = 207785

Pleats, Limited - see Thames Valley Traction Company, Limited

Prince Omnibus Company, Limited = 220048 (file destroyed)

Pro Bono Publico, Limited = 207926 (file destroyed)

Queen Line Coaches & Baldock Motor Transport, Limited = 247739 (file destroyed)

Red Line Coaches, Limited = 249845 (file destroyed)

Red Rover Omnibus, Limited = 223515 (incorporated 28 July 1927, name changed to Tarifminor Limited on 13 April 1988, company dissolved on 15 September 1992)

Reliance Omnibus Company, Limited = 210062 (file destroyed)

Renown Traction Company, Limited = 216929 (file destroyed)

Road Motors (Luton) Limited - company acquired by National Omnibus and Transport Company, Ltd in May 1925 (Barker/Robbins Vol 2, page 484/485) company number might be 109519?

Robert Hawkins & Company, Limited = 218968

Robert Thackray, Limited = 210941 (company in liquidation 10 April 1995)

Royal Highlander Omnibus Company, Limited - although some secondary sources mention a company with this title, it would appear that the proposal to set it up was never carried into effect. See: London's Buses Volume One, by Blacker, Lunn & Westgate, page 208, paragraph three)

St George Omnibus Company, Limited = 211524 (file destroyed)

Shepherd's Bush Exhibition Limited = 99936

Sphere Omnibus Company, Limited = 216726 (file destroyed)

Sunset Pullman Coaches, Limited = 239539 (file destroyed)

Sunshine Saloon Coaches, Limited = 269455 (file destroyed)

Supreme Motor Omnibus Company, Limited = 220450 (file destroyed)

Tarifminor, Limited - see Red Rover Omnibus Company, Limited

Thames Valley Traction Company, Limited = 168948 (name changed to Pleats, Limited on 24 March 1988, company dissolved on 10 July 1989)

Thomas Tilling, Limited = 52492 (incorporated 12 May 1897, company still trading)

Tilbury Coaching Services, Limited = 258381 (file destroyed March 1964)

Tilbury Safety Coaches, Limited = 265500 (file destroyed)

Tillingbourne Bus Company, Limited = 259480 (incorporated on 7 October 1931 as Tillingbourne Valley Bus Services, Limited. Name changed to Tillingbourne Valley Services, Limited on 13 April 1935 and again to Tillingbourne Bus Company, Limited on 25 October 1972. Company still trading.)

Tillingbourne Valley Bus Services, Limited - see Tillingbourne Bus Company, Limited

Tillingbourne Valley Services, Limited - see Tillingbourne Bus Company, Limited

Union Jack (Luton) Omnibus Company, Limited = 234961 (file destroyed 1971)

United Omnibus Company, Limited = 211707

Upminster Services, Limited = 266213 (file destroyed)

Varsity Omnibus Company, Limited - see Fairway Coaches, Limited

Victory Omnibus Company, Limited = 222854

W Eggleton, Limited = 230106 (file destroyed)

Watford Omnibus Company, Limited = 254991 (file destroyed)

Wells & Son (Transport), Limited - see G H Allitt & Sons, Limited

Westcliff-on-Sea Motor Services, Limited = 135399

Western General Omnibus Company, Limited = 246031 (file destroyed)

West Herts. Motor Services, Limited = 247394 (file destroyed December 1964)

West Kent Motor Services, Limited = 225314 (file destroyed)

Yellow Line Coaches, Limited = 249852

BT31 was checked up to the end of 1965 for box numbers relating to the section above.

BT31 - Companies taken over in whole or in part by, or otherwise associated with London Transport and its predecessors, but for which company numbers were not found:

Southern Motor Omnibus Company - may be a limited company? (taken over by the LGOC in 1913)

William Allen, Limited (incorporated circa 1923?)

Government Department Records etc:

BT31 - NOTE 1: the following companies had their Registered Office at 55 Broadway prior to the formation of the LPTB, but were not affected by the 1933 act:

Earls Court Grounds, Limited = 138679 (incorporated 18 December 1914)
Rushton Tractors, Limited = 30370/234852 (see also: Rushton Tractors (1929), Limited = 30548/242323)

BT31 - NOTE 2: the following companies have their Registered Office at 55 Broadway (unless otherwise stated) as at 1 January 1996, or have been dissolved or ceased trading whilst having their registered office there:

Bexleybus Limited = 02158491 (incorporated 28 August 1987) company dissolved on 24 April 1990.
Harrow Buses Limited = 02158473 (incorporated 28 August 1987) company dissolved on 25 July 1989. (This company should not be confused with another, which changed its name to Harrow Buses Limited on 16 October 1995. This other company, number 00091413, was incorporated on 24 December 1906 as Harrogate Road Car Company Limited. It has undergone several changes of name, to: Harrogate and District Road Car Company Ltd on 22 December 1924; West Yorkshire Road Car Company Ltd on 14 December 1927; AJS Developments Ltd on 8 August 1989; Associated Bus & Coach Investments Ltd on 7 October 1991 and then to Harrow Buses Limited on 16 October 1995. This company has no connection with London Regional Transport).
Kingston Buses Limited = 02123684 (incorporated 15 April 1987) company dissolved on 19 September 1989.
London Buses Limited (registered office 172 Buckingham Palace Road, London, SW1W 9TN) = 01900906 (incorporated 29 March 1985) ceased trading on 4 March 1995 and assets transferred to LT.
London Dial-A-Ride Limited = 02602192 (incorporated 17 April 1991) since ceased trading.
London Forest Travel Limited = 02328491 (incorporated 14 December 1988), company dissolved on 29 August 1995.
London Transport Insurance (Guernsey) Limited (registered office 4th Floor, The Albany, South Esplanade, St Peter Port, Guernsey) = 28442 (incorporated 2 August 1994 in Guernsey).
London Transport International Incorporated (Delaware) = dissolved (not registered in England).
London Transport International Services Limited = 01274664 (incorporated 24 August 1976), ceased trading 31 March 1992.
London Transport Pension Fund Trustees Limited (The) = 00941331 (incorporated 29 October 1968), company dissolved on 21 March 1995.
London Transport Trustee Company Limited = 00320689 (incorporated 14 November 1936).
London Underground Limited = 01900907 (incorporated 29 March 1985).
LRT Medical Services Limited = 02246967 (incorporated 22 April 1988) company dissolved on 29 August 1995.
LRT Pension Fund Trustee Company Limited = 02338675 (incorporated 24 January 1989).
LTM Enterprises Limited = 02306312 (incorporated 18 October 1988 as Austbase Limited, name changed 8 November 1989) company dissolved on 29 August 1995.
Metropower Limited = 02557760 (incorporated 13 November 1990) since ceased trading, company dissolved on 11 June 1996.
Orpington Buses Limited (registered office 172 Buckingham Palace Road, London, SW1W 9TP) = 01983863 (incorporated 29 January 1986 - subsidiary of London Buses, Limited), company dissolved on 22 August 1995.
PB Buses Limited = 02034838 (incorporated 7 July 1986 - subsidiary of London Buses, Limited) company dissolved on 8 August 1989.
Victoria Coach Station Limited (registered office 164 Buckingham Palace Road, London, SW1W 9TP) = 00205610 (incorporated 30 April 1925) company acquired from the former National Bus Company, on 31 October 1988.
Waterloo & City and Underground Extensions Railways Limited = 02911960 (incorporated 18 March 1994) company transferred to the LRT Group in April 1994, since ceased trading.
Wimbledon Buses Limited = 02171093 (incorporated 30 September 1987) company dissolved on 25 July 1989.

Transport History Research Trust = 02329418 (incorporated 12 December 1988 as The London Transport Museum Limited, name changed 3 May 1991) This company was set up by independent trustees with a view to taking over the running of the London Transport Museum.

BT31 - NOTE 3: the following companies were at one time wholly owned subsidiaries of LRT, but have now been sold off to private enterprise:

Centrewest London Buses Limited = 02328596 (incorporated 14 December 1988) was sold on 2 September 1994 to Centrewest Limited.
Data Networks PLC = 02002981 (incorporated 21 March 1986) only about 30% of the equity capital was held by LRT. This interest was sold to CAP Group PLC in May 1987. The company name was changed to Sema Group Facilities Management PLC on 7 May 1990 and again to Sema Group Outsourcing PLC on 16 March 1995.
Docklands Light Railway Limited = 02052677 (incorporated 4 September 1986), initially funded jointly by LRT and the London Docklands Development Corporation. LRT's shareholding was sold to the LDDC for a nominal consideration of £1 on 1 April 1992. A small portion of the DLR at Bank station was transferred to London Underground Limited at about the same time.

Government Department Records etc:

BT31 - NOTE 3: the following companies were at one time wholly owned subsidiaries of LRT, but have now been sold off to private enterprise: *continued....*

East London Bus and Coach Company Limited = 02328402 (incorporated 14 December 1988) was sold 6 September 1994 to Stagecoach Holdings PLC.

Leaside Bus Company Limited = 02328559 (incorporated 14 December 1988) was sold 29 September 1994 to Cowie Group PLC.

London Central Bus Company Limited = 02328565 (incorporated 14 December 1988) was sold 17 October 1994 to Go Ahead Group PLC.

London Coaches Limited = 02328599 (incorporated 14 December 1988), was sold to its own management on 1 April 1992 and is a part of Pullmans Group Limited.

London General Transport Services Limited = 02328489 (incorporated 14 December 1988) was sold 2 November 1994 to Mokett Limited.

London Northern Bus Company Limited = 02328608 (incorporated 14 December 1988) was sold 26 October 1994 to MTL Trust Holdings Limited. The company name was changed to MTL London Northern Limited on 20 March 1995.

London United Busways Limited = 02328561 (incorporated 14 December 1988) was sold 5 November 1994 to London United Busways 1994 Limited.

LRT Bus Engineering Limited = 01900908 (incorporated 29 March 1985) was sold to Frontsource Limited in January 1988. The company name was changed to Belmanton Limited on 31 March 1988 and the company was subsequently dissolved on 5 October 1993.

LTA Advertising Limited = 02866133 (incorporated 26 October 1993) was sold in August 1994 to Transportation Displays Incorporated. The company name was changed to TDI Advertising Limited on 5 April 1995.

Metroline Travel Limited = 02328401 (incorporated 14 December 1988) was sold 7 October 1994 to Gravitas 1058 Limited.

Routemaster Reinsurance Limited (registered office 80 Harcourt Street, Dublin, Republic of Ireland) = 214501 (incorporated 14 March 1994 in Dublin) was sold to owners of ten of the former London Bus Companies, ie: Centrewest London Buses Limited; East London Bus and Coach Company Limited; South East London & Kent Bus Company Limited; Leaside Bus Company Limited; Metroline Travel Limited; London Central Bus Company Limited; London Northern Bus Company Limited; London General Transport Services Limited; London United Busways Limited; South London Transport Limited. Since each of these companies had a 10% interest in Routemaster Reinsurance Limited, LT's interest ceased when the last of these companies, South London Transport Limited was sold on 10 January 1995.

South East London & Kent Bus Company Limited = 02328595 (incorporated 14 December 1988) was sold 6 September 1994 to Stagecoach Holdings PLC.

South London Transport Limited = 02328467 (incorporated 14 December 1988) was sold 10 January 1995 to Cowie Group PLC.

Stanwell Buses Limited (trading as Westlink) = 01983867 (incorporated 29 January 1986 - subsidiary of London Buses, Limited) was sold to its own management on 19 January 1994. The company was subsequently sold to West Midlands Travel Limited on 11 April 1994. West Midlands Travel Limited was then merged with National Express in March 1995, but Stanwell Buses Limited was subsequently sold to London United Busways Limited on 14 September 1995.

BT31 - NOTE 4: the following companies have taken over sections of the LRT business, including staff:

Aramark, PLC = 00983951 (incorporated 7 July 1970 as Ara Services, PLC, name changed on 10 October 1994) took over part of the catering activities of LRT in March 1993. It is understood that LRT's catering staff were actually made redundant, but were all allowed to apply for new positions with Ara Services.

GEC Alsthom NL Service Provision, Limited = 2849400 (incorporated 1 September 1993 as GEC Alsthom Train Leasing, Limited. Name later changed to GEC Alsthom Northern Line Service Provision, Limited. Name changed again on 13 January 1995 to GEC Alsthom NL Service Provision, Limited) was associated with the tender submission for supplying new rolling stock for the Northern Line. Another GEC Group company actually took over former LUL staff etc - see entry below.

GEC Alsthom Railway Maintenance Services, Limited = 2849471 (incorporated on 1 September 1993 as GEC Alsthom Train Maintenance, Limited, name changed on 1 June 1994) took over the staff at Golders Green and Morden railway depots on 26 November 1995 as part of its involvement in the provision of new rolling stock for the Northern Line, to be leased to London Underground Limited. The same company is understood to have taken a long lease on the Golders Green Depot site from the same date.

BT34 = Board of Trade, Companies Registration Office, Liquidators' Accounts:

Allen Omnibus Company, Limited = 4007/135369
Aro Omnibus Company, Limited = 5090/213445
Associated Omnibus Company, Limited = 2959/67942
Biss Brothers, Limited = 4986/201611
Brailey, Limited = 5073/210893
Bromley Autocar Company, Limited = 1790/71435
Burlington Omnibus Company, Limited = 4968/199918

Government Department Records etc:

BT34 = Board of Trade, Companies Registration Office, Liquidators' Accounts:
continued....

City & Suburban Motor Omnibus Company, Limited = 2037/85315
Electric Traction Company, Limited = 970/40798
Gearless Motor Omnibus Company, Limited = 2084/88234
Great Eastern London Motor Omnibus Company, Limited = 2080/88044
Great Eastern London Suburban Tramways and Omnibus Company, Limited = 1300/51310
H L Omnibus Company, Limited = 5158/226101
Henslowe Bus Company, Limited = 4971/200164
Highgate Hill Tramways Company, Limited = 1214/48333
Hooker & Irvine, Limited = 5086/212792
Kew, Richmond & Kingston Tramways Company, Limited = 88/5908
London & District Motor Bus Company, Limited = 2013/83760
London Electric Omnibus Company, Limited = 1202/47990
London Electrobus Company, Limited = 3229/88381
London Exhibitions, Limited = 2684/41536
London General Omnibus Company, Limited = 2431/1376
London Motor Omnibus Company, Limited = 1894/76670
London Motor Omnibus Company, Limited = 2004/83158
London Power Omnibus Company, Limited = 2014/83844
London Public Omnibus Company, Limited = 5142/222970
London Road Car Company, Limited = 316/17734
London Tramways Company, Limited = 79/5198
London United Tramways, Limited = 990/41621
Metropolitan District Electric Traction Company, Limited = 1776/70843
Metropolitan Steam Omnibus Company, Limited = 2129/91540
Metropolitan Tower Construction Company, Limited = 794/34612
Motor Bus Company, Limited = 2027/84647
Motor Car Emporium, Limited = 2804/54970
Motor Traction Company, Limited = 1486/58017
New Central Omnibus Company, Limited = 3725/119497
New London & Suburban Omnibus Company, Limited = 1068/44094
Passenger Transport, Limited = 4834/188443
Railway Equipment and Construction Company, Limited = 1720/68029
Red Rose Motor Services, Limited = 4912/194888
Samuelson Transport Company, Limited = 4662/174223
Sear Bros, Limited = 5160/226676
Shamrock Traction Company, Limited = 4958/198936
Star Omnibus Company, Limited = 2871/61088
Thomson Motor Services, Limited = 5052/208549
Timpson's Omnibus Services, Limited = 5085/212643
Vanguard Motor Bus Company, Limited = 2129/91529
Waltham Motor Services, Limited = 5077/211383
Ward Electrical Car Company, Limited = 555/27503

BT41 = Companies Registration Office Files of Joint Stock Companies Registered under the 1844 and 1856 Acts:
Piece number 386/2191 = London General Omnibus Company, Limited
Piece number 395/2246 = London Omnibus Company, Limited
Piece number 395/2247 = London Omnibus Tramway Company, Limited
Piece number 451/2530 = Metropolitan Saloon Omnibus Company, Limited

BT58 = Companies Department. Correspondence and Papers:
Piece number 56/COS656 = London United Tramways. Bill to confer various powers, 1918

NATIONAL BUS COMPANY:

FH4 = National Bus Company: Staff Department. Registered files and unregistered files:
Piece number 17 = National Council for the Omnibus Industry (NCOI): Arbitration awards: Industrial Courts Act 1919: Board of Arbitration; difference between two sides of NCOI and London Transport Executive rates of pay and conditions of service for drivers and conductors, country buses and coach and central road services, 1940-1960.
Piece number 20 = National Council for the Omnibus Industry (NCOI): Arbitration awards: Wage awards: NBC, Municipal and London Passenger Transport Board; transcripts of claims, 1943.

HOME OFFICE AND MINISTRY OF HOME SECURITY:

HO45 = Home Office: Registered Papers:

Piece number 3333 = Omnibuses - Carrying excess passengers (prosecution of omnibus proprietoress at Bow Street Police Court on 24 October 1850 for having a seat for passengers along the roof, contrary to Sections 13 and 14 of 5 & 6 Vic., Cap.79), 1850.

Piece number 4621 = Setting down passengers in the middle of the street: Suggestion respecting Penny Omnibuses for the labouring classes, 1853.

Piece number 9638/A32915 = Report on explosion on Underground (District) Railway, 1883-1884.

Piece number 9744/A56338B = Advertisements on public carriages, London General Omnibus Co. summons against police dismissed, 1895.

Piece number 9762/B670 = Latimer Road and Acton Railway Bill, 1887.

Piece number 9909/B20975 = London Cabs and Omnibuses (Consolidation) Bill 1896-97.

Piece number 9957/V15442A = City and South London Railway (Islington Extension) Bill 1892, 1891-1892.

Piece number 9957/V15442B = City and South London Railway Bill, 1893.

Piece number 9957/V15442D = City and South London Railway Bill, 1896.

Piece number 9958/V15442E = City and South London Railway Bill and Act, 1898.

Piece number 10271/79523 = Metropolitan and District Railways (City Lines and Extensions) Bill and Act 1879, 1878-1902.

Piece number 10271/79523A = Bill to amend Metropolitan and District Railways (City Lines and Extensions) Act 1879, 1879-1880.

Piece number 10271/79523B = Bill to extend time for purchasing lands under Metropolitan and District Railways (City Lines and Extensions) Act 1879, 1880.

Piece number 10281/105947 = Apprehension of Whittaker Wright, reward, information, expenses etc., suicide after trial, 1903-1904.

Piece number 10288/110360 = Hackney Carriages and Omnibuses, General, Metropolitan, 1903-1907.

Piece number 10332/136072 = Advertisements on omnibus horses or their harnesses, 1906.

Piece number 10366/156419 = Metropolitan Omnibus Traffic - Statistics, 1907.

Piece number 10366/156525 = Motor Omnibuses - London, 1908-1909.

Piece number 10373/160395 = Metropolitan Electric Tramways Bill, 1908-1909.

Piece number 10517/135214 = London Traffic Problem, 1905-1914.

Piece number 10710/243128 = Omnibus Strike to secure recognition of Union of Licensed Vehicle Workers (newspaper cuttings regarding Tilling's and London General Omnibus Company and London and Provincial Union of Licensed Vehicle Workers industrial action), September 1913.

Piece number 10723/250050 = Licensing of Assistant Conductors of Metropolitan Stage Carriages, 1914.

Piece number 10772/276048 = London County Council Tramways - Alteration and extension of tracks - effect on traffic, 1915-1916.

Piece number 15572/231163 = London General Omnibus Company Limited: issue of licences and regulation of fares. Pirate buses. Proposal that London County Council should operate buses, 1912-1926.

Piece number 16617/585901 = **Parts 1-23:** London Passenger Transport Act, 1933, 18 Feb 1931 - 16 June 1933.

Piece number 16618/585901 = **Parts 24-44:** London Passenger Transport Act, 1933, 23 June 1933 - 18 Mar 1936.

Piece number 18218/704135 = Underground Railways: Protection from flooding by sewage, 1938-1939.

Piece number 18540/704198 = Tubes, use as shelters (various files), 1936-1941.

Piece number 21326/920325 = Transport Bill 1947, 1946.

HO186 = Ministry of Home Security - Air Raid Precautions 1939, (ARP GEN) Registered files:

Piece number 16 = Exercises, blackouts and displays: held by forty-five counties and boroughs in England and Wales and by Leyland Motors Ltd and London Passenger Transport Board, 1938-1939.

Piece number 17 = Exercises, blackouts and displays: held by forty-five counties and boroughs in England and Wales and by Leyland Motors Ltd and London Passenger Transport Board, 1938-1939.

Piece number 18 = Exercises, blackouts and displays: held by forty-five counties and boroughs in England and Wales and by Leyland Motors Ltd and London Passenger Transport Board, 1938-1939.

Piece number 149 = Use of tube tunnels as shelters in wartime, 1939.

Piece number 287 = Reporting of damage to London Passenger Transport Board's services, 1940.

Piece number 321 = Use of tube stations during air raids and improvement of shelter position in London, 1940.

Piece number 341 = Government Evacuation Scheme: transport of children from Greater London, Thameside and the Medway towns, 1940.

Piece number 342 = Government Evacuation Scheme: application to the East End of London, 1940.

Piece number 639 = Air Raids - London Region: enquiry into Bank tube station bomb incident, 1941.

Piece number 652 = Immobilisation of damaged trolley buses, trams and buses, 1941.

Piece number 1447 = Use of railway property for shelter purposes, 1939-1944.

Government Department Records etc:

HO186 = Ministry of Home Security - Air Raid Precautions 1939, (ARP GEN) Registered files: *continued....*

Piece number 1636 = Visits by members of the Royal Family to various parts of the country, 1940-1944 (Contains details of Royal visit to Southwark Deep Tunnel Air-Raid Shelter in old City & South London Railway running tunnels).

Piece number 1668 = Deep underground shelters, 1942-1944.

Piece number 1763 = Shelters (including use of deep tube shelters) as protection against flying bombs and rockets, 1944.

Piece number 1832 = Decentralisation of air raid warning system: withdrawal of teleprinter broadcast of air raid warnings to railways and London Passenger Transport Board, 1943-1944.

Piece number 1879 = Tube shelters in London: provision, 1942-1944.

Piece number 2125 = River Thames Emergency Service: organisation, 1939-1945.

Piece number 2272 = Closing of tube railway flood gates against flying-bombs and rocket attacks and special warning to transport authorities, 1944-1945.

Piece number 2324 = River Emergency Service: formation and exercises, 1941-1945.

Piece number 2419 = Tube incidents statistics, 1941-1945.

HO192 = Ministry of Home Security, Research and Experiments Dept, Registered Papers:

Piece number 8 = REPORTS - Regional Technical Intelligence Officers, Damage to underground railways, 1940-1943.

Piece number 1505 = Underground Stores and Tunnels: Molins Machine Co Ltd, Deptford: 8/9 September 1940, 1944. (This file contains a plan which shows the position of impact of a High Explosive Bomb dropped on the East London line tracks on the night of 7/8 September 1940).

HO194 = Ministry of Home Security and Home Office: Finance Divisions: Civil Defence Grants: Registered files:

Piece number 30 = Bethnal Green shelter disaster: settlement of compensation claims, 1945-1955.

HO196 = Ministry of Home Security, Research and Experiments Department, Notes:

Piece number 11, paper number 151 = Notes on damage to railway tunnels by high explosive weapons, Section 1. Tube railways. Dr. Phillips. 26 Mar 1942.

Piece number 11, paper number 156 = Notes on damage to railway tunnels by high explosive weapons. Part II. Tunnels other than tube railways. Dr. Phillips. 6 Apr 1942.

Piece number 11, paper number 201 = Report of blast tests on three windows and a door of types used in L.P.T.B. rolling stock. 24 Dec 1942.

HO197 = Ministry of Home Security, Chief Engineer's Dept, Registered Files:

Piece number 20 = Provision of baffle walls and ventilation in the Gainsborough Road, Leytonstone underground station, 1941-1942.

Piece number 34 = Home Defence Committee Working Party: adaption of new underground railways as communal shelters, 1942-1949.

Piece number 46 = Deep shelter in south tunnel at Goodge Street underground station: ventilation, 1943-1944.

Piece number 47 = Deep shelter in south tunnel at Goodge Street underground station: adaption, 1942-1945.

Piece number 48 = Deep shelter in west tunnel at Chancery Lane underground station: accommodation, 1944.

Piece number 49 = Deep tunnel shelter at Clapham Common underground station: adaption for use by the Ministry of Works, 1943-1945.

Piece number 50 = Safety measures proposed for Bethnal Green underground station to provide additional safeguards for shelterers, 1943-1945.

HO199 = Ministry of Home Security, Intelligence Branch, Registered Files:

Piece number 114 = Bethnal Green shelter disaster during air raid on London 3 Mar 1943: announcements made on foreign radio programmes, 1943.

HO200 = Ministry of Home Security, Tube Shelter Committee, Registered Files:

Piece number 1 = Public shelter occupancy statistics, 1940-1942.

Piece number 2 = General organisation and directive policy, 1941-1943.

Piece number 3 = Agreements for use of tubes with the London Passenger Transport Board, 1941-1943.

Piece number 4 = Access and emergency opening arrangements, 1941-1943.

Piece number 5 = Monthly reports, January to August 1943 by the Secretary of the Tube Shelter Committee, 1943.

Piece number 6 = Agenda and minutes of meetings 1941-1943 and correspondence, 1941-1944.

Piece number 7 = Maintenance agreements with the London Passenger Transport Board, 1942-1944.

Piece number 8 = Deep tube shelters: Manager's reports January to July 1944, 1944.

Piece number 9 = Allocation of tickets for deep tube shelters, 1944-1945.

Piece number 10 = Construction and maintenance of deep tube shelters, 1944-1945.

Government Department Records etc:

HO205 = Ministry of Home Security, "O" Division, Correspondence and Papers:

Piece number 28 = Bethnal Green underground station shelter accident: Secretary of State reports on inquiry by Mr Lawrence Dunne, 1943.

Piece number 29 = Bethnal Green underground station shelter accident: suggestions for improvements in access to shelters from lessons learnt, 1943.

Piece number 36 = Bethnal Green underground station shelter accident: proposal to construct an additional entrance to control access, 1943.

Piece number 124 = Chalmers Kearney: proposed tube-railway construction for use as air-raid shelter in wartime, 1940-41.

Piece number 134 = Deep tunnel shelters: protection for War Cabinet and War Rooms, 1939-1943.

Piece number 187 = Publicity on London's tube shelters, 1942.

Piece number 189 = Indemnity and Agreement with the London Passenger Transport Board on provision of tunnel shelters, 1940-1943.

Piece number 190 = Underground railway shelters: management and control in London, 1941-1945.

Piece number 191 = Eight new tube shelters in London, 1942-1944.

Piece number 192 = New tube shelters: access through underground railway stations, 1942-1944.

Piece number 193 = Tube shelters: arrangements for the supply of water, 1942-1945.

Piece number 194 = New Tube Shelter Committee: progress reports, 1942.

Piece number 195 = Tube tunnel shelters: use for war production, 1942-1943.

Piece number 196 = Tube shelters: use in London as sleeping accommodation for British and American service personnel, 1942-1945.

Piece number 197 = Tube shelters: anti-flooding precautions, 1943-1944.

Piece number 198 = Goodge Street South underground station tunnel: use as Supreme Allied Command Headquarters, 1943-1945.

Piece number 199 = Chancery Lane underground station tunnel: adaption as citadel accommodation, 1944-1945.

Piece number 200 = Clapham Common underground station tunnel: use as citadel accommodation, 1944-1945.

Piece number 201 = Safety measures at the entrances to tube shelters, 1943-1945.

Piece number 202 = Chancery Lane deep tube shelter: use by Public Record Office for storage of documents, 1945.

Piece number 203 = Survey of locations in and around London suitable for tunnelling to provide shelters, 1940-1944.

Piece number 208 = Liverpool Street Central Line railway tunnel: use as underground shelter, 1943-1945.

Piece number 209 = Stratford-Leyton Central Line railway tunnel: use as underground shelter, 1943.

Piece number 223 = Shelter provision: policy for London, 1939-1944.

Piece number 224 = Bethnal Green and Mile End: use of this section of underground tunnel as shelter not approved due to risk of flooding, 1944.

Piece number 225 = Underground railways in London: safety measures to minimise risks to shelterers, 1939-1945.

Piece number 226 = Underground railways in London: withdrawal of shelter facilities, 1941-1945.

Piece number 227 = Bethnal Green tube shelter disaster: setting up enquiry and warrant appointing Mr Laurence Rivers Dunne as Chairman, 1943.

Piece number 228 = Bethnal Green tube shelter disaster: offers by members of the public to give evidence, 1943.

Piece number 229 = Bethnal Green tube shelter disaster: claims for expenses of witnesses attending official enquiry, 11 to 17 March, 1943.

Piece number 230 = Bethnal Green tube shelter disaster: police statements, 1943.

Piece number 231 = Bethnal Green tube shelter disaster: letters from the public, 1943.

Piece number 232 = Bethnal Green tube shelter disaster: draft report, 1943.

Piece number 233 = Bethnal Green tube shelter disaster: Dunne Report, 1943.

Piece number 234 = Bethnal Green tube shelter disaster: requests for copies of official report, 1943.

Piece number 235 = Bethnal Green tube shelter disaster: papers and memoranda compiled for Mr. Dunne.

Piece number 236 = Bethnal Green tube shelter disaster: letters from the public, 1943.

Piece number 237 = Bethnal Green tube shelter disaster: requests from "Daily Herald" to take photographs at the enquiry, 1943.

Piece number 238 = Bethnal Green tube shelter disaster: publication concerning the Dunne enquiry, 1943.

Piece number 252 = London Passenger Transport Board tube stations and new tube shelters: number of shelterers: weekly returns 9 July 1944 to 30 June 1945, 1944-1945.

Piece number 253 = Clapham North, Clapham South and Stockwell: diagrams of deep tube shelters. Undated.

Piece number 256 = Tunnel shelters: plans. Undated.

Piece number 266 = Shelters in underground railways in London: contracts and costs, 1940-1946.

Piece number 267 = Shelters in underground railways in London: contracts and costs, 1940-1946.

Piece number 268 = Shelters in underground railways in London: contracts and costs, 1940-1946.

Piece number 269 = Deep tube shelters: accountant's reports, 1941-1943.

Piece number 270 = Deep tube shelters: accountant's reports, 1944-1946.

HO205 = Ministry of Home Security, "O" Division, Correspondence and Papers: *continued..*

Piece number 271 = Underground railway shelters in London: accommodation arrangements, 1941-1946.

Piece number 272 = Tube shelters: arrangements for the supply of electricity, 1942-1946.

Piece number 273 = Tube shelters: use as rest centres and for housing the homeless, 1945-1946.

Piece number 274 = Goodge Street South underground shelter: use as Army headquarters, 1942-1946.

Piece number 284 = Deep tube shelters: transfer to Ministry of Works and War Office, 1945-1947.

Piece number 303 = Deep tube shelters: financial administration and control, 1940-1948.

Piece number 306 = Underground railways in London: withdrawal of shelter equipment: post-war restoration, 1945-1948.

Piece number 319 = Underground shelters: allocation to and use by General Post Office, 1949.

Piece number 337 = Requisitioning of premises in London for the construction of deep level shelters, 1940-1950.

Piece number 338 = Agreement with the London Passenger Transport Board for the maintenance of equipment, 1942-1950.

Piece number 358 = Bethnal Green tube shelter disaster: claims by members of the public for personal injury, 1941-1955.

Piece number 359 = Bethnal Green tube shelter disaster: claims by members of the public for personal injury, 1941-1955.

Piece number 364 = London: tube railways: use of uncompleted sections as deep shelters, 1941.

HO206 = Ministry of Home Security, Regional Technical Adviser's and Regional Work Adviser's Registration Files:

Piece number 1 = Southwark Borough: disused tube tunnels, 1939-1940.

Piece number 4 = Southwark Borough: Borough High Street tunnel shelter, 1939-1943.

Piece number 5 = Southwark Borough: Old City and South London Tube; disused tube tunnels, 1939-1943.

Piece number 6 = Bethnal Green: tube shelter, 1940-1943.

Piece number 7 = Stepney Borough: disused underground station at St. Mary's, Whitechapel, 1940-1943.

Piece number 8 = Finsbury Borough: disused tube station in City Road, 1941-1943.

Piece number 9 = Holborn Borough: British Museum disused tube station, 1941-1943.

Piece number 10 = Aldwych tube station, 1941-1943.

Piece number 11 = West Ham Borough: disused tube tunnels, 1941-1943.

Piece number 13 = Smithfield: disused railway tunnel, 1939-1944.

Piece number 15 = Liverpool Street tube station, 1940-1945.

HO207 = Home Office and Ministry of Home Security, Civil Defence Regions Headquarters and Regional files:

Piece number 10 = River Thames Tunnels: use as air raid shelters in event of war, 1935-1939.

Piece number 92 = Chancery Lane deep tunnel: reserve war room accommodation, 1944-1945.

Piece number 226 = Special survey showing occupancy of tube station shelters for periods between Sept 1940 and May 1945, 1940-1945.

Piece number 227 = Number of shelterers in tube stations for periods Jan to Dec 1944, 1944.

Piece number 346 = New Tube Shelter Committee: offices for manager and staff, 1943.

Piece number 350 = Tube Shelter Committee: responsibilities, 1941-1944.

Piece number 354 = Deep tunnel shelters: allocation of accommodation, 1944.

Piece number 357 = Tube stations and certain other large public shelters: revised standard of medical supplies available, 1941-1943.

Piece number 359 = Vermin in shelters: special action necessary in tube shelters, 1940-1944.

Piece number 363 = Living conditions in certain air raid shelters including trenches and tube station shelters: reports, 1940-1941.

Piece number 386 = Public Shelters, tube stations and deep shelters: reports on welfare and general conditions, 1940-1945.

Piece number 401 = Tube station shelters: provision; report of meeting between members of Ministry of Transport, London Passenger Transport Board and Home Secretary, 1940-1941.

Piece number 402 = Tube shelters, Chiselhurst caves and tunnels at Coulsdon, Epsom and Kenley: authority for requisitioning, 1943.

Piece number 404 = Tube stations: use as public shelters, 1940-1944.

Piece number 405 = Tube station shelters: disposal of sewage, 1940-1943.

Piece number 406 = Tube station shelters: reports by London Passenger Transport Board on sanitary arrangements and provision of bunks and first aid posts, 1940-1943.

Piece number 407 = Tube shelters: maintenance of latrines and bunks, 1940-1941.

Piece number 408 = Tube stations: control of shelterers; draft rules for guidance of local authorities, shelter wardens and police, 1943-1945.

Piece number 409 = Underground tube stations: issue of tickets to people sheltering, 1940-1941.

Piece number 410 = Disused tube tunnels and stations: use as additional shelter accommodation, 1940-1941.

Piece number 411 = Tube station shelters: first aid facilities, 1940-1941.

Government Department Records etc:

HO207 = Home Office and Ministry of Home Security, Civil Defence Regions Headquarters and Regional files: *continued....*

Piece number 412 = Tube station shelters: closing owing to traffic difficulties, 1942.

Piece number 413 = Tube station shelters: closing for economy reasons, 1941-1943.

Piece number 414 = Tube stations: post-war arrangements for clearing of shelter equipment, 1945.

Piece number 415 = Tube station shelters: form of indemnity approved by Treasury, 1940-1943.

Piece number 416 = Tube stations: bunks, 1940-1943.

Piece number 417 = Tube station shelters: provision of amenities, 1941-1943.

Piece number 418 = Tube station shelters: anti-gas measures, 1941-1943.

Piece number 419 = Interdepartmental Committee on London Tube Shelter Accommodation: terms of reference, 1941.

Piece number 420 = Tube stations used as shelters: floodgates and watertight doors, 1942-1943.

Piece number 431 = Shelter accommodation: scheme for issue of tickets, 1940.

Piece number 442 = New Tube Shelter Committee: appointment and powers; correspondence and papers, 1941-1944.

Piece number 443 = Tube station shelters: equipment and stores, 1941-1945.

Piece number 444 = Tube station shelters: liaison with other government departments about supplies for canteens, 1941-1945.

Piece number 445 = Tube station shelters: medical aid posts, 1941-1943.

Piece number 446 = Tube station shelters and equipment: maintenance, 1941-1943.

Piece number 447 = Tube station shelters: progress reports for 19 May and 16 June 1942 and reports of Superintendents' 40th and 42nd to 50th meetings about general administration, 1942-1945.

Piece number 448 = Tube station shelters: special conference called with local authorities; co-operation in management and control, 1942-1944.

Piece number 449 = Tunnel shelters by the New Tube Shelter Committee: administration*, 1942-1944.
    * See also HO200.

Piece number 450 = New tube shelters: reports on access and construction work, 1941-1943.

Piece number 451 = Deep tube shelters: opening, 1944.

Piece number 471 = Goodge Street Station tunnel shelter: use by American army personnel, 1942.

Piece number 475 = Tube stations and tunnel shelters: special reports on expenditure, 1941-1944.

Piece number 503 = Tube station shelters: police report on condition and behaviour of the public, 1940 (closed for 75 years).

Piece number 513 = London Bridge Station: tube shelter, 1941-1944.

Piece number 518 = Bethnal Green - Tube shelter disaster: newspaper cuttings, 1943.

Piece number 519 = Bethnal Green - Emergency entrance to tube shelter after the disaster in March 1943, 1943-1945.

Piece number 618 = Finsbury - City Road Underground Station Shelter, 1940-1944.

Piece number 625 = Greenwich - Deep tunnel shelters, 1940-1942.

Piece number 636 = Hampstead - Tube station shelters, 1943-1944.

Piece number 651 = Holborn - Chancery Lane old tube station as public shelter, 1940.

Piece number 653 = Holborn - Disused British Museum tube station: use as shelter, 1940-1945.

Piece number 654 = Holborn tube station and Aldwych tunnel as air raid shelters, 1941.

Piece number 656 = Hornsey - Deep tunnel shelters, 1940-1941.

Piece number 660 = Islington - Tubes and Underground railways: use as shelters, 1939-1940.

Piece number 664 = Deep tunnel shelters: provision in association with tube system, 1940.

Piece number 676 = Islington - Tube station shelters, 1941-1943.

Piece number 981 = South Kensington Station: public shelter in sub-way under Exhibition Road, 1940-1946.

Piece number 685 = Kensington - Tube station shelters, 1941-1943.

Piece number 710 = Lambeth - Underground and trench shelters: complaints, 1940-1942.

Piece number 711 = Lambeth - Tube station shelters, 1942-1944.

Piece number 721 = Leyton - Tunnel shelters, 1940-1945.

Piece number 723 = London: City. Public shelters including basements and tunnels: addresses of public shelters requisitioned in private premises, 1938-1941 (1959).

Piece number 727 = Smithfield: public shelter in disused railway tunnel, 1939-1945.

Piece number 731 = Liverpool Street Station: tunnel shelter, 1940-1945.

Piece number 740 = Liverpool Street tunnel shelter: substitution of steel for timber bunks, 1940-1944.

Piece number 760 = Merton and Morden - Tube station shelters, 1943.

Piece number 781 = Paddington - Station subway: agreement with London Passenger Transport Board for use as public shelters, 1941.

Piece number 784 = Tube station shelters, 1943-1944.

Piece number 820 = South Kensington tube station: use of disused station as shelter, 1941-1945.

Piece number 835 = Southwark - Shelters: use of disused railway tunnels, 1939-1942.

Piece number 845 = Southwark - Tube station shelters, 1941-1944.

Piece number 859 = St. Mary's Underground Station, Whitechapel Road: public shelter in disused station, 1940-1945 (1953).

Piece number 919 = Wandsworth - Tube station shelters, 1943-1944.

Piece number 994 = Aldwych tube station shelters, 1941-1946.

Piece number 997 = Bethnal Green - Tube shelter, 1939-1947.

Piece number 1020 = Tube shelter disaster in Mar 1943, 1939-1945 (closed for 75 years).

HO228 = Home Office: Scientific Adviser's Branch: Reports (Z Series):

Piece number 1 = Notes on the occupancy of shelters during attack by V1 weapons on London, 1944.

Government Department Records etc:

METROPOLITAN POLICE:

MEPO 1 = Office of the Commissioner, Letter Books:
Piece number 56 = From Public Carriage Office to Various. Volume 1 (Indexed), 30 Apr 1850 - 6 Mar 1855.

Piece number 57 = From Public Carriage Office to Home Office. Volume 2 (Indexed), 21 Nov 1860 - 6 Oct 1880.

MEPO 2 = Metropolitan Police, Office of the Commissioner, Correspondence and Papers:
Piece number 241 = Traffic statistics: Central London, City and West End Railways, 1890-1903.

Piece number 280 = Omnibuses: improper ventilation, 1891-1902.

Piece number 322 = Omnibuses: fare increases without notice, 1893-1907.

Piece number 423 = Explosion at Aldersgate Street Station, 1897.

Piece number 678 = Omnibuses - registration marks, 1904-1905.

Piece number 695 = Stations: use of police lavatories by tramwaymen, 1904.

Piece number 780 = Light Railways Act 1903: licensing of electric tramcars as stage carriages, 1905-1920.

Piece number 790 = Tramcars: overcrowding, 1905.

Piece number 792 = Metropolitan electric tramways: excess passengers Bye Law, 1905-1906.

Piece number 793 = Tramcars: whether subject to provisions of Motor Car Acts, 1905.

Piece number 819 = Traffic: motor omnibuses without lights, 1905-1907.

Piece number 907 = Street collections on omnibuses, 1905.

Piece number 925 = London County Council tramcars: experimental use of trailer cars, 1905-1912.

Piece number 926 = Middlesex County Council (Tramways) Bill, 1906.

Piece number 972 = Traffic: motor bus drivers; leaving vehicle with engine running, 1906.

Piece number 985 = West Ham Corporation tramways: drivers and conductors; suggested transfer of licensing to local authority, 1906.

Piece number 989 = Tramcars: suitability of brakes, 1906.

Piece number 1009 = Cabs and omnibuses: Report of Select Committee (1906), 1906.

Piece number 1027 = Motor omnibuses: unlicensed drivers, 1906.

Piece number 1069 = Tramcars: period of renovation, 1907.

Piece number 1076 = Motor omnibus testing: annoyance caused at Wimbledon, 1907-1912.

Piece number 1077 = Tramways Bill: House of Commons Committee; attendance of officers, 1907.

Piece number 1123 = Commendations: Metropolitan railway collision - awards, 1907-1908.

Piece number 1159 = London United Tramways Bill 1908: observations on Draft Bill, 1908.

Piece number 1240 = Traffic: dangerous tramway standards, 1907-1915.

Piece number 1248 = Public service vehicles, tramcars and cars: 1908-1909.

Piece number 1253 = London United Tramways Bill 1909 (printed): 1909-1910.

Piece number 1254 = Central London Railway Bill 1909: 1909.

Piece number 1255 = London County Council Tramways and Improvements Act 1909: 1909-1910.

Piece number 1278 = Motor cab and omnibus drivers' licences: testing of applicants, 1909.

Piece number 1291 = Tramcars (Disabled) Regulations: 1909-1916.

Piece number 1327 = London County Council tramway improvements, 1909-1920.

Piece number 1386 = Motor Omnibuses: examination by Noise Committee, 1910.

Piece number 1412 = Metropolitan Electric Tramways Bill 1911, 1910-1911.

Piece number 1428 = Greater London Railway Bill 1911, 1911.

Piece number 1509 = Tramways: passengers refusing to pay fares - Police Powers, 1912-1914.

Piece number 1600 = Traffic: Refuges in connection with London County Council tramways, 1913-1914.

Piece number 1601 = London County Council trams: employment of youths as conductors assistants, 1914.

Piece number 1709 = Erith Urban District Council: purchase of tramcars from Hull, 1915-1918.

Piece number 1735 = Air Raids - Shelters: Underground Railway Stations, 1917-1918.

Piece number 1736 = Air Raids - Shelters: excessive numbers using during raids, 1918.

Piece number 1806 = Proposals for the construction of pedestrian subways: London County Council district. Includes traffic returns and plans, 1909-1913, **AND** Ditto for Westminster City Council, 1911-1912.

Piece number 2094 = London Traffic Act, 1924: preparation of schedules, 1924-1926.

Piece number 2105 = London County Council (Tramways and Improvements) Bill, 1915, 1914-1922.

Piece number 2106 = Beaconsfield-Strand-Omnibus route No 98, 1926 1927.

Piece number 2108 = London General Omnibus Company centenary celebrations: operation of three horse-drawn buses, 1929.

Piece number 2109 = London Electric Railway Act, 1923: Piccadilly Circus and Leicester Square Stations, 1922-1929.

Piece number 2116 = London "General" Omnibus Company: failing to display table of fares inside buses, 1923.

Piece number 2139 = Piccadilly Circus: regrading of roadway and waterproofing of "Underground Railway" station roof, 1931-1932.

Piece number 2141 = London Tramways: weather protection screens for passengers at Charing Cross and Waterloo, 1923-1925.

Government Department Records etc:

MEPO 2 = Metropolitan Police, Office of the Commissioner, Correspondence and Papers:
    continued....

Piece number 2142 = Omnibus and tramcar stopping places: Ealing Common Railway Stations, 1924-1933.

Piece number 2147 = Public Service Vehicles: Prohibition of police officers giving certificates of character, 1920.

Piece number 2149 = Fatal accident: motor omnibus destroyed by fire, 30 August 1924.

Piece number 2150 = Smoking inside omnibuses, 1924.

Piece number 2151 = Endorsement of proprietors licences on appointment of new general manager of London County Council Tramways, 1925.

Piece number 2152 = Obsolete public carriage badges, 1927-1928.

Piece number 2153 = Public Service Vehicles: Disqualification for driving under the influence of drink or drugs, 1931-1933.

Piece number 2154 = Road Traffic Act, 1930: licensing of conductors and drivers of public service vehicles in the City and Metropolitan Police District, 1931-1933.

Piece number 2155 = London Passenger Transport Bill, 1931-1932.

Piece number 2156 = Conditions of fitness for Metropolitan short-stage carriages, 1931-1933.

Piece number 2157 = Metropolitan short stage Carriage Order 1931, 1931-1933.

Piece number 2158 = Drivers and Conductors: issue of composite licences to act as either, 1931.

Piece number 2159 = Public Service Vehicles: Appeals against decisions of Traffic Commissioners, 1931-1932.

Piece number 2161 = Fire extinguishers: approval of types "Protex" "Taxex" and "Dominion", 1929-1931.

Piece number 2162 = Fitting of pneumatic tyres to omnibuses licensed on and after 1 Jan. 1930, 1929.

Piece number 2163 = Municipal Mutual Insurance Ltd. Commissioner authorised acceptance of policies for public carriages within the Metropolitan Police District, 1930.

Piece number 2166 = Public Service Vehicles: Direction indicators, 1930-1932.

Piece number 2167 = Standing passengers in stage carriages, 1915-1922.

Piece number 2168 = Hoods for double deck omnibuses: six wheeled public service vehicles (the "NS" Type), 1923-1928.

Piece number 2169 = Single deck omnibus: new type low loading "Dennis" chassis, 1925-1927.

Piece number 2170 = London "General" Omnibus: New type "S.T.1", 1929-1930.

Piece number 2171 = Omnibus destroyed by fire in Rotherhithe Tunnel 16 May 1931, 1931.

Piece number 2172 = The "one man" tramcar, 1922-1925.

Piece number 2173 = Coupled tramcar unit: trial and experiment with magnetic brakes, 1923-1927.

Piece number 2174 = Study of provincial tramway systems and headlights on London tramcars, 1909-1924.

Piece number 2175 = Stability of tramcars: explanatory memoranda, 1924.

Piece number 2177 = Woman fatally injured by "Green Line" coach: carrying of lifting jacks and tools, 1930.

Piece number 2178 = Medical examination of public service vehicle and motor cab drivers from the age of 50 years and upwards, 1911-1922.

Piece number 2179 = The "Pirate" Bus era: dangerous driving caused by "shadowing" or "sandwiching", 1922-1923.

Piece number 2180 = Applicants for public carriage licences: supply of information by Ministry of Labour, 1923-1924.

Piece number 2182 = Lost Property: silk scroll of 12 Chinese paintings of the 17th-18th century left on omnibus and subsequently destroyed by fire, 1926-1928.

Piece number 2183 = Refusal of public service licence on medical grounds: successful appeal and costs against police, 1931.

Piece number 2184 = Operation of tramcars and other vehicles in various exhibition grounds, 1909-1923.

Piece number 2185 = Fire extinguishing appliances for use on public service vehicles, 1927-1932.

Piece number 2229 = Property found in public carriages: payment of awards to drivers and conductors, 1910-1932.

Piece number 2255 = Photographic record of 'B' type omnibus driving tests carried out at New Scotland Yard, 1923.

Piece number 3133 = Public Carriage licensed Drivers and Conductors convicted for offences during the General Strike, 1926-1927.

Piece number 3153 = Metropolitan Police Traffic Manual, 1933-1940.

Piece number 3327 = Donation of 4% stock accruing from the "Daily Express" Horse-omnibus Drivers Fund, 1934-1936.

Piece number 3391 = Police at Tube and Railway stations, 1938-1940.

Piece number 3426 = Offer of closed Tube stations for police use, 1939-1940.

Piece number 3466 = Lighting of Underground trains, destination panels and depots, 1940-1945.

Piece number 3483 = Fog lamps on tram cars, 1940.

Piece number 3534 = Group Reserve Centre - Knightsbridge Underground Station, 1939-1942.

Piece number 3546 = Provision of respirators etc for London Transport drivers and conductors, 1939-1942.

Piece number 3568 = War Reserves recruited from London Passenger Transport Board, 1939.

Piece number 3720 = River Emergency Service, 1939-1942.

Piece number 3722 = Use of Underground Stations and railway tunnels during air raids, 1940.

Government Department Records etc:

MEPO 2 = Metropolitan Police, Office of the Commissioner, Correspondence and Papers: *continued....*

Piece number 3853 = Telephone line between Underground station and Marble Arch Police Station, 1934.

Piece number 4014 = Various methods of familiarising horses to dustcarts, pigeons, bearskins and London Passenger Transport Board tower wagons, 1937-1939.

Piece number 4550 = Disqualification of premises at Putney Sports Club: subsequent application for use as a Transport Board Canteen, 1939-1941.

Piece number 4687 = Omnibus routes: printed booklets of approved routes for public carriages, 1925-1935.

Piece number 4689 = Commissioner's approval of routes under Section 6 of London Traffic Act 1924: legal aspect, 1929-1938.

Piece number 4697 = Withdrawal of bridge guards by London General Omnibus Company Limited on economy grounds, 1926-1932. (The guards were placed at certain specific points at bridges on double decker omnibus routes).

Piece number 4714 = Census of traffic undertaken by Metropolitan and City Police and the Port of London Authority, 1934-1937.

Piece number 4726 = Routes operated by public service vehicles: where and where not to stop, 1936.

Piece number 4727 = Pedestrian guard rails at tram stopping places ("Head Stops"), 1936-1938.

Piece number 4728 = Preparation of omnibus routes: approvals for routes, types, accessories and restrictions, 1923-1939.

Piece number 4745 = Lay out and subway at Swan and Edgar's corner, Piccadilly Circus, 1926-1936.

Piece number 4747 = Junction of Bethnal Green Road - Brick Lane: removal of stalls, 'bus stop etc to facilitate traffic, 1930-1942.

Piece number 4766 = East Hill, Wandsworth: dangerous conditions for pedestrians caused by old tram track, 1933-1937.

Piece number 4775 = London Passenger Transport Board Bill 1934 (1), 1933-1936.

Piece number 4776 = London Passenger Transport Board Bill 1935 (2), 1935.

Piece number 4779 = The A.E.C. Renown type six wheeler omnibus in single and double decker form, 1930-1932.

Piece number 4780 = Route 238: enlargement of Turnpike Lane Station and use of double decker buses, 1935-1937.

Piece number 4781 = Route revision in Eastern Area (Barking, Becontree and Romford), 1936-1951.

Piece number 4782 = Routes 22, 108 and 208: approval and alterations, 1931-1937.

Piece number 4783 = Approval of various 409 S.S. (Special service routes), 1937-1950.

Piece number 4784 = Special service 402: Watford and Queens Rangers ground, 1937-1953.

Piece number 4785 = Special service 341: Watford and Crystal Palace, 1937-1953.

Piece number 4786 = Special service 454: Redhill and Imber Court, 1938-1954.

Piece number 4787 = Re-introduction of Special service 455 (Redhill and Sutton), 1938-1955.

Piece number 4788 = Special service number 60 (Associated Equipment Company Limited staff) Leyton to Southall, 1938-1952.

Piece number 4806 = Device enabling trolley buses to pass over Fire Brigade hoses on roadway, 1931-1933.

Piece number 4811 = Piccadilly widening involving section of Green Park: new booking hall, adjustments of cab ranks and stopping places, 1930-1950.

Piece number 4814 = Closure of railway crossing at Churchfield Road, Acton, during reconstruction, 1936-1954.

Piece number 4815 = Finchley Memorial bus stand and suggested turning point at Regents Park Road, 1935-1955.

Piece number 4816 = Stopping Places: Development of Eccleston Place Motor Coach Station, 1932-1938.

Piece number 4866 = Dangerous driving by overtaking tramcar when passengers alighting: Transport Board Police request assistance in identifying driver, 1935.

Piece number 4886 = Standing passengers in public service vehicles, 1928-1937.

Piece number 4887 = Committee of Enquiry into London Motor Coach Services, 1932-1933.

Piece number 4888 = Method of dealing with unfitness of public service vehicles and Metropolitan short stage carriages, 1932.

Piece number 4893A = Use of a ten seater passenger vehicle at Bromley and the contravention of the Road Traffic Act 1930, 1932-1933.

Piece number 4893B = Public service vehicle drivers and conductors and taxicab drivers: certain restrictions and medical certificates, 1927-1936.

Piece number 4897 = Public Carriage Passing Stations: standard specification of requirements, 1937.

Piece number 4898 = The work of a Public Carriage Office Passing Station: locations and improvements, 1931-1940.

Piece number 4899 = Public Service Vehicle Insurance: "named driver" limitation, 1925-1935.

Piece number 4900 = All metal taxi and 'bus bodies: specification, advantages of construction and observations, 1930-1937.

Piece number 4907 = London United Tramways trackless trolley 'buses: design, blueprints, routes and inspection, 1930-1945.

Piece number 4908 = Employment of men of colour as cab drivers, 'bus drivers and conductors, 1917-1932.

Government Department Records etc:

MEPO 2 = Metropolitan Police, Office of the Commissioner, Correspondence and Papers: *continued....*

Piece number 4912 = London Passenger Transport Act 1933: obsolete and new forms of licence for drivers and conductors, 1935.

Piece number 4913 = Operation of clerestory (N.S. type) double deck 'buses through Blackwall Tunnel: blueprints and tests, 1926-1938.

Piece number 4914 = London Passenger Transport Board Bill 1937 and extension of time order 1940 for compulsory purchase of lands etc, 1936-1940.

Piece number 4915 = London Passenger Transport Board Bill 1938 and extension of time order 1941, 1937-1941.

Piece number 4916 = Discussions between London Passenger Transport Board, local authorities and other bodies, 1938-1939.

Piece number 4917 = Experimental operation of a 30 foot public service vehicle on coach route A 1, 1939.

Piece number 4918 = Complaints about Public Carriage Service during wartime: decision to establish direct police - Transport Board - local authority contacts, 1939.

Piece number 5101 = Lost property in public service vehicles: Public Service Vehicle (Lost Property) (Amendment) Regulations 1958, 1931-1959.

Piece number 5103 = Handling of property found by omnibus garage employees and cleaners to conductors, 1932.

Piece number 5104 = Damage caused through property being left on 'bus: furnishing owner's name and address, 1933.

Piece number 5171 = Diaries for Public Carriage officers (new pattern), 1938.

Piece number 5185 = First aid treatment for Lambeth staff and persons attending Public Carriage and Lost Property Offices, 1926-1927.

Piece number 5332 = Lost property: summonses against bus drivers and conductors failing to promptly deposit, 1925.

Piece number 5337 = Public Carriage Office: standardisation of forms on removal to Lambeth, 1927.

Piece number 5351 = Public Carriage Office: registration improvements, 1932-1936.

Piece number 5359 = Public Carriage Office staff: adjustment of strength between civilians and police, 1933-1936.

Piece number 5360 = "B.1", "B.3" and "B.5" Branches: adjustments caused through London Passenger Transport Bill, 1933.

Piece number 5380 = Public Carriage Office: civilian establishment, 1935-1942.

Piece number 5411 = Transfer of Lost Property and Public Carriage Offices to 109, Lambeth Road, 1919-1928.

Piece number 5418 = Alterations in accommodation at Lambeth and Public Carriage premises following London Passenger Transport Bill, 1933.

Piece number 5531 = Policing of public subways as affected by the London Passenger Transport Board Act 1939, 1938-1957.

Piece number 5532 = Erection of barriers in the vicinity of Piccadilly Underground Station to facilitate crowd control, 1936-1937.

Piece number 5548 = Impressment of horses and transport in time of National Emergency, 1924-1934.

Piece number 6354 = War Measures: Use of underground railway stations as air raid shelters: protective measures and control, 1941-1945.

Piece number 6363 = War Measures: Immobilisation of buses and trams in the event of invasion, 1941-1943.

Piece number 6391 = War Measures: Control of tunnels under Thames, 1938-1946.

Piece number 6437 = War Measures: Public Service Vehicles and heavy goods vehicles: issue of permits to drivers instead of licences, 1939-1946.

Piece number 6479 = War Measures: Evacuation of school children from London: arrangements with London County Council, Ministry of Health and London Passenger Transport Board, 1940-1944.

Piece number 6481 = War Measures: Buses and trolleybuses: police supervision of headlamps designed to comply with lighting restrictions, 1940-1944.

Piece number 6657 = Proposal by London Passenger Transport Board to have earlier and more uniform closing hours: Home Office requests police observations, 1942-1943.

Piece number 6717 = Omnibus struck by falling road-side tree, three passengers killed: Solicitors Department notes on legal position, 1938-1945.

Piece number 6766 = Road works in Blackwall Tunnel vicinity: re-routing of bus services, 1935-1966.

Piece number 6768 = Traffic arrangements during the reconstruction of Kings Cross station, 1936-1942.

Piece number 6772 = Stopping places: Route 408: Green (country) route south of Thames, 1940-1965.

Piece number 6773 = Stopping places: Substitution of buses for railway services interrupted by enemy action, 1940-1942.

Piece number 6774 = Stopping places: Marking of omnibus stopping places on roadway, 1938-1964.

Piece number 6775 = Stopping places: Laws requiring public transport passengers to wait in lines or queues, 1938-1955.

Piece number 6776 = Stopping places: Route 312: Green (country) route north of Thames, 1936-1964.

Piece number 6777 = Stopping places: Route 37: Red (central) route south of Thames, 1938-1966.

Government Department Records etc:

MEPO 2 = Metropolitan Police, Office of the Commissioner, Correspondence and Papers:
continued....

Piece number 6778 = Stopping places: Route 310: Green (country) route north of Thames, 1935-1964.

Piece number 6779 = Stopping places: Route 455: Green (country) Amersham re-organisation scheme, 1936-1965.

Piece number 6780 = Stopping places: Route 228: Red (central) route south of Thames, 1939-1966.

Piece number 6781 = Stopping places: Route 12: Red (central) route crossing Thames, 1939-1966.

Piece number 6782 = Stopping places: Route 68: Red (central) route crossing Thames, 1937-1966.

Piece number 6783 = Stopping places: Route 230: Red (single deck) route north of Thames, 1941-1964.

Piece number 6784 = Stopping places: Route 227: Red (single deck) route south of Thames, 1942-1964.

Piece number 6785 = Stopping places: Green Line coach operation in central London: preparation and resumption after wartime suspension, 1942-1947.

Piece number 6786 = Stopping places: Introduction of gas producer buses on certain routes: selection of turning points to allow for gas trailer, 1943-1944.

Piece number 6787 = Stopping places: Route 13: Red (central) route north of Thames, 1943-1965.

Piece number 6788 = Stopping places: Route 210: Red (single deck) route north of Thames, 1937-1965.

Piece number 6789 = Stopping places: Construction of tramway loop at Woolwich to provide better service for war-workers, 1944.

Piece number 6801 = Traffic Legislation: London Passenger Transport Act, 1933: transfer of powers and duties, 1933-1934.

Piece number 6812 = Public Service Vehicles (Equipment and Use) Regulations: specification of equipment to be carried and authority to dispense with conductor, 1931-1944 (See MEPO 2/8982 for Part II).

Piece number 6814 = Public Service Vehicles: suggested increase in length and suitable routes in the Metropolitan traffic area, 1944-1949.

Piece number 6816 = Restriction of fuel: wartime control of coach journeys from evacuation areas to reception areas, 1939-1940.

Piece number 6818 = Alien public carriage drivers: issue of permits, 1940-1944.

Piece number 6820 = Speed of omnibuses during wartime "black-out" hours: result of survey carried out by Traffic Branch in relation to 20 m.p.h. speed limit, 1940.

Piece number 6821 = Returns of public service vehicle drivers and conductors' licences and badges, 1929-1953.

Piece number 6826 = Mechanically propelled public carriages other than electric tramcars, licensed at the Public Carriage Office: quarterly returns of vehicles, 1921-1959.

Piece number 6828 = London Passenger Transport Board Bill, 1939: Commissioner's views, 1938-1945.

Piece number 6829 = Express bus services: operation on selected routes during peak travel hours, 1939-1941.

Piece number 6830 = Information kiosks erected by London Passenger Transport Board to assist the public after air raids, 1940-1945.

Piece number 6831 = Public Service Vehicle licences and certificates: annual requisitions to Ministry of Transport, 1931-1966.

Piece number 6833 = Taxi cab drivers and drivers and conductors of public service vehicles: extension of licences, 1932-1942.

Piece number 6838 = Private hire vehicles: question of legislation, 1935-1938.

Piece number 6841 = Licensing of drivers and conductors of public service vehicles, tramcars and trolley vehicles: transfer of powers to the Commissioner of Police, 1933-1959.

Piece number 6842 = Trolley bus route Barnet to Finsbury Square: inspection report, 1938.

Piece number 6844 = Drivers and conductors of the London Passenger Transport Board: employed for short periods without a licence or permit as a wartime measure, 1941-1945.

Piece number 6845 = Suggested amendments to Public Service Forms 16 and 16A and Public Carriage Forms 17 and 17A: war measures, 1943-1944.

Piece number 6849 = Applications by ex-soldiers for Public Service Vehicle licences: introduction of new character and health certificates, 1921-1949.

Piece number 6982 = Commissioner's ruling to grant a pedlar's certificate to the holder of a public service vehicle or a cab-driver's licence, 1945-1947.

Piece number 7204 = Protection of tunnels under Thames during first world war, 1914-1918.

Piece number 7209 = Public Carriages: grant of public carriage licences to men suffering from partial physical disability: Committee reports and correspondence, 1915-1941.

Piece number 7360 = Accidents to persons boarding or alighting from public service vehicles, 1936-1946.

Piece number 7376 = Omnibus and coach services in inner London: scheme for through green line services crossing central areas, short working turning points and "The Wheel Plan", 1935-1954.

Piece number 7377 = Traffic conditions in the vicinity of Victoria railway station, 1929-1958.

Piece number 7381 = Metropolitan and City of London Police annual census of vehicular traffic, 1919-1946.

Piece number 7382 = Road Vehicles Registration and Licensing Regulations, 1925-1949.

Piece number 7383 = Gas propelled vehicles: legislative measures covering taxation, speed limits, drawing of producer trailers, etc., 1933-1954.

Piece number 7386 = Omnibus workings: routes 244 and 603 approved, 1932-1965.

Piece number 7387 = Inter station bus services: special routes between main line railway stations, 1936-1964.

Government Department Records etc:

MEPO 2 = Metropolitan Police, Office of the Commissioner, Correspondence and Papers: *continued....*

Piece number 7388 = Special bus services to and from central London and various airports prior to development of Heathrow (London) Airport, 1939-1949.

Piece number 7397 = Stencil plates for public carriage approval marks: imprints from 1872 attached, 1928-1962.

Piece number 7399 = Conditions of Fitness Regulations, 1936 and 1941 for public service vehicles, 1930-1955.

Piece number 7400 = Public Carriage Office: census of work in connection with licensing and inspecting of public carriages and cost incurred, 1931-1966.

Piece number 7401 = Insurance of public carriages, 1931-1961.

Piece number 7403 = Public service vehicles over 27ft 6ins: Ministry of Transport directions respecting routes in the London area, 1933-1958.

Piece number 7404 = London Transport buses: suggestions for the safety of passengers, 1937-1946.

Piece number 7408 = Licensing Committee: representation of drivers and conductors by union official or solicitor when appearing before the Committee, 1921-1960.

Piece number 7492 = Public carriage licensees: supply of addresses to private persons, 1909-1924.

Piece number 7517 = London and Home Counties Traffic Advisory Committee: constitution and nomination of Metropolitan Police representative, 1924-1963.

Piece number 7521 = Traffic Control: Omnibus routes 104A, 131 and 551 - North London, 1921-1930.

Piece number 7522 = Traffic Control: Omnibus routes 78, 82, and 112 - South East London, 1931-1966.

Piece number 7523 = Traffic Control: Omnibus tours of London arranged by London Passenger Transport Board, 1935-1939.

Piece number 7524 = Traffic Control: Omnibus routes Alexandra Park and Wood Green Station, 1935-1964.

Piece number 7525 = Traffic Control: Croydon Aerodrome: Purley Way, 1929-1963.

Piece number 7526 = Stopping Places: Trolleybus turning circles: various routes, 1936-1939.

Piece number 7530 = Classification of public service vehicles, 1932-1965.

Piece number 7531 = Fitting of radio receiving sets in motor cabs and omnibuses, 1933-1956.

Piece number 7559 = Railway police recruits to visit a Metropolitan Police station as part of training, 1946-1948.

Piece number 7673 = Hire of buses to transport police to scenes of political meetings, etc., 1934-1935.

Piece number 7674 = Legal agreements between London Passenger Transport Board and Receiver for buses to transport police on special occasions, 1936-1965.

Piece number 7685 = Abstract of laws relating to proprietors, drivers, conductors of public carriages within the Metropolitan Police District and the City of London: instructions for reprinting, 1935-1950.

Piece number 7700 = War Measures: Thames road tunnels: lighting restrictions, 1940-1945.

Piece number 7705 = Wartime lighting restrictions on road vehicles, 1939-1947.

Piece number 7769 = Southgate Underground Station: traffic congestion, provision and parking facilities, 1938-1965.

Piece number 7798 = Oxford Circus: traffic conditions, 1932-1966.

Piece number 7801 = Peak Hour traffic: staggering of working hours, 1946-1957.

Piece number 7802 = Bus terminal, Sidcup Railway Station: operators appeal against decision of licensing authority, 1931-1966.

Piece number 7806 = Erection of refuges on routes where trams have been replaced by trolley vehicles, 1937-1940.

Piece number 7807 = Lists of special events which may affect traffic: half-yearly returns to Ministry of Transport, 1939-1950

Piece number 7810 = Approved bus routes: operation of double deck vehicles on certain routes, 1937-1963.

Piece number 7811 = Kings Cross motor coach station: selection of new site due to termination of lease, 1946-1966.

Piece number 7815 = Driving tests for new cab and public service drivers: policy, 1935-1966.

Piece number 7819 = Public Service Vehicles (Conduct of Drivers, Conductors and Passengers) Regulations 1931, 1933, 1936 and (Amendment) Regulations 1935 and 1946.

Piece number 7820 = "Green Line" coaches: destination indicator blinds to show black lettering on old gold coloured background, 1946.

Piece number 8039 = Refuges in tramway streets, 1932-1947.

Piece number 8045 = London Passenger Transport Board bye-laws 1947, 1947.

Piece number 8047 = London public service vehicles: licensing statistics from 1896, 1947-1953.

Piece number 8048 = Trolley vehicle requirements: draft revision of 1932 regulations, 1947-1961.

Piece number 8142 = Thames tunnels: control of speed of vehicles, 1934-1955.

Piece number 8148 = Blackwall and Rotherhithe tunnels: traffic conditions and proposed amendments to bye-laws, 1929-1968.

Piece number 8151 = London tramways: speed limit and stopping place regulations, 1932-1948.

Piece number 8152 = Property left on public service vehicles belonging to the London Passenger Transport Board: procedure, 1933-1936; 1947.

Government Department Records etc:

MEPO 2 = Metropolitan Police, Office of the Commissioner, Correspondence and Papers:
continued....

Piece number 8274 = Traffic accidents caused by road conditions or defective public service vehicles, 1934-1957.

Piece number 8286 = Victoria Station area: proposed improvement of traffic conditions, 1948-1956.

Piece number 8291 = Kingsway tunnel: conversion from tramway to normal traffic use, 1948-1966.

Piece number 8295 = Stopping Places: Coach operations: approved routes, 1948-1960.

Piece number 8301 = London Hackney Carriages Act, 1843, Sec.8: abstract of laws issued to drivers and conductors, 1948-1966.

Piece number 8303 = Public service vehicles: fitting of direction indicators and stop lights, 1937-1961.

Piece number 8306 = Trolley buses: general policy regarding traffic restrictions and speed limits, 1937-1950.

Piece number 8307 = Control of the number and frequency of omnibus journeys in London, 1933-1958.

Piece number 8370 = Parliamentary Questions: Examination of public service vehicles by Public Carriage Office, 1932.

Piece number 8372 = Parliamentary Questions: Provision of fareboards on top deck of London buses, 1932.

Piece number 8376 = Parliamentary Questions: Bus and tramcar stopping places, 1934.

Piece number 8385 = Parliamentary Questions: Obstruction caused by buses from Trafalgar Square stopping in Duncannon Street, 1936.

Piece number 8404 = Parliamentary Questions: Control of pedestrians by means of a level crossing gate at Victoria Embankment junction with Kingsway tunnel, 1939.

Piece number 8406 = Parliamentary Questions: Disused tube railway tunnel in Southwark: proposed air raid shelter, 1939.

Piece number 8447 = Medical examinations: applicants for public service vehicle drivers' and conductors' and motor cab drivers' licences - revised scale of fees for second opinion, 1948-1949, 1962-1965.

Piece number 8451 = Public Carriage Office Inspecting Staff: refreshment allowance and special allowances for technical skill, 1910-1922, 1949-1956.

Piece number 8463 = Horse drawn vehicles: licensing, 1932-1949.

Piece number 8464 = London Traffic Act, 1924 (Approval of Routes) Order, 1933.

Piece number 8471 = Revised procedure for recording licences issued by the Public Carriage Office, 1932-1934.

Piece number 8528 = London Passenger Transport Board Act, 1935: re-construction of Aldgate East, 1936-1947.

Piece number 8530 = Stopping Places: Proposed consultation on conditions of pedestrian safety before construction of London Transport Executive railway stations, 1949-1957.

Piece number 8531 = South London tramway conversion scheme: replacement of trams by omnibuses, 1949-1952.

Piece number 8532 = 1949 Police report on public service vehicles for the Metropolitan Traffic Area, 1949-1950.

Piece number 8568 = Census of vehicles passing over Waterloo Bridge on 18 July 1939 and 12 July 1949, 1949-1950.

Piece number 8585 = Traffic congestion in London: measures to reduce, 1910-1950.

Piece number 8599 = Traffic census in Metropolitan and City Police Districts: 1937, 1939, 1949, 1952 and 1954.

Piece number 8604 = Issue of licences to taxi drivers and public service vehicle drivers and conductors, 1931-1961.

Piece number 8662 = Festival of Britain, 1951: Traffic: arrangements and publicity campaign, 1950-1951.

Piece number 8694 = Use of London Transport Board breakdown lorries for the removal of heavy vehicles: police procedure, 1929-1969.

Piece number 8699 = South London tramway conversion scheme: bus route No.57 replacing tram route No.20 (Specimen), 1950-1965.

Piece number 8700 = Introduction of 8 feet wide omnibuses to central London: opposition and subsequent approval, 1950.

Piece number 8703 = Licensing of cabs and cab drivers, and public service vehicle drivers and conductors, etc: Commissioner's powers, 1948-1954.

Piece number 8942 = Accident on Emett miniature railway at the Festival Gardens Fun Fair on 11 July: list of casualties, 1951.

Piece number 8958 = Instructions to police in the event of a railway accident, 1951-1957.

Piece number 8974 = Bus stand: Green Man public house, Leytonstone, 1950-1966.

Piece number 8982 = Public service vehicles: specification of equipment to be carried and authority to dispense with conductors, 1950-1965 (See MEPO 2/6812 for Part I).

Piece number 8985 = Public service drivers and conductors: annual return of convictions, 1951-1966.

Piece number 8986 = Coach services for air terminals: applications for road service licences, 1947-1965.

Piece number 9290 = Fatal accident at miniature railway, Alexandra Park, N10, 1952-1954.

Piece number 9295 = Development of London Airport: internal layout and traffic arrangements, 1952-1953.

Piece number 9299 = Effect on accidents and congestion by the replacement of trams by buses from 1950 to 1952, 1952-1953.

MEPO 2 = Metropolitan Police, Office of the Commissioner, Correspondence and Papers: *continued....*

Piece number 9300 = Research into traffic flow to facilitate passage of buses and other vehicles, 1952-1954.

Piece number 9303 = Victoria Embankment: removal of tram tracks and layout as dual carriageway, 1952-1954.

Piece number 9305 = Stopping Places: Long North/South bus service No.21 - Wood Green to Farningham, Kent, with later variations: specimen route, 1935-1966.

Piece number 9306 = Omnibus excursions including circular tour of London promoted by London Transport Executive, 1951-1966.

Piece number 9309 = London and Home Counties Traffic Advisory Committee: history and policy of Stopping Places Committee, 1952-1967.

Piece number 9320 = Investigation of, and action to prevent obstruction by, slow moving omnibuses, 1952-1954.

Piece number 9323 = Public Service Vehicle driver who was indicted on a manslaughter charge and based his defence on defective eyesight: Jury's rider on renewal of driving licences for Public Service Vehicles, 1952-1953. **Note: This file is closed for 75 years**.

Piece number 9426 = Supply of information to private persons concerning licensed owners and drivers, 1931-1955.

Piece number 9428 = Police evidence to the Thesiger Committee on the licensing of road passenger vehicles and the operation of contract coaches in Central London, 1952-1956.

Piece number 9574 = Public carriages: policy regarding diabetic drivers, 1954-1958.

Piece number 9972 = Licensing of drivers and conductors of public service vehicles: policy, 1957-1968.

Piece number 9981 = Organisation and staffing of Public Carriage Office, 1955-1967.

Piece number 10258 = Licensing of drivers of public service vehicles: restrictions on issue of licences, 1963-1969.

Piece number 10460 = Robbery with violence at the London Transport Executive generating station, Lots Road, SW10 on 17 August 1961, 1961-1962.

Piece number 10544 = Inquest and police investigation into derailment of train between Dagenham East and Elm Park on 29 March 1965: Ministry of Transport report; police report, material and non-material statement, 1965 (see also MEPO 2/10545;10546;10547;10548;10549 for related statements, plans, photographs, inquest notes etc. Some LT equipment beside their adjacent tracks was damaged as a result of this BR accident).

MEPO 3 = Metropolitan Police, Office of the Commissioner, Correspondence and Papers, Special Series:

Piece number 214 = London tramways and underground railway maps (1911).

Piece number 521 = Counterfeit coin: woman wrongly given in to custody for "knowingly uttering" a counterfeit florin in payment of a London County Council tram fare, 1921.

Piece number 575 = Evacuation of Government Departments and conveyance by London Passenger Transport Board, 1939.

Piece number 775 = Transport Board employee, injured whilst conveying police: Receiver's refusal to meet claim, 1936-1937.

Piece number 777 = War Reserve involved in 'bus accident' off duty: Receiver's claim for pay, 1940-1941.

Piece number 987 = Importuning cases brought by London Passenger Transport Police: magisterial comment on evidence, 1935.

Piece number 1726 = Shooting with intent to do grievous bodily harm to Police Constable Carmichael by Charles Walter Browne at Dollis Hill Railway Station on 28 November 1937, 1937-1939.

Piece number 2501 = Evacuation of Children from London in wartime: transport arrangements, 1938. **Note: This file is closed for 75 years**.

MEPO 4 = Metropolitan Police, Office of the Commissioner, Miscellaneous Books and Papers:

Piece number 45 = Metropolitan traffic manual 1922 (Containing law on road, river and air traffic in London and elsewhere).

Piece number 77 = Coronation of their Majesties King George VI and Queen Elizabeth: Omnibus turning points, 1937.

Piece number 78 = Coronation of their Majesties King George VI and Queen Elizabeth: London Passenger Transport Board's booklet: traffic arrangements, 1937.

Piece number 83 = Coronation of their Majesties King George VI and Queen Elizabeth: London Transport's folder map, 1937.

Piece number 137 = Drivers and conductors of tramcars and trolley vehicles in Metropolitan Police District: abstract of laws, 1949 (booklet).

Piece number 142 = Coronation of H.M. Queen Elizabeth II: London Transport folder showing processional route and coronation area, etc, 1953.

Piece number 155 = Census of traffic: Metropolitan and City of London police, 1966.

MEPO 4 = Metropolitan Police, Office of the Commissioner, Miscellaneous Books and Papers: *continued....*

Piece number 173 = Public Carriage Office: notice to omnibus proprietors operating on approved routes, 1925.

Piece number 269 = Hackney carriage and Metropolitan stage carriage standings: notices to drivers and conductors, 1886-1939.

Piece number 495 = Abstract of laws relating to drivers and conductors of tramcars and trolley vehicles within the Metropolitan Police District, 1949 (booklet).

MINISTRY OF HEALTH:

MH76 = Emergency Medical Services:

Piece number 67 = Shelter policy: use of tube stations: matters raised by Committee of Imperial Defence, 1938-1941.

Piece number 537 = Public Air Raid Shelters: Civil Defence Region 5 (London): visits to medical aid posts in tube shelters, 1941-1944.

Piece number 538 = Public Air Raid Shelters: Civil Defence Region 5 (London): reports on vermin at tube station shelters, 1940-1945.

Piece number 539 = Civil Defence Region 5 (London): medical subjects relevant to new tube shelters, 1941-1942.

Piece number 546 = Mosquitoes in underground railways, 1940-1945.

Piece number 553 = Financial arrangements with London Passenger Transport Board regarding tube station shelters, 1940-1943.

Piece number 577 = Correspondence with London Passenger Transport Board concerning tube shelters, 1940-1942.

MINISTRY OF TRANSPORT:

MT1 = London Passenger Transport Arbitration Tribunal (See also PRO10/1000-1009):

Piece number 1 = Amounts claimed and awarded. Table (alphabetical). With <u>duplicate</u> (1936?)/ Awards. Main. (Arranged alphabetically.) <u>Copies</u> 1934-1936.

Piece number 2 = Awards. Extent of transfer. (Arranged alphabetically.) <u>Copies</u>. 1934./Claims. Analysis, etc. (1933?)./Costs. Taxation, etc. Correspondence and papers. 1934-1936./Minute book. 3 October 1933 - 6 April 1936./Observations in the form of memoranda delivered by the tribunal. (Arranged alphabetically.) (May 1934-July 1935)./Orders (original). Pooling scheme (railways) and Premier Omnibus Co., Ltd. (18 June 1935-10 July 1935)./Procedure. Forms. <u>Copies</u>. 1933-(1936).

Piece number 3 = Proceedings. Shorthand reports. A - Bi*, April-Nov 1935.

* For the Ambassador Bus Co., Ltd., <u>see</u> the report of the joint case of this company and the Sphere Omnibus Co., Ltd., <u>in</u> M.T.1/14.

Piece number 4 = Proceedings. Shorthand reports. Br - C. Feb 1934 - Feb 1936.

Piece number 5 = Proceedings. Shorthand reports. E - H, March 1934 - Nov 1935./Proceedings. Shorthand reports. Ilford borough council. 25 June 1935./Proceedings. Shorthand reports. Lewis Omnibus Co., Ltd. 12-24 June 1935.

Piece number 6 = Proceedings. Shorthand reports. M - Pe. Feb 1934 - March 1936./Proceedings. Shorthand reports. Pooling scheme (railways). March - May 1935.

Piece number 7 = Proceedings. Shorthand reports. Pr - Pu. March 1934 - Nov 1935.

Piece number 8 = Proceedings. Shorthand reports. Ra - Rel. Feb 1934 - Nov 1935.

Piece number 9 = Proceedings. Shorthand reports. Renown Traction Co., Ltd. 5-28 Nov 1934.

Piece number 10 = Proceedings. Shorthand reports. Renown Traction Co., Ltd. 3 Dec 1934 - 14 Jan 1935.

Piece number 11 = Proceedings. Shorthand reports. Renown Traction Co., Ltd. 15 - 29 Jan 1935.

Piece number 12 = Proceedings. Shorthand reports. Renown Traction Co., Ltd. 4 Feb - 9 Apr 1935.

Piece number 13 = Proceedings. Shorthand reports. Ro - Ru. May 1935 - March 1936.

Piece number 14 = Proceedings. Shorthand reports. Ry - S. March 1934 - Nov 1935.

Piece number 15 = Proceedings. Shorthand reports. Tilling and British Automobile Traction, Ltd. 11 Feb 1935./Proceedings. Shorthand reports. Thomas Tilling, Ltd. 28 May - 7 June 1934.

Piece number 16 = Proceedings. Shorthand reports. Thomas Tilling, Ltd. 11-27 June 1934.

Piece number 17 = Proceedings. Shorthand reports. Thomas Tilling, Ltd. 2-11 July 1934.

Piece number 18 = Proceedings. Shorthand reports. Thomas Tilling, Ltd. 16-19 July 1934 and 8 - 15 Oct 1934.

Piece number 19 = Proceedings. Shorthand reports. Thomas Tilling, Ltd. 17-31 Oct 1934 and 28 Nov 1934 and 11 Feb 1935.

Piece number 20 = Proceedings. Shorthand reports. U - W. March 1934 - Nov 1935./Rules. <u>Signed copy</u>. 3 Oct 1933./Schemes. Examination by interested parties. List (chronological). Oct 1933 - March 1936./Seal. <u>Upper and lower matrix</u>. (Oct 1933)./Seal. Formal impressions. List (chronological). Oct 1933 - June 1936./Sittings. List (chronological). Dec 1933 - April 1936./Staff. List. (1933-1936?).

Government Department Records etc:

MT6 = Board of Trade/Ministry of Transport, Railways: Correspondence and Papers. See APPENDIX 1 on pages 81-96 (Note: There is a two volume index by place and Company with the MT6 class lists. This index can be used to locate most of the relevant material, although it does contain a few errors. All references which are thought to relate to London Transport have been abstracted and appear as an appendix to this list. In a few cases these descriptions might prove not to be relevant. It was not possible to check these peripheral references by requesting the actual documents themselves. There are also many other files with general titles, which might also have a relevance to London Transport. Once again the two volume index should be checked for other possible material. This listing cannot be exhaustive.

MT9 = Board of Trade, Marine Department: Correspondence and Papers:
Piece number 2365 = Thames Passenger Service: Public Enquiry Report, 1932-1934.

MT14 = Light Railways Commission: Out Letters, 1896-10 Mar 1922 (For indexes see MT16).

MT16 = Light Railways Commission: Indexes to Out-letters, 1896-1916.

MT17 = Light Railways Commission: Registers to in-letters, 21 Sept 1896-18 Feb 1922 (For indexes see MT18).

MT18 = Light Railways Commission: Indexes to In-letters, 21 Sept 1896-1914.

MT24 = Transport Arbitration Tribunal:
Piece number 11 = Applications for Valuation of Railway and Canal Securities under Section 17 of the Transport Act, 1947 - Hammersmith & City Railway Company, 27.2.1948 (Final order made 2.4.1948).

MT29 = Board of Trade/Ministry of Transport: Railway Inspectorate - Inspectors' Reports (a full list of material relevant to London Transport is in preparation).

MT33 = Road Transport: Correspondence and Papers:
Piece number 4 = London, Middlesex and Hertfordshire County Councils; Tramways and Improvements Bills, 1919-1920.
Piece number 21 = Appeals (Passenger): East Surrey Traction Co. v Reigate Rural District Council, 1920.
Piece number 121 = Commissions, Committees and Conferences: Committee of Inquiry into London Motor Coach Services (Amulree), 1931-1935.
Piece number 135 = London Passenger Transport Act, 1933 - vehicle construction in special areas, 1932-1949.
Piece number 136 = Examination of London Passenger Transport Board's vehicles, 1933-1937.
Piece number 137 = London Passenger Transport: Lost property; Provisional Regulations, 1933-1949.
Piece number 138 = Public Service Vehicles: Routes and Stopping Places: London Passenger Transport Board: central area, 1933-1937.
Piece number 140 = London Passenger Transport: Services; Traffic Commissioners' jurisdiction, 1933-1934.
Piece number 179 = London Passenger Transport Board Bill 1934, 1933-1934.
Piece number 182 = London Passenger Transport Board Bill 1935, 1935-1946.
Piece number 183 = London Passenger Transport Board Bill 1936, 1935-1946.
Piece number 184 = London Passenger Transport Board Bill 1937, 1936-1945.
Piece number 185 = London Passenger Transport Board Bill 1939, 1938-1947.
Piece number 186 = London Passenger Transport Board Bill 1947, 1946-1947.
Piece number 189 = London Passenger Transport: Facilities; North and North East London; Public Inquiry, 1924-1930.
Piece number 190 = London Passenger Transport: Facilities; East London; Public Inquiry, 1925-1935.
Piece number 191 = Co-ordination of passenger transport services in London, 1926-1929.
Piece number 193 = London Passenger Transport: Deputation to Minister; co-operation of London transport undertakings, 1927.
Piece number 196 = London Passenger Transport: Use of River Thames transport facilities to relieve street congestion, 1929-1939.
Piece number 197 = London Passenger Transport: Transport services on River Thames; Public Inquiry, 1934-1935.
Piece number 198 = Amalgamation; London General Omnibus Company and others, 1927-1932.
Piece number 199 = London Passenger Transport: Coach services in Inner London, 1935-1940.
Piece number 201 = London Passenger Transport Board Bill 1938, 1937-1938.
Piece number 203 = London Passenger Transport Bills, 1931, 1932 and 1933; co-ordination of passenger transport, 1930-1933.
Piece number 213 = Appeals (Passenger): Eastern Traffic Area, London General Country Services Ltd, 1932.

MT33 = Road Transport: Correspondence and Papers: *continued....*

Piece number 246 = London Passenger Transport: Minutes of Meetings with the London County Council and Underground Group of Companies, 1920-1921.

Piece number 415 = London Passenger Transport Bill 1938, 1937-1946.

Piece number 462 = Employees (Passenger): Improvements in working conditions for road passenger transport workers: in relation to London Passenger Transport Board, 1946-1949.

Piece number 469 = Effect of nationalisation on London Passenger Transport Board, 1946-1947.

Piece number 470 = Effect of nationalisation on London Passenger Transport Board, 1948-1949.

Piece number 478 = Appeals (Passenger): W H Smith v London Transport Executive, 1948-1950.

Piece number 484 = Public Service Vehicles: Supply: Bus replacement programme: London Passenger Transport Board, 1947.

Piece number 485 = Public Service Vehicles: Supply: Priority of delivery for London Transport Executive, 1948-1949.

Piece number 493 = Licensing position in Metropolitan area after passing of London Passenger Transport Act 1933, 1932-1934.

MT36 = Committees and Commissions, Advisory Committee on London Traffic:

Piece number 1 = Formation of Committee, 1919-1921.

Piece number 2 = Minutes of meetings 1-16, 1919-1920.

Piece number 3 = Financial position of London Transport undertakings: special meeting on December 18; minutes and papers, 1919.

Piece number 4 = Technical Sub-Committee (known later as Technical Committee): terms of reference, 1919.

Piece number 5 = Technical Sub-Committee: Sub-Committee No.1 (Traffic regulation); markets and fairs, 1919-1920.

Piece number 6 = Technical Sub-Committee: Sub-Committee No.2 (Improvement of street facilities); minutes and papers, 1919-1920.

Piece number 7 = Technical Sub-Committee: Sub-Committee No.3 (Future development); minutes and papers, 1919-1920.

Piece number 8 = Technical Sub-Committee: minutes of meetings 1-16, 1919-1920.

Piece number 9 = Technical Sub-Committee: Sub-Committee No.1; minutes of meetings 1-45, 1919-1924.

Piece number 10 = Proposed London Traffic Authority, 1920-1921.

Piece number 11 = London Traffic Bill, 1920-1924.

Piece number 12 = Technical Sub-Committee: Sub-Committee No.1; Minister's request for report, 1924.

Piece number 13 = Technical Sub-Committee: Sub-Committee No.1; report to the London and Home Counties Traffic Advisory Committee, 1924-1925.

Piece number 14 = Advisory Committee on London Traffic: signed report to Minister, 1920.

MT37 = Committees and Commissions, London and Home Counties Traffic Advisory Committee:

Piece number 1 = Appointments, rules of procedure, 1924-1928.

Piece number 2 = Sub-Committee on Travelling Facilities, 1925-1927.

Piece number 5 = Sub-Committee on omnibus competition with tramways: appointment and terms of reference, 1929-1932.

Piece number 6 = Third annual report, 1927-1928, 1928-1929.

Piece number 7 = Appointments of Chairman, members and secretariat members, 1928-1932.

Piece number 9 = Fifth annual report, 1929-1930, 1930-1931.

Piece number 10 = Inquiry into London traffic and highway improvements, 1930-1935.

Piece number 11 = Sixth annual report, 1930-1931, 1931-1932.

Piece number 12 = Rules of procedure, 1924-1951.

Piece number 13 = London Traffic (Joint Committee*): rules of procedure, 1933-1947. (* A committee of representatives of local authorities to choose members of the L & H.C.T.A.C.)

Piece number 14 = London Passenger Transport Act: re-constitution of Committee, 1933-1936.

Piece number 15 = Meeting with London Passenger Transport Board (1933), 1933-1938.

Piece number 16 = Eleventh annual report, 1935-1936, 1937.

Piece number 17 = Twelfth annual report, 1936-1937, 1936-1939.

Piece number 18 = Thirteenth annual report, 1937-1938, 1938-1939.

Piece number 19 = Fourteenth annual report, 1938-1939, 1938-1944.

Piece number 20 = Suspension of meetings during the War, 1939-1946.

Piece number 21 = Fifteenth annual report, 1939-1940, 1940.

Piece number 22 = Sixteenth annual report, 1940-1941, 1941.

Piece number 23 = Seventeenth annual report, 1941-1942, 1941-1943.

Government number 24 = Extension of period of office of the Committee, 1942-1948.

Piece number 25 = Eighteenth annual report, 1942-1943, 1942-1943.

Piece number 26 = Nineteenth annual report, 1943-1944, 1944.

Piece number 27 = Twentieth annual report, 1944-1945, 1945-1946.

Piece number 28 = Twenty-first annual report, 1945-1946, 1946-1948.

MT37 = Committees and Commissions, London and Home Counties Traffic Advisory Committee: *continued....*

Piece number 29 = Twenty-second annual report, 1946-1947, 1947-1948.

Piece number 30 = Twenty-third annual report, 1947-1948, 1948-1949.

Piece number 31 = Minutes of meetings 1-109, 1924-1929.

Piece number 32 = Minutes of meetings 110-181, 1930-1933.

Piece number 33 = Minutes of meetings 1-50, 1933-1937.

Piece number 34 = Minutes of meetings 51-73, 1938-1940.

Piece number 35 = Minutes of meetings 74*-118, 1946-1950. (* Minutes of Meeting 74 are not available, and it is not known if a meeting was in fact held)

Piece number 36 = Minutes of meetings 119-167, 1951-1955.

Piece number 37 = Minutes of meetings 168-215, 1956-1959.

Piece number 38 = Minutes of meetings 216-239, 1960-1963.

Piece number 39 = Sub-Committee no.1 (Regulations): minutes of meetings 1-72, 1925-1929.

Piece number 40 = Sub-Committee no.1 (Regulations): minutes of meetings 73-107, 1930-1933.

Piece number 41 = Sub-Committee no.2 (Alternative Routes): minutes of meetings 1-98, 1925-1929.

Piece number 42 = Sub-Committee no.2 (Alternative Routes): minutes of meetings 99-159, 1930-1933.

Piece number 43 = Sub-Committee on Omnibus Regulations: minutes of meetings 1-4, 1925-1926.

Piece number 44 = Sub-Committee on Omnibus Workings: minutes of meetings 1-41, 1926-1929.

Piece number 45 = Sub-Committee on Omnibus Workings: minutes of meetings 42-91, 1930-1933.

Piece number 46 = First statutory meeting with London Passenger Transport Board: minutes, 1933.

Piece number 47 = Sub-Committee "A" (Road Traffic): minutes of meetings 1-70, 1933-1939.

Piece number 48 = Sub-Committee "A" (Road Traffic): minutes of meetings 71-112, 1946-1950.

Piece number 49 = Sub-Committee "A" (Road Traffic): minutes of meetings 113-156, 1951-1955.

Piece number 50 = Sub-Committee "A" (Road Traffic): minutes of meetings 157-169, 1956-1957.

Piece number 51 = Sub-Committee "B" (Passenger Transport Facilities): minutes of meetings 1-11, 1933-1936.

Piece number 52 = Sub-Committee "B" (Passenger Transport Facilities): minutes of meetings 12-20, 1937-1939.

Piece number 53 = Sub-Committee "C" (Road Works): minutes of meetings 1-28, 1933-1936.

Piece number 54 = Sub-Committee "C" (Road Works): minutes of meetings 29-40, 1937-1939.

Piece number 55 = Traffic Circulation Sub-Committee: minutes of meetings 1-40, 1957-1961.

Piece number 56 = Traffic Regulation Sub-Committee: minutes of meetings 1-32, 1957-1962.

Piece number 57 = Road Development Sub-Committee: minutes of meetings 1-7, 1958-1959.

Piece number 58 = Sub-Committee No.1 (Regulations): sandwichmen, 1925-1933.

Piece number 59 = Memoranda on work of Committee; procedure in connection with Committee, 1928-1939.

Piece number 60 = General Purposes Sub-Committee: minutes of meeting, 1936.

MT45 = Ministry of Transport Establishment and Organisation: Correspondence and Papers:

Piece number 312 = Additional members: appointments under London Passenger Transport Act 1933, 1933-1949.

Piece number 417 = British Transport Commission; scheme of delegation: London Transport Executive, 1947-1948.

Piece number 487 = Transport Users Consultative Committee for London: appointment of chairman and additional members, 1949-1950.

Piece number 501 = London Transport Executive: appointment of chairman and members, 1947.

Piece number 503 = National Insurance (modification of the London Transport and Railway Pension Schemes) Regulations 1956: drafts, 1947-1956.

MT46 = Co-ordination of London Passenger Transport, 1927-1933: Correspondence and Papers:

Piece number 1 = London County Council (Co-ordination of Passenger Traffic) Bill, 1929: London Electric Railway Companies (Co-ordination of Passenger Traffic) Bill 1929, 1929-1930.

Piece number 2 = London Passenger Transport Bill, 1929-1932.

Piece number 3 = Negotiations: Metropolitan Railway Company, 1930-1931.

Piece number 4 = Negotiations: Metropolitan Railway Company, 1932.

Piece number 5 = Negotiations: Local authorities other than London County Council, 1930-1931.

Piece number 6 = Negotiations: Local authorities other than London County Council, 1931-1933.

Piece number 7 = Negotiations: Sir William McLintock's Report, 1930.

Piece number 8 = Negotiations: Sir William McLintock's Report, 1930-1931.

Piece number 9 = Negotiations: Four main line amalgamated Railway Companies, 1930-1932.

Piece number 10 = Negotiations: Underground, including Common Fund Companies, 1930-1931.

Piece number 11 = Negotiations: Underground, including Common Fund Companies, 1931-1932.

Piece number 12 = Negotiations: Independent bus owners, 1931-1933.

MT46 = Co-ordination of London Passenger Transport, 1927-1933: Correspondence and Papers: *continued....*

Piece number 13 = Negotiations: Messrs. Thomas Tillings Ltd, 1930-1933.

Piece number 14 = Negotiations: Sir William McLintock on Trustee Securities, 1930.

Piece number 15 = Negotiations: Railway Clerks Association, National Union of Railwaymen and Associated Society of Locomotive Engineers and Firemen, 1930-1931.

Piece number 16 = Negotiations: Effects on London Traffic Advisory Committee, 1930-1931.

Piece number 17 = Negotiations: Middlesex County Council Tramways, 1930-1933.

Piece number 18 = Negotiations: London County Council Tramways, 1930-1931.

Piece number 19 = Negotiations: London County Council Tramways, 1931-1932.

Piece number 20 = Negotiations: General valuations etc. of undertakings, 1930-1931.

Piece number 21 = London Passenger Transport Bills: General, 1930-1931.

Piece number 22 = London Passenger Transport Bills: General, 1931-1932.

Piece number 23 = London Passenger Transport Bills: General, 1932-1933.

Piece number 24 = London Passenger Transport Bills: General, 1933.

Piece number 25 = London Passenger Transport Bills: Amendments approved by Minister, 1931-1933.

Piece number 26 = London Passenger Transport Bills: Draft of proposed White Paper and Cabinet papers, 1933.

Piece number 27 = London Passenger Transport Bills: Indices relating to clause files etc, 1929-1933.

Piece number 28 = Establishment of London Passenger Transport Board, 1931-1932.

Piece number 29 = Establishment of London Passenger Transport Board, 1932-1933.

Piece number 30 = Incorporation, proceedings and officers of Board, 1931.

Piece number 31 = General duty of Board as to passenger transport, 1931-1933.

Piece number 32 = Provisions as to members of Board, 1931-1933.

Piece number 33 = Transfer to Board of passenger transport undertakings, 1931-1932.

Piece number 34 = Transfer to Board of passenger transport undertakings, 1932-1933.

Piece number 35 = Provisions relating to Associated Equipment Company Ltd, 1929-1933.

Piece number 36 = Consideration for transfer of undertakings other than local authorities undertakings: Consideration for transfer of local authorities undertakings, 1931.

Piece number 37 = Consideration for transfer of undertakings other than local authorities undertakings: Consideration for transfer of local authorities undertakings, 1931-1933.

Piece number 38 = Determination of amount of consideration and terms of transfer of all undertakings except the Underground, 1931-1933.

Piece number 39 = Payments on account to be made by the Board, 1931-1933.

Piece number 40 = Constitution and procedure of Arbitration Tribunal, 1931-1933.

Piece number 41 = Staff and expenses of tribunal, 1931-1933.

Piece number 42 = Rules to be applied in determining compensation, 1931-1933.

Piece number 43 = Power of Board to run public service vehicles, 1930-1933.

Piece number 44 = Restriction on carriage of road passengers on certain journeys in special areas, 1930-1933.

Piece number 45 = Provisions relating to provincial operating companies, 1931-1933.

Piece number 46 = Working agreements, 1931-1933.

Piece number 47 = Provision of service of passenger vessels on River Thames, 1930-1933.

Piece number 48 = Power of Board to lease or sell surplus lands, 1931-1933.

Piece number 49 = Restriction on power to manufacture, 1931-1933.

Piece number 50 = Restriction on power of Board to establish garages, 1931-1933.

Piece number 51 = Power to abandon tramway systems, 1931.

Piece number 52 = Power to abandon tramway systems, 1931-1933.

Piece number 53 = Supply of electricity by local authorities, 1931-1933.

Piece number 54 = Statutory charging powers of the Board, 1931-1933.

Piece number 55 = Road service fares and charges of the Board, 1931-1933.

Piece number 56 = Fares in force on appointed day, 1931-1933.

Piece number 57 = Notification of alterations in fares, 1931-1933.

Piece number 58 = Revision of fares of the Board, 1931-1933.

Piece number 59 = Representations by local authorities as to the services or facilities of the Board, 1931-1933.

Piece number 60 = Co-ordination of services of Board and amalgamated railway companies, 1931-1933.

Piece number 61 = Application of provisions relating to amalgamated railway companies, 1931-1933.

Piece number 62 = Charging powers of amalgamated railway companies, 1931-1933.

Piece number 63 = Revision of fares of amalgamated railway companies, 1931-1933.

Piece number 64 = Representations by local authorities as to services or facilities of amalgamated railway companies, 1931-1933.

Piece number 65 = Transfer of powers of Railway and Canal Commission etc, 1931-1933.

Piece number 66 = Transport fund, 1931-1933.

Piece number 67 = Power of Board to borrow for capital purposes, 1931-1933.

MT46 = Co-ordination of London Passenger Transport, 1927-1933: Correspondence and Papers: *continued....*

Piece number 68 = Issue of transport stock, 1931-1933.

Piece number 69 = Dealings with transport stock by local authorities, 1931-1933.

Piece number 70 = Power of Board to borrow temporarily, 1931-1933.

Piece number 71 = Reserve fund, 1931-1933.

Piece number 72 = Insurance fund, 1931-1933.

Piece number 73 = Tramway Debt Liquidation fund, 1931-1933.

Piece number 74 = Continuance of grants under London Traffic Act 1924, 1931-1933.

Piece number 75 = Application of revenues of Board, 1931-1933.

Piece number 76 = Annual reports, statistics and returns, 1931-1933.

Piece number 77 = Accounts and audit, 1931-1933.

Piece number 78 = Enactments relating to accounts of railway or tramway undertakings not to apply to the Board, 1931-1933.

Piece number 79 = Amendments of Road Traffic Act, 1930 and London Traffic Act, 1924, 1931-1933.

Piece number 80 = Amendments of Road Traffic Act, 1930 and London Traffic Act, 1924, 1931-1933.

Piece number 81 = Amendments of Road Traffic Act, 1930 and London Traffic Act, 1924, 1931-1933.

Piece number 82 = Wages and conditions of service, 1930-1932.

Piece number 83 = Wages and conditions of service, 1932-1933.

Piece number 84 = Staff and superannuation, 1930-1931.

Piece number 85 = Staff and superannuation, 1931.

Piece number 86 = Staff and superannuation, 1931-1932.

Piece number 87 = Staff and superannuation, 1933-1934.

Piece number 88 = Exemption from stamp duties, 1930-1933.

Piece number 89 = Maintenance of transferred undertakings until appointed day, 1931-1933.

Piece number 90 = Documents of transferred undertakings to be surrendered, 1931-1933.

Piece number 91 = Inspection of works etc, 1931-1933.

Piece number 92 = Pending proceedings and existing contracts, 1931-1933.

Piece number 93 = Provisions as to substituted stock, 1931-1933.

Piece number 94 = Dissolution of transferred companies, 1931-1933.

Piece number 95 = Dissolution of the Underground Electric Railways Company of London Limited and the London and Suburban Traction Company Limited, 1931-1933.

Piece number 96 = Provisions as to certain stocks of the Metropolitan Railway Company, 1931-1933.

Piece number 97 = Protection for holders of Debenture Stock of London United Tramways Limited, 1931-1933.

Piece number 98 = Costs of Act, 1931-1933.

Piece number 99 = Valuation for rating purposes of heriditaments occupied by the Board, 1930-1933.

Piece number 100 = Protection for statutory gas and water undertakers, 1931-1933.

Piece number 101 = Protection for Great Western Railway Company, London Midland and Scottish Railway Company and London and North Eastern Railway Company, 1931-1933.

Piece number 102 = Saving for London County Council, 1931-1933.

Piece number 103 = Provisions as to undertaking of Surplus Lands Committee, 1931-1933.

Piece number 104 = Sale of part of undertaking to Southern Railway Company, 1931-1933.

Piece number 105 = Application to Board of Tramways Act, 1870.

Piece number 106 = Powers of Board as to Bills in Parliament and provisional orders, 1931-1933.

Piece number 107 = Inquiries by Minister, 1931-1933.

Piece number 108 = Protection for Postmaster General, 1931-1933.

Piece number 109 = Proof of signed map, 1931-1933.

Piece number 110 = Saving for existing bye-laws etc, 1931-1933.

Piece number 111 = Custody of lost property, 1931-1933.

Piece number 112 = Interpretation, 1931-1933.

Piece number 113 = Repeals, 1931-1933.

Piece number 114 = Short title, 1931-1933.

Piece number 115 = Undertakings to be transferred, 1931-1933.

Piece number 116 = Issue of Transport Stock to companies owning the Underground undertakings and distribution of that stock, 1931-1933.

Piece number 117 = Issue of Transport Stock to the Metropolitan Railway Company and distribution of that stock, 1931-1933.

Piece number 118 = Distribution of Transport Stock issued as consideration for transfer of undertakings to the Board and the winding up of certain companies whose undertakings are transferred, 1931-1933.

Piece number 119 = Issue of Transport Stock to certain local authorities, 1931-1933.

Piece number 120 = London Passenger Transport Area, 1931-1933.

Piece number 121 = Provisions relating to purchase of property of provincial operating companies etc, 1931-1933.

Piece number 122 = Provisions with respect to Railway Rates Tribunal, 1931-1933.

Piece number 123 = Provisions which are to form the basis of the pooling scheme, 1931-1933.

MT46 = Co-ordination of London Passenger Transport, 1927-1933: Correspondence and Papers: *continued....*

Piece number 124 = Consequential and minor amendments to be made in the Road Traffic Act 1930, 1931-1933.

Piece number 125 = Constitution of the London and Home Counties Traffic Advisory Committee, 1931-1933.

Piece number 126 = Consequential and minor amendments to be made in the London Traffic Act 1924, 1931-1933.

Piece number 127 = Provisions as to the making and approval of schemes applying the Railways (Valuation for Rating) Act, 1930, to the undertakings of the Board, 1931-1933.

Piece number 128 = Enactments repealed, 1931-1933.

Piece number 129 = Arrangement of clauses, 1931-1933.

Piece number 130 = Clauses withdrawn, 1931-1933.

Piece number 131 = Cabinet memoranda: reasons for carrying on the bill, 1931.

Piece number 132 = Carry-over motion: Cabinet memorandum, 1931-1932.

Piece number 133 = Appointment of Board by a selection committee and other amendments designed to remove opposition prior to House of Commons Committee stage, 1931-1932.

Piece number 134 = Formation of London Passenger Transport Board: Correspondence with Appointing Trustees, 1931-1933.

Piece number 135 = London Passenger Transport Act, 1933: licensing of drivers and conductors of public service vehicles, tramcars and trolley vehicles, 1933.

Piece number 136 = London Passenger Transport Act, 1933: delegation of powers; Metropolitan Traffic Area, 1933.

Piece number 137 = London Passenger Transport Act, 1933: Section 28; regulations re alteration in London Passenger Transport Board fares, 1933-1939.

Piece number 138 = London Passenger Transport Act, 1933: Section 10(2); date for submission of agreements to Tribunal, 1933-1934.

Piece number 139 = London Passenger Transport Act, 1933: Arbitration Tribunal; preliminary proceedings, 1933-1934.

Piece number 140 = London Passenger Transport Act, 1933: date and form of annual accounts, 1934-1948.

Piece number 141 = Lord Ashfield: appointments, 1931-1948.

Piece number 142 = Mr. Frank Pick: appointments, 1933-1942.

Piece number 143 = Transfer of licensing of vehicles to Metropolitan Traffic Area: delegation of licensing of drivers and conductors to the Metropolitan Police, 1932-1936.

Piece number 144 = Chairman and members: appointments, 1933-1937.

Piece number 145 = London Passenger Transport Act, 1933: Arbitration Tribunal; appointment of members, 1931-1936.

MT47 = Finance Correspondence and Papers:

Piece number 35 = Uniformity and improvement of railways: Lord Ashfield's proposals to Trades Facilities Committee, 1921-1922.

Piece number 72 = Trade Facilities Act Advisory Committee: London Underground Railways; proposed £6,000,000 grant, 1923.

Piece number 105 = Underground: accounts and statistical returns, 1925-1929.

Piece number 144 = Agreement with Treasury, London Passenger Transport Board, Great Western Railway and London and North Eastern Railway: Financing of transport extensions, 1935-1938.

Piece number 145 = Agreement with Treasury, London Passenger Transport Board, Great Western Railway and London and North Eastern Railway: Financing of transport extensions, 1939.

Piece number 146 = Agreement with Treasury, London Passenger Transport Board, Great Western Railway and London and North Eastern Railway: Financing of transport extensions, 1940-1947.

Piece number 158 = Railways (Agreement) Act, 1935 and London Passenger Transport Board (Agreement) Act, 1935: railway development programme; possible extension of financial arrangements, 1938.

Piece number 218 = Nationalisation of Railways, Canals and London Passenger Transport Board: Compensation, 1946.

Piece number 219 = Nationalisation of Railways, Canals and London Passenger Transport Board: Compensation, 1946-1947.

Piece number 220 = Nationalisation of Railways, Canals and London Passenger Transport Board: Liability which will pass to the Commission to pay interest and dividends on guaranteed securities, 1947.

Piece number 221 = Nationalisation of Railways, Canals and London Passenger Transport Board: Valuation of securities: orders made by the Minister fixing conversion dates, 1948.

Piece number 226 = London Passenger Transport Board: valuation of 4 1/2% "LA" stock, 1946-1948.

Piece number 276 = Government Control of Railways and London Transport: Agreement with Controlled Undertakings: 1939-1940.

Piece number 277 = Government Control of Railways and London Transport: Agreement with Controlled Undertakings: 1940-1941.

Piece number 278 = Government Control of Railways and London Transport: Agreement with Controlled Undertakings: 1941.

Government Department Records etc:

MT47 = Finance Correspondence and Papers: *continued....*
Piece number 279 = Government Control of Railways and London Transport: Agreement with Controlled Undertakings: 1941-1945.
Piece number 374 = Investment Programmes Committee: London Transport Central Line: east-west extension, 1947-1948.
Piece number 534 = London Transport Board: draft of annual accounts; comments on the draft; grant payments, 1964-1967.

MT49 = Geddes' Papers (Sir Eric Campbell Geddes, 1875-1937):
Piece number 22 = London Underground Railways: revision of season ticket rates, 1921.
Piece number 34 = London Electric Railways Bills, 1919-1920.
Piece number 60 = London Tube Railways and Railway settlement, 1919-1920.
Piece number 74 = London Electric (Fares) Bill 1920, 1920.
Piece number 148 = Traffic Advisory Committee (London), 1919-1920.
Piece number 171 = London County Council Tramways Scheme: deputation from London County Council, 1919.

MT54 = Light Railway Plans, 1896-1947, which includes some relevant plans (See MT58 for copies of the Orders themselves).
Note: An index to both Light Railway Plans and the Orders themselves will be found in the PRO class lists, immediately after MT54).

MT55 = Emergency Road Transport Organisation:
Piece number 244 = London Passenger Transport Board and emergency organisation of road transport, 1939.
Piece number 245 = London Passenger Transport Board and emergency organisation of road transport, 1940-1942.
Piece number 246 = London Passenger Transport Board: fuel rations and withdrawal of services, 1941-1945.
Piece number 252 = Public Service Vehicles - Special transport arrangements for London, 1940-1941.
Piece number 408 = London Passenger Transport Board: manpower problems, 1942-1946.

MT56 = Rates and Charges: Correspondence and Papers:
Piece number 74 = Main line railways and London Passenger Transport Board: 1st application for increases: memoranda, 1940.
Piece number 75 = Main line railways and London Passenger Transport Board: 2nd application for increases, 1940-1942.
Piece number 76 = Main line railways and London Passenger Transport Board: 3rd application for increases, 1940-1942.
Piece number 77 = Main line railways and London Passenger Transport Board: policy and memoranda on increases, 1945-1946.
Piece number 78 = Main line railways and London Passenger Transport Board: policy and memoranda on increases, 1946.
Piece number 79 = Main line railways and London Passenger Transport Board: policy and memoranda on increases, 1946-1947.
Piece number 80 = Charges Consultative Committee: Inquiry into charges of main line railways and L.P.T.B: reports: revenue estimates: memoranda, 1946-1947.
Piece number 81 = Charges Consultative Committee: Inquiry into charges of main line railways and L.P.T.B: reports: revenue estimates: memoranda, 1947.
Piece number 120 = London Passenger Transport Board coaches used as ambulances, 1939-1944.
Piece number 263 = London Passenger Transport Board: increased fares on country routes operated by home counties bus companies, 1940-1941.
Piece number 264 = London Passenger Transport Board: extension of availability of workmen's tickets, 1941-1945.
Piece number 266 = London Passenger Transport Board: fuel economy: adjustment of fares to discourage non-essential travel, 1941-1946.
Piece number 370 = London Passenger Transport Act 1933: proposed revision, 1959-1960.
Piece number 527 = London Area (Interim) Passenger Charges Scheme: policy, 1949-1950.
Piece number 568 = London Transport Executive: New Victoria - North East London Line: policy, 1957-1961.

MT57 = Highways: Maps and Plans:
Piece number 52 = Great West Road, Bath Road to Syon Lane; Bridge over Metropolitan District Railway, 1923.
Piece number 77 = Western Avenue. Bridge over Metropolitan District Railway at Acton. L. G. Mouchel and Partners Ltd. 8 sheets, 1929.
Piece number 78 = Western Avenue. Bridge over Central London Railway at Acton. L. G. Mouchel and Partners Ltd. 11 sheets, 1929.

Government Department Records etc:

MT58 = Light Railway Orders, 1896-1937 (See MT54 for accompanying plans).
Note: An index to both Light Railway Orders and the accompanying plans will be found in the PRO class lists, immediately after MT54).

MT62 = Port and Transit Executive Committee:
Piece number 31 = Statutory control of main line railway companies and London Passenger Transport Board charges: Minister's brief, c.1940.

MT67 = Railway Rates Tribunal:
Piece number 32 = Application by the London Passenger Transport Board under the London Passenger Transport Act 1933 to increase charges, Jan-June 1939.

Piece number 83 = Applications for approval of agreed charges 1934: GWR, LNER, LMSR, SR and London Passenger Transport Board (LPTB) with C and T Harris (Colne) Ltd, No.51, 1934.

Piece number 86 = Applications for approval of agreed charges 1935: GWR, LNER, LMSR, SR and LPTB with C and T Harris (Colne) Ltd and all persons and companies whom it may concern, No.42, 1935.

Piece number 91A = Applications for approval of agreed charges 1943: Amalgamated railway companies and LPTB: with Midland Electric Manufacturing Company Ltd, No.1102, 1943.

Piece number 91B = Applications for approval of agreed charges 1943: Amalgamated railway companies and LPTB: with Monkhouse and Glasscock Ltd, No.1103, 1943.

Piece number 93 = Applications for approval of agreed charges 1943: Amalgamated railway companies and LPTB: with H. F. O'Brien and Company Ltd, No.1105, 1943.

Piece number 94 = Applications for approval of agreed charges 1943: Amalgamated railway companies and LPTB: with Thomas Parkinson Ltd, No.1106, 1943.

MT70 = London Traffic Branch (August 1907-June 1916):
Piece number 1 = Register of correspondence, c.1907-1910 (Shown as Wanting).
Piece number 2 = Register of correspondence, 1910-1914.
Piece number 3 = Register of correspondence, 1914-1916.
Piece number 4 = Index to registers, 1910-1916.
Piece number 5 = Annual report, 1908.
Piece number 6 = Annual report, 1909.
Piece number 7 = Annual report, 1910.
Piece number 8 = Annual report, 1911.
Piece number 9 = Annual report, 1912.
Piece number 10 = Annual report, 1913.
Piece number 11 = Annual report, 1914.
Piece number 12 = Annual report, 1915.

MT74 = Transport Act 1947, Bill Files and Papers:
Piece number 132 = London Passenger Transport Board: dissolution, 1946-1947.
Piece number 133 = River Thames passenger service: proposals, 1947.
Piece number 144 = Nationalisation. B.T.C. Records and the Public Record Office, 1946.

MT77 = Transport Charges Consultative Committee:
Piece number 1 = Charges (railway control) consultative committee: proceedings of an inquiry into charges on road services of the London Passenger Transport Board, May 1940.

Piece number 2 = Charges (railway control) consultative committee: proceedings of inquiries 1) to increase charges of the railway owned docks, harbours, piers and wharves and 2) into charges of the railway companies and of the London Passenger Transport Board, July-Sept 1940.

Piece number 4 = Charges consultative committee: proceedings of an inquiry into adjustment of fares on the railways and road services of the London Passenger Transport Board, July-August 1946.

MT80 = Transport Tribunal Proceedings:
Piece number 4 = London area (interim) passenger charges scheme: minutes of evidence, May - July 1950.
Piece number 25 = London fares and miscellaneous charges division: 1963-1964: applications Nov 1962 - July 1964.
Piece number 26 = London fares and miscellaneous charges division: 1964: applications, Aug 1964 - Feb 1965.
Piece number 27 = London fares and miscellaneous charges division: 1966: applications, Feb 1966 - July 1966.
Piece number 28 = London fares and miscellaneous charges division: 1968: applications, Mar - Aug 1968.
Piece number 34 = Applications - London Transport Board (LTB) for amendment of the Nationalised Transport (London Fares) Order 1962, 1963.
Piece number 35 = Applications - LTB for an order cited as the London Fares (LT) Order 1963, 1963.
Piece number 37 = Applications - LTB for the alteration of the London Fares (LT) Order 1963, 1964.
Piece number 38 = Applications - British Railways Board and LTB for the alteration of London Fares Orders: objections and exhibits, 1964.

Government Department Records etc:

MT84 = Roads Department: Unregistered files:

Piece number 16 = Entrances and exits: doors, especially emergency exits, on public service vehicles including comments on the 'pay as you board' bus, 1945, 1936-1945 (includes information on a central entrance power operated door fitted on STL1793 in 1945, as an experiment)

MT87 = Nationalised Transport Division: NTA (Files):

Piece number 6 = London Transport Board: capital investment; reconstruction of Euston Underground station, 1960-1965.

Piecc number 9 = London Transport Board: Manufacturing activities and powers: procedure for approval of proposals under Transport Act 1962 s. 13(4), 1962-1963.

Piece number 10 = London Transport Board: Financial Targets, 1962-1963.

Piece number 11 = London Transport Board: capital investment: policy, 1962-1965.

Piece number 12 = London Transport Board: capital investment: proposed new rolling stock; Roding Valley, Epping-Ongar and Aldwych lines, 1962.

Piece number 13 = London Transport Board: capital investment: London Bridge provision of escalators, 1962-1965.

Piece number 14 = London Transport Board: capital investment: criteria, 1962-1963.

Piece number 15 = London Transport Board: legislation: London Government Bill, 1963.

Piece number 41 = London Transport Board. Appointments: chairmen and board members, 1963-1964.

Piece number 42 = London Transport Board. Victoria Line: extension of Green Park Station, 1962-1964.

Piece number 43 = London Transport Board: Victoria Line: Gibson Square ventilation shaft; petition and complaints against construction, 1963-1965.

Piece number 44 = London Transport Board: Bakerloo Line: extension to Camberwell and Lewisham; proposals and comments, 1963-1964.

Piece number 45 = London Transport Board: Labour relations: staff negotiation consultation method, 1951-1963.

Piece number 46 = London Transport Board: Labour relations: bus staff; wages and conditions claim 1962, 1962-1963.

Piece number 47 = London Transport Board: Labour relations: busmen - Committee of Inquiry (Phelps-Brown); general correspondence, 1963-1964.

Piece number 48 = London Transport Board: Press cuttings, 1963.

Piece number 49 = London Transport Board: Property: policy, control of sale and commercial development, 1965.

Piece number 52 = London Transport pictorial posters: purchase tax, 1963-1964.

Piece number 67 = Transport Tribunal: application 1963 No.1 - tolls; London Transport Board, buses through the Blackwall Tunnel, 1963-1964.

Piece number 68 = Transport Tribunal: Transport Act 1962; implementation, draft rules and procedure, 1963-1965.

Piece number 92 = Re-location of Covent Garden Market: effect on London Transport Board and Transport Holding Company, 1963-1966.

MT94 = Tramway Inspection Registers (a full list of information relevant to London Transport is in preparation).

MT95 = Registered Files: Highways Engineering (HE Series):

Piece number 687 = Construction: reconstruction of Oxford Circus Station, <u>with plans</u>, 1962-1967.

Piece number 773 = Bridges - Tottenham Hale Station: Victoria Line; new flyover, <u>with photographs</u>, 1963-1965.

Piece number 774 = Bridges - Tottenham Hale Station: Victoria Line; new flyover, <u>with photographs</u>, 1963-1965.

MT96 = General Division: Registered Files (G and GD Series):

Piece number 6 = Application of Pensions (Increase) Acts to former local authority employees transferred to the London Passenger Transport Board, 1952-1960.

Piece number 37 = British Transport Commission: London Transport Executive, 1953-1960.

Piece number 82 = Committee for Staggering of Working Hours in Central London: publicity sub-committee, 1956-1957.

Piece number 83 = Committee for Staggering of Working Hours in Central London: publicity sub-committee, 1957-1958.

Piece number 91 = Transport Users Consultative Committee: London area; nomination and appointment of members, 1958-1961.

Piece number 107 = Staggering of working hours in Central London: publicity sub-committee, 1958-1966.

Piece number 123 = Nationalised boards: remuneration of board members and senior executives; policy, 1959-1962.

MT96 = General Division: Registered Files (G and GD Series):   *continued....*

Piece number 147 = British Transport Commission: London Transport Executive; appointment of Chairman and members, 1961-1962.

Piece number 205 = "Drink and Driving" exhibition at Charing Cross underground station site, with plans, 1964-1965.

Piece number 223 = Modernisation and electrification of Great Northern Suburban lines; economic benefit studies, 1963.

Piece number 224 = Modernisation and electrification of Great Northern Suburban lines; economic benefit studies, 1963-1964.

Piece number 235 = Private Bills: London Transport (no 2) Bill 1967, authorisation of the Piccadilly tube line to Heathrow Airport; General Division involvement; with House Committee amendments, 1966-1967.

MT97 = Registered Files: Road Transport (RT Series):

Piece number 97 = Trams and Trolley Vehicles: Byelaws: London Transport Executive, 1939-1959.

Piece number 98 = Replacement of trams and trolley buses by diesel oil buses, 1950-1971.

Piece number 142 = Lost property: revision of regulations; London Transport Executive, 1950-1961.

Piece number 168 = London Transport Board: approval of routes, 1952-1957.

Piece number 180 = Committee of Inquiry into London Transport (Chambers report): consideration of report, 1955-1958.

Piece number 181 = Committee of Inquiry into London Transport (Chambers report): bus operations in central London, 1953-1958.

Piece number 230 = Replacement of trams and trolleybuses by diesel oil buses: British Transport Commission: London Transport Executive, 1950-1961.

Piece number 267 = Metropolitan Traffic Area (Drivers and Conductors Licences) Order 1934: revision, 1957-1962.

Piece number 277 = London Transport Board: bus problems in London, 1956-1963.

Piece number 339 = London Transport Executive: reduction of services, 1958-1962.

Piece number 397 = Rights of appeal against the refusal by the London Transport Executive of consent for other service operators, 1959.

Piece number 398 = London Transport Executive: deficiencies in bus services due to crew shortage, 1959-1961.

Piece number 503 = Transport Bill 1961/62: clauses 7 and 8; powers of London Transport Board, 1961-1962.

Piece number 504 = Transport Bill 1961/62: document folder, 1961-1962.

Piece number 505 = Transport Bill 1961/62: clauses 59 & 60; running powers into and out of London Passenger Transport Area, 1961-1962.

Piece number 513 = London Transport Executive: Victoria Line tube railway, 1959-1961.

Piece number 514 = London Transport Executive: deficiencies in bus service due to crew shortages, 1961-1962.

Piece number 529 = Licensing of drivers and conductors by Commissioner of Police for the Metropolis, 1961-1971.

Piece number 535 = London Transport Board: consent to other operators to run services in London "Special Area"; policy, 1961-1966.

Piece number 573 = Transport Bill 1961: certificate of routes available to London Transport Board outside the London Passenger Transport area, with plans, 1962.

Piece number 574 = Transport Bill 1962: procedure on appeals to Minister against decision of Metropolitan Traffic Commissioners on refusal of consent by London Transport Board; drafting of regulations, 1962.

Piece number 785 = Passimeters: proposed by London Transport Board to install on public service vehicles, 1964-1965.

Piece number 797 = Bus fuel grants: London Transport Board; granting of fuel tax relief; correspondence with Greater London Council (GLC), 1965-1970.

MT98 = Registered Files: Vehicle Safety (VS Series):

Piece number 4 = London Passenger Transport Act: operation in the special area; directions to Traffic Commissioners, 1933-1948; 1949-1959.

Piece number 107 = Special buses for conveyance of cyclists through Dartford Tunnel, 1955-1966.

MT102 = Registered Files: Mechanical Engineering (ME Series):

Piece number 15 = Fuel supply systems and lubricants: gas producer vehicle tests - L.T.E. bus, 1952-1956.

Piece number 26 = London Transport double deck bus in Knightsbridge, collided into bus shelter after turning from Grosvenor Place, resulting in casualties, 1953-1954.

Piece number 69 = Special vehicles for use in Dartford tunnel, 1955-1963.

Piece number 116 = Bus accident Oxford St. Harewood Place, causing eight deaths: revised question of "dead man's handle" for Public Service Vehicles, 1957-1958.

Piece number 227 = Special vehicles for use in Dartford tunnel, 1961-1963.

Piece number 228 = Special vehicles for use in Dartford tunnel, 1961-1964.

Government Department Records etc:

MT105 = Registered Files: Highways Land Division (HL and HLL Series):

Piece number 147 = Land Acquisition for Roads: Forms used by land branch staff: shortened procedure agreement used by British Railways Board and London Passenger Transport Board, 1958-1971.

MT106 = Registered Files, London Highways Division (LH Series):

Piece number 41 = Strand underpass, using part of Kingsway Subway, 1947-1959.

Piece number 42 = Strand underpass, using part of Kingsway Subway, plans, 1961-1963.

Piece number 70 = Victoria Line: report of the London Travel Committee to Minister of Transport and Civil Aviation, 1956-1959.

Piece number 71 = Mono-rail service to London Airport, 1958-1964.

Piece number 75 = Transport facilities between Central London and London Airport: proposed extension of Piccadilly Line, 1959-1970.

Piece number 133 = London CC: Strand underpass using part of Kingsway Subway, 1960-1964.

Piece number 134 = London CC: Strand underpass using part of Kingsway Subway, 1965-1970.

Piece number 135 = London CC: Strand underpass using part of Kingsway Subway, with plans, 1965-1970.

Piece number 136 = London CC: Strand underpass using part of Kingsway Subway, 1960-1962.

Piece number 137 = London CC: Strand underpass using part of Kingsway Subway, with plans, 1960-1962.

Piece number 138 = London CC: Strand underpass using part of Kingsway Subway, with plans, 1960-1962.

Piece number 159 = Highway consequences of Victoria Line underground railway construction, with plans, 1961-1965.

Piece number 165 = Relief for London Transport buses delayed through traffic congestion, 1961-1964.

Piece number 258 = London Transport Board (LTB): parliamentary proposals; London Transport Bill 1964/65, 1964-1965.

Piece number 260 = London Transport Bill 1965/66, 1965-1966.

Piece number 314 = Public transport in London: priorities for buses; reserved lanes; experimental traffic scheme on Tottenham High Road, 1965-1970.

Piece number 369 = Blackfriars Bridgehead underpass: London City Corporation, renewing of London Transport's District Line tunnel (2 parts) with plans and drawings, 1962-1963.

Piece number 370 = Blackfriars Bridgehead underpass: London City Corporation, renewing of London Transport's District Line tunnel (2 parts) with plans and drawings, 1961-1970.

Piece number 389 = Proposed Neasden underpass: intersection of A406 North Circular Road with Neasden Lane A4088; bus stopping places; effect of scheme on London Transport electricity mains (2 parts) with plans and drawings, 1964-1968.

MT114 = Registered Files, Railway Inspectorate (RI Series):

Piece number 79 = Deep level shelters adjacent to railway (Goodge Street Station), 1956-1959.

Piece number 109 = Wembley Park: passing loop Metropolitan Line, 1954.

Piece number 110 = Remote control at Aldersgate from Farringdon signal box, 1954-1955.

Piece number 111 = Chorley Wood: conversion of main line running signals from semaphore to coloured light, 1954-1956.

Piece number 112 = Speed control signalling of District Line, 1955-1956.

Piece number 113 = Camden Town: control from push button desk; modernization programme, 1955.

Piece number 114 = Queensway Station: new high speed lifts, 1956-1958.

Piece number 133 = Permanent way maintenance: facing point equipment; experiments by London Transport Board with French railway layout, 1954-1956.

Piece number 138 = London Transport: approval and inspection of new rolling stock; including A60-C69 surface line stock, 1954-1970.

Piece number 170 = Safety: Waterloo and City railway: trav-o-lators at Bank station, 1957-1960.

Piece number 178 = Automatic train driving: tests on underground, 1957-1964.

Piece number 199 = Cromwell Road - South Kensington: re-arrangement of tracks, 1957-1959.

Piece number 200 = District and Circle line: re-arrangement of tracks, 1957-1962.

Piece number 201 = Notting Hill Gate: reconstruction of station, 1957-1960.

Piece number 202 = South Harrow: modernisation of signalling control, 1957.

Piece number 203 = Highgate station: new escalator, 1957-1961.

Piece number 212 = Signals and telecommunications: London Transport signalling interference from traction current, 1957-1958.

Piece number 320 = London Transport Executive: fire in Central Line tube train between Shepherds Bush and Holland Park, 28 July 1958 (with plans and photographs), 1958-1960.

Piece number 321 = London Transport Executive: fire in Central Line tube train between Gants Hill and Redbridge, 11 Aug 1960, 1960-1962.

Piece number 322 = London Transport Executive: fire in Central Line tube train between Gants Hill and Redbridge, 11 Aug 1960 (with plans), 1960-1961.

Piece number 323 = London Transport Executive: fire in Central Line tube train between Gants Hill and Redbridge, 11 Aug 1960 (with plans and photographs), 1960-1961.

Piece number 324 = London Transport Executive: collision of tube trains between Victoria and St James's Park, 22 Nov 1962, 1962-1969.

Government Department Records etc:

MT114 = Registered Files, Railway Inspectorate (RI Series):   *continued....*

Piece number 325 = London Transport Executive: collision of tube trains between Victoria and St James's Park, 22 Nov 1962, 1962.

Piece number 326 = London Transport Executive: collision of tube trains between Victoria and St James's Park, 22 Nov 1962 (with plans), 1962-1963.

Piece number 342 = Underground railways: transport of heavy fuel oil near London Transport lines, 1960-1962.

Piece number 525 = Working of single line branches: comprehensive undertakings submitted by British Rail Board and London Transport Board (with plans), 1936-1965.

Piece number 531 = Great Northern Electrics: Kings Cross suburban electrification and take-over of Northern (City) London Transport lines (Drayton Park to Moorgate) (with plans), 1954-1970.

Piece number 573 = Farringdon-Liverpool Street. Metropolitan Line modernisation programme 1956: control from Farringdon (with plans), 1956-1979.

Piece number 574 = Kennington, Northern Line: automatic signalling, introduction of 'programme machines' with reports on signalling at Leicester Square and Euston, 1957-1958.

Piece number 575 = Kensington Olympia - West Kensington junction, District Line: conversion to single line (with plans), 1958.

Piece number 576 = Metropolitan line improvements: signalling, stations and track (with plans), 1959-1983.

Piece number 577 = Metropolitan line improvements: signalling, stations and track (with plans), 1959-1983.

Piece number 578 = Metropolitan line improvements: signalling alterations at Chesham, 1960.

Piece number 579 = Parsons Green and Putney Bridge, District line: machine control with supervision from Earls Court, 1960.

Piece number 580 = Parsons Green and Putney Bridge, District line: machine control with supervision from Earls Court (plan folder), 1960.

Piece number 581 = Harrow and south of Rickmansworth - Metropolitan Line: provision of four tracks and runaway catchpoints (with plans), 1961-1962.

Piece number 582 = Harrow and south of Rickmansworth - Metropolitan Line: provision of four tracks and runaway catchpoints (with plans), 1961-1962.

Piece number 583 = Tower Hill station: resiting; question of clearances, 1963-1968.

Piece number 584 = Tower Hill station: resiting; question of clearances (plan folder), 1963-1968.

Piece number 585 = Victoria Line: financial report, inspectors report, signal data and information for chief inspector (with plans), 1963-1968.

Piece number 586 = Victoria Line: financial report, inspectors report, signal data and information for chief inspector (with plans), 1963-1968.

Piece number 587 = Victoria Line: financial report, inspectors report, signal data and information for chief inspector (with plans), 1963-1968.

Piece number 588 = Turnham Green - District and Piccadilly Line: modernisation of signalling (with plans), 1963.

Piece number 589 = LHD type escalators: upgrading and modernisation; installation of new prototype escalators at Oval underground station, 1963-1971.

Piece number 590 = Hammersmith area - District Line: modernisation of signalling (with plans), 1963-1964.

Piece number 591 = Modernisation of lifts at Bank, Tufnell Park and Chalk Farm: installation of prototype lifts (with plans), 1954-1973.

Piece number 624 = London Transport: rolling stock programme policy; replacement of tube stock, single manning, braking circuits, emergency lighting and other issues (with photographs and plans), 1960-1971.

Piece number 640 = London Transport: power supply modernisation; report by London Transport Executive and Central Electricity Generating Board Working Party (with plans), 1968-1969.

MT115 = Registered Files, Railways and Inland Waterways Division (RIW Series):

Piece number 20 = London Plan Working Party Report, 1949-1955.

Piece number 21 = London Plan Working Party Report: North London travel facilities, 1950-1955.

Piece number 22 = London Plan Working Party Report: Bakerloo Tube extension to Camberwell, 1949-1960.

Piece number 23 = London Plan Working Party Report: Bakerloo Tube extension to Camberwell, 1960-1963.

Piece number 59 = Inquiry into London Transport: publication of report, 1955-1958.

Piece number 60 = Staggering of working hours in London Transport Executive area, 1954-1956.

Piece number 93 = EWC Kearney's High Speed Tube Railway invention: Private Office correspondence with Ministry of Works, 1951-1964.

Piece number 94 = British Transport Commission re-organisation: position of London Transport Executive, 1954-1959.

Piece number 142 = Staggering of working hours in London Transport Executive area, 1955-1956.

Piece number 143 = Staggering of working hours in London Transport Executive area, 1949-1958.

Piece number 145 = Appointment of Committee for Staggering of Working Hours in Central London, 1956-1957.

Piece number 146 = Appointment of Committee for Staggering of Working Hours in Central London, 1958.

Piece number 147 = Committee for Staggering of Working Hours in Central London: minutes and reports, 1958.

MT115 = Registered Files, Railways and Inland Waterways Division (RIW Series):
   continued....

Piece number 148 = Committee for Staggering of Working Hours in Central London: meetings of Zone Sub-Committees; Zone 2, London West End, 1957.

Piece number 149 = Rail facilities to air terminals, 1957-1964.

Piece number 177 = London Travel Committee: Main Committee: policy, 1959-1961.

Piece number 178 = London Travel Committee: Appointment of committee (Part 1), 1958-1960.

Piece number 179 = London Travel Committee: Appointment of committee (Part 2), 1960-1961.

Piece number 180 = London Travel Committee: Working papers, 1958-1960.

Piece number 181 = London Travel Committee: Reports, 1959.

Piece number 182 = London Travel Committee: First meeting: circulated papers and minutes, 1958-1959.

Piece number 183 = London Travel Committee: Second meeting: circulated papers and minutes, 1958-1959.

Piece number 184 = London Travel Committee: Third meeting: circulated papers and minutes, 1959.

Piece number 185 = London Travel Committee: Fourth meeting: circulated papers and minutes, 1959.

Piece number 186 = London Travel Committee: Fifth meeting: circulated papers and minutes, 1959.

Piece number 187 = London Travel Committee: Sixth meeting: circulated papers and minutes, 1959.

Piece number 188 = London Travel Committee: Parliamentary briefs: preparation, 1959-1960.

Piece number 189 = London Travel Committee: Seventh meeting: circulated papers and minutes, 1959.

Piece number 190 = London Travel Committee: Publication of reports, 1959-1960.

Piece number 191 = London Travel Committee: Eighth meeting: circulated papers and minutes, 1959.

Piece number 192 = London Travel Committee: Ninth meeting: circulated papers and minutes, 1959.

Piece number 193 = London Travel Committee: Tenth meeting: circulated papers & minutes, 1959-1960.

Piece number 194 = London Travel Committee: First Annual Report: preparation, 1960.

Piece number 195 = London Travel Committee: Committee functions: re-appraisal, 1960-1961.

Piece number 196 = London Travel Committee: Staggering of Hours Sub-Committee: working papers, 1959-1960.

Piece number 197 = London Travel Committee: Staggering of Hours Sub-Committee: working papers, 1960-1961.

Piece number 198 = London Travel Committee: Staggering of Hours Sub-Committee: meetings and minutes, 1959-1961.

Piece number 199 = London Travel Committee: Staggering of Hours Sub-Committee: circulated papers, 1959-1960.

Piece number 200 = London Travel Committee: Staggering of Hours Sub-Committee: reports issued, 1959-1960.

Piece number 201 = London Travel Committee: Staggering of Hours Sub-Committee: ministerial correspondence and parliamentary questions, 1959-1961.

Piece number 202 = London Travel Committee: Staggering of Hours Sub-Committee: meeting of Chairman of the Zone Committee, 1958-1959.

Piece number 203 = London Travel Committee: Road Traffic Sub-Committee: meetings and minutes, 1959-1960.

Piece number 204 = London Travel Committee: Road Traffic Sub-Committee: circulated papers, 1959-1960.

Piece number 205 = London Travel Committee: Road Traffic Sub-Committee, reports issued, 1959-1960.

Piece number 206 = London Travel Committee: Road Traffic Sub-Committee: working party on football fixtures, 1959-1960.

Piece number 207 = London Travel Committee: Railway Development Sub-Committee: working papers, 1959-1960.

Piece number 208 = London Travel Committee: Railway Development Sub-Committee: meetings and minutes, 1959-1961.

Piece number 209 = London Travel Committee: Railway Development Sub-Committee: circulated papers, 1959-1960.

Piece number 210 = London Travel Committee: Railway Development Sub-Committee: reports issued, 1959.

Piece number 211 = London Travel Committee: Railway Development Sub-Committee: meeting with Local Authorities' representatives about Victoria Line, 2 June 1959, 1959-1960.

Piece number 212 = London Travel Committee: New Developments Sub-Committee: working papers, 1959-1960.

Piece number 213 = London Travel Committee: New Developments Sub-Committee: meetings and minutes, 1959-1960.

Piece number 214 = London Travel Committee: New Developments Sub-Committee: circulated papers, 1959-1960.

Piece number 215 = London Travel Committee: New Developments Sub-Committee: reports issued, 1959-1960.

Piece number 216 = Committee of Inquiry into London Transport: Materials for draft report, 1953-1955.

Piece number 217 = Committee of Inquiry into London Transport: Chairman's preliminary draft report, 1954.

Piece number 218 = Committee of Inquiry into London Transport: Signed copy of final report, 1955.

Piece number 219 = Committee of Inquiry into London Transport: Report: part 2, 1954.

Piece number 220 = Committee of Inquiry into London Transport: Report: part 2, 1953-1954.

Government Department Records etc:

MT115 = Registered Files, Railways and Inland Waterways Division (RIW Series):
continued....

Piece number 221 = Committee of Inquiry into London Transport: Transcripts of meetings: 26 Feb - 7 May, 1954.

Piece number 222 = Committee of Inquiry into London Transport: Transcripts of meetings: 17 May - 14 December 1954.

Piece number 223 = Committee of Inquiry into London Transport: Minutes of meetings, 1953-1955.

Piece number 224 = Committee of Inquiry into London Transport: Agenda and arrangements for meetings, 1953-1955.

Piece number 225 = Committee of Inquiry into London Transport: Correspondence with London Transport Executive, 1953-1955.

Piece number 226 = Committee of Inquiry into London Transport: Oral evidence: London Transport Executive, 1954-1955.

Piece number 227 = Committee of Inquiry into London Transport: Oral evidence: Ministry of Transport, 1954.

Piece number 228 = Committee of Inquiry into London Transport: Oral evidence: London Area Transport User's Consultative Committee and Central Transport Consultative Committee for Great Britain, 1952-1955.

Piece number 229 = Committee of Inquiry into London Transport: Written evidence: members of the public, 1939; 1953-1954.

Piece number 230 = Committee of Inquiry into London Transport: Written evidence: members of the public, 1953-1954.

Piece number 231 = Committee of Inquiry into London Transport: Evidence submitted by organisations (S to Z), 1953-1954.

Piece number 232 = Committee of Inquiry into London Transport: Conditions of employment of public transport staff, 1947-1954.

Piece number 233 = Committee of Inquiry into London Transport: Papers circulated to committee: Inquiry London Transport 1-40 and index to series, 1953.

Piece number 234 = Committee of Inquiry into London Transport: Papers circulated to committee: Inquiry London Transport 41-54, 1953.

Piece number 235 = Committee of Inquiry into London Transport: Papers circulated to committee: Inquiry London Transport 55-82, 1953.

Piece number 236 = Committee of Inquiry into London Transport: Papers circulated to committee: Inquiry London Transport 83-130, 1953-1954.

Piece number 237 = Committee of Inquiry into London Transport: Papers circulated to committee: Inquiry London Transport, 131-151, 1934-1954.

Piece number 238 = Committee of Inquiry into London Transport: Papers circulated to committee: Inquiry London Transport 152-170, 1953-1954.

Piece number 239 = Committee of Inquiry into London Transport: Papers circulated to committee: Inquiry London Transport 171-196, 1954.

Piece number 240 = Committee of Inquiry into London Transport: Papers circulated to committee: Inquiry London Transport 197-228, 1953-1954.

Piece number 241 = Committee of Inquiry into London Transport: Papers circulated to committee: Inquiry London Transport 229-254, 1954.

Piece number 242 = Committee of Inquiry into London Transport: Papers circulated to committee: Inquiry London Transport 255-270, 1950-1954.

Piece number 243 = Committee of Inquiry into London Transport: Papers circulated to Committee: Inquiry London Transport 271-304, 1951-1954.

Piece number 244 = Committee of Inquiry into London Transport: Papers circulated to Committee: Inquiry London Transport 305-350, 1954.

Piece number 245 = Committee of Inquiry into London Transport: Papers circulated to Committee: Inquiry London Transport 351-379, 1954.

Piece number 246 = Committee of Inquiry into London Transport: Papers circulated to Committee: Inquiry London Transport 380-408, 1954.

Piece number 247 = Committee of Inquiry into London Transport: Papers circulated to committee: Inquiry London Transport 409-460, 1954-1955.

Piece number 292 = Monorails: proposed monorail to London Airport based on Alweg Monorail System by Air Rail Ltd, 1958-1963.

Piece number 293 = Monorails: Railplanes Ltd; proposed suspended monorail system, 1960-1964.

MT118 = Ministry of Transport, Bridges Engineering Division, Registered Files (BE Series):

Piece number 51 = London Transport Board: Trunk Road 36 (A406) Neasden bridge No.29 Hean Dog Lane; London Borough of Brent, 1952-1975.

Piece number 52 = London Transport Board: Trunk Road 36 (A406) Neasden bridge No.29 Hean Dog Lane; London Borough of Brent: plans (1952-1975).

Government Department Records etc:

MT119 = Registered Files, Highways (Classified Roads) Division (HC Series):
Piece number 4 = Festival of Britain 1951: inter-departmental working party and selection of site, 1946-1948.
Piece number 5 = Festival of Britain 1951: new works proposal, 1948-1949.

MT120 = Ministry of Transport, Registered Files, Highways General Planning Division (HGP and GPH Series):
Piece number 5 = Road Investment Programme: Removal of tram lines in London, 1950-1954.

MT124 = Registered Files, Railways and Inland Waterways Divisions A, B and C (RA, RB and RC Series):
Piece number 11 = Policy on London Plan: railway works including British Transport Commission's Route C proposals (Victoria Line), 1951-1953.
Piece number 12 = Policy on London Plan: railway works including British Transport Commission's Route C proposals (Victoria Line), 1953-1958.
Piece number 40 = Passenger Traffic: Rail link to London Airport, 1950-1959.
Piece number 87 = Policy on London Plan: railway works including British Transport Commission Route C proposals (Victoria Line), 1958-1961.
Piece number 126 = Passenger Traffic: rail link to London Airport, 1959-1962.
Piece number 143 = London Transport: new rolling stock for Central and Piccadilly lines, 1960-1961.
Piece number 168 = Re-enactment of British Transport Commission (BTC) and London Transport Executive (LTE) general byelaws, 1953-1961.
Piece number 169 = Re-enactment and revision of BTC and LTE explosives byelaws, 1959-1967.
Piece number 209 = Pensions: statutory undertakings; pensions funds of British Transport Commission controlled companies, British Transport Commission Group Pension Funds Regulations 1962, 1959-1962.
Piece number 252 = Transport Bill 1961-1962: Joint Ministry - British Transport Commission Working Party Recommendations. No. 12: London Transport, 1961.
Piece number 256 = Transport Bill 1961-1962: Joint Ministry - British Transport Commission Working Party Recommendations. No. 15: criteria to be applied to determination of London fares, 1961-1962.
Piece number 288 = Transport Bill 1961-1962: London Transport Board: policy, 1961-1962.
Piece number 289 = Transport Bill 1961-1962: London Transport Board: proposed changes in area of operation and powers, 1961-1962.
Piece number 334 = Transport Bill 1961-1962: Representations: London County Council, 1961-1962.
Piece number 350 = Transport Bill 1961-1962: Representations: West Ham County Borough Council, 1962.
Piece number 402 = Transport Bill 1961-1962: Parliamentary Proceedings: Commons Amendments Clause 7: London Board's duties and powers, 1961-1962.
Piece number 403 = Transport Bill 1961-1962: Parliamentary Proceedings: Commons Amendments Clause 8: London Board's powers to run road passenger services outside the London Passenger Transport Area, 1961-1962.
Piece number 431 = Transport Bill 1961-1962: Parliamentary Proceedings: Commons Amendments including: Clause 45: Transport Tribunal to make orders regulating charges for passengers in London area, 1961-1962. **AND** Clause 46: London fares orders procedures, 1961-1962. **AND** Clause 47: London fares' reviews, 1961-1962. **AND** Clause 48: quick procedure for raising London fares, 1961-1962.
Piece number 436 = Transport Bill 1961-1962: Parliamentary Proceedings: Commons Amendments Clause 55: British Railways and London Transport Boards to give notice of service withdrawals, 1962.
Piece number 440 = Transport Bill 1961-1962: Parliamentary Proceedings: Commons Amendments Clause 59: appeal rights of other bus operators against London Transport refusal to allow them to operate services in London "special area", 1961-1962 **AND** Clause 60: appeal procedure for application by London Transport to operate bus services outside its area, 1961-1962.
Piece number 444 = Transport Bill 1961-1962: Parliamentary Proceedings: Commons Amendments including: Clause 67: London Transport lost property services: 1961-1962.
Piece number 449 = Transport Bill 1961-1962: Parliamentary Proceedings: Commons Amendments Clause 77: compensation to members of Commission or London Transport Executive who retire in special circumstances, 1961-1962.
Piece number 460 = Transport Bill 1961-1962: Parliamentary Proceedings: Commons Amendments Seventh Schedule: transitional provisions relating to Transport Stock, Passenger Fares in London and Transport Users Consultative Committees, pensions and the dissolution of the Commission, 1961-1962.
Piece number 485 = Transport Bill 1961-1962: Parliamentary Proceedings: Lords Amendments Clause 7: London Board's duties and powers, 1962.
Piece number 486 = Transport Bill 1961-1962: Parliamentary Proceedings: Lords Amendments Clause 8: London Boards' powers to run road passenger services outside London Passenger Transport Area, 1962.
Piece number 508 = Transport Bill 1961-1962: Parliamentary Proceedings: Lords Amendments Clause 43: removal of control of charges (except passenger fares in London area and docks charges) from Boards; Railway and Dock Boards not to be common carriers, 1962.

MT124 = Registered Files, Railways and Inland Waterways Divisions A, B and C (RA, RB and RC Series): *continued....*

Piece number 509 = Transport Bill 1961-1962: Parliamentary Proceedings: Lords Amendments including: Clause 45: Transport Tribunal to make orders regulating charges for passengers in London Area, 1962 **AND** Clause 46: London fares orders procedure, 1962 **AND** Clause 47: London fares reviews, 1962 **AND** Clause 48: quick procedure for raising London fares, 1962.

Piece number 513 = Transport Bill 1961-1962: Parliamentary Proceedings: Lords Amendments Clause 54: Railways and London Transport Boards to give notice of service withdrawals, 1962.

Piece number 517 = Transport Bill 1961-1962: Parliamentary Proceedings: Lords Amendments including: Clause 58: appeal by other bus operators against London Transport's refusal to allow them to operate in London "Special Area", 1962 **AND** Clause 59: appeal procedure for applications by London Transport to operate bus services outside its area, 1962.

Piece number 521 = Transport Bill 1961-1962: Parliamentary Proceedings: Lords Amendments Clause 67: Railways and London Transport Board; powers to make bye-laws, 1962 **AND** Clause 68: London Transport lost property services, 1962.

Piece number 524 = Transport Bill 1961-1962: Parliamentary Proceedings: Lords Amendments including: Clause 79: compensation to Commission of London Transport members who are retired prematurely, 1962.

Piece number 527 = Transport Bill 1961-1962: Parliamentary Proceedings: Lords Amendments including: Clause 87: use and development of Commission's and Board's surplus land in London, 1962.

Piece number 534 = Transport Bill 1961-1962: Parliamentary Proceedings: Lords Amendments Seventh Schedule: transitional provisions relating to stock, passenger fares in London, Transport Users' Consultative Committees, pensions and the dissolution of Commission, 1962.

Piece number 539 = Transport Bill 1961-1962: Parliamentary Proceedings: Lords Amendments including: New Clauses: power for London Board to enter into certain agreements or arrangements; Title and commencement of Act; repeals and savings effected as result of Act; restrictions on Transport Boards' powers to develop land in London, 1962.

Piece number 584 = Transport Users Consultative Committee: Nomination and Appointment of Chairman and Members: London area, 1962-1964.

Piece number 604 = Transport Act 1962: Implementation: Passenger fares in London: Nationalised Transport (London Fares) Order 1962, 1962.

Piece number 613 = Transport Act 1962: Implementation: Policy on London plan: railway works including British Transport Commission route C proposals, 1961.

Piece number 614 = Transport Act 1962: Implementation: Policy on London plan: railway works including British Transport Commission route C proposals, 1961-1962.

Piece number 638 = Railway Investment Programme: Capital investment: replacement of London Transport trolley buses, 1961.

Piece number 806 = Withdrawal of unremunerative services: London Transport Board: correspondence on agreed procedures for future closure proposals, 1963.

Piece number 820 = Transport Users' Consultative Committee (TUCC): London area: minutes of meetings: Jan 1961-July 1961, 1961-1968.

MT125 = Ministry of Transport, Bill Papers:

Piece number 15 = London Traffic Bill 1924: Draft bills and bills in various stages through Parliament, 1924.

Piece number 16 = London Traffic Bill 1924: Discussions in both houses <u>Printed</u>, 1924.

Piece number 17 = London Traffic Bill 1924: Commons' amendments, 1924.

Piece number 18 = London Traffic Bill 1924: Lords' amendments, 1924.

Piece number 49 = London Passenger Transport Bill 1933: Minutes of proceedings before joint committee <u>Printed</u>, 1931.

Piece number 50 = London Passenger Transport Bill 1933: Bill showing amendments made in Commons, 1931-1932.

Piece number 51 = London Passenger Transport Bill 1933: Bill showing amendments made in Lords, 1933.

Piece number 52 = London Passenger Transport Bill 1933: Petitions <u>Printed</u>, 1933.

Piece number 53 = London Passenger Transport Bill 1933: Printed papers of amendments <u>Printed</u>, 1933.

Piece number 54 = London Passenger Transport Bill 1933: London County Council (Co-ordination of Public Transport) Bill 1929, 1929.

Piece number 55 = London Passenger Transport Bill 1933: Proceedings before joint committee <u>Printed</u>, 1931.

Piece number 56 = London Passenger Transport Bill 1933: Proceedings other than before joint committee <u>Printed</u>, 1931-1933.

Piece number 57 = London Passenger Transport Bill 1933: Amendments and briefs: Commons' recommittal stage, 1932.

Piece number 58 = London Passenger Transport Bill 1933: Amendments and briefs: Commons' consideration stage, 1933.

Piece number 59 = London Passenger Transport Bill 1933: Amendments and briefs: Lords' committee stage, 1933.

Government Department Records etc:

MT125 = Ministry of Transport, Bill Papers: *continued....*
Piece number 60 = London Passenger Transport Bill 1933: Amendments and briefs: Lords' report and other stages, 1933.
Piece number 61 = London Passenger Transport Bill 1933: Miscellaneous papers, 1927-1931.

MT129 = Ministry of Transport, Registered Files, London Traffic Division (LT Series):
Piece number 42 = Traffic Policy: Holborn MBC: Kingsway Subway, 1951-1958.
Piece number 81 = Schemes to improve London Transport: consultations with London Transport executive, 1955-1962.

MT130 = Light Railway Orders, Hearing of Objections:
Piece number 1 = Evidence and Notes: 1898-1899 (includes: London United).
Piece number 3 = Evidence and Notes: 1900 (includes: Waltham Cross and Enfield).
Piece number 4 = Evidence and Notes: 1900 (includes: Dartford District; County of Middlesex).
Piece number 6 = Evidence and Notes: 1902 (includes: Walthamstow and District).
Piece number 7 = Evidence and Notes: 1903 (includes: Barking (Extensions); London United; County of Middlesex; Waltham Cross and Enfield).
Piece number 9 = Evidence and Notes: 1905 (includes: County of Middlesex (Extension of time); Tottenham and Walthamstow).
Piece number 10 = Evidence and Notes: 1906-1907 (includes: County of Middlesex).

MT132 = Ministry of Transport, Registered Files, Finance, Transport and Shipping Division (FTS Series):
Piece number 49 = London Transport financial position: proposed reorganization, 1965.

MT135 = Ministry of Transport: London Policy Division: Registered Files (LP Series):
Piece number 1 = British Transport historical relics: preservation schemes and museum, 1963-1967.
Piece number 2 = Investment: electrification of Great Northern Suburban Services, 1960-1963.
Piece number 3 = Investment: social benefit of methods of modernisation; study with calculation and analysis, 1962-1963.
Piece number 4 = Investment: social benefit of methods of modernisation; study with calculation and analysis, 1960-1963.
Piece number 5 = London Transport Board, Board membership: selection and appointment, 1964-1966.
Piece number 6 = London Transport Board, Victoria Line: investment and progress, 1963-1966.
Piece number 7 = London Transport Board, Victoria Line: proposed extension to Brixton, 1963-1966.
Piece number 8 = London Transport Board, Automatic fare collection: investment analysis and proposals, 1963-1967.
Piece number 9 = London Transport Board, Victoria Line: automatically controlled tube trains; introduction, 1963-1968.
Piece number 10 = London Transport Board, Tower Hill tube station: reconstruction; capital investment, 1963-1967.
Piece number 11 = London Transport Board, Proposed Brixton-Walthamstow Line (Victoria Line): social benefit study, 1962-1970.
Piece number 12 = London Transport Board, Underground tube power supply: modernisation of Greenwich power plant, 1962-1968.
Piece number 13 = Heathrow Airport access: monorail and other rapid transit systems; proposals with brochures, 1963-1967.
Piece number 14 = Heathrow Airport rail link: discussion between British Railways and British European Airways with maps, 1961-1965.
Piece number 15 = London transportation study: phase 3; financial and contractual aspects, 1963-1966.
Piece number 16 = London traffic survey 1962/3: financial arrangements, 1961-1962.
Piece number 17 = Divisional arrangements and procedures: re-organisation of London Policy (LP) Division, 1965-1966.
Piece number 18 = Divisional arrangements and procedures: setting up of LP registry and filing system, 1966.
Piece number 20 = British Railways Board (BRB): electrification of Great Northern Suburban services, 1965-1967.
Piece number 21 = London Transport Board (LTB), Organisation and management: London Transport's bus plan, 1966-1967.
Piece number 22 = London Transport Board (LTB), Investigation into London Transport's problems: future financial position and prospects, 1965.
Piece number 23 = London Transport Board (LTB), Investigation into London Transport's problems: future financial position and prospects, 1965.
Piece number 24 = London Transport Board (LTB), Investigation into London Transport's problems: future financial position and prospects, 1965.

MT135 = Ministry of Transport: London Policy Division: Registered Files (LP Series): *continued....*

Piece number 25 = Capital Investment: Railway investment proposals: Fleet Line - social benefit study, 1966-1967.

Piece number 37 = Transport Co-Ordinating Council for London (TCCL) - Meetings: agenda, minutes and papers, 1966-1967.

Piece number 38 = Transport Co-Ordinating Council for London (TCCL) - Public Transport Investment Group (MOT, LTB, BRB and GLC): agenda, papers and minutes, 1966.

Piece number 39 = Transport Co-Ordinating Council for London (TCCL) - Public Transport Investment Group (MOT, LTB, BRB and GLC): consideration of investment in transport in London as a whole with plans and maps, 1967.

Piece number 40 = Transport Co-Ordinating Council for London (TCCL) - Committees, conferences and working parties: Crown Estate Commissioners, Regent Street Committee; redevelopment plans and traffic implications; minutes of meetings with plans, 1964.

Piece number 41 = Transport Co-Ordinating Council for London (TCCL) - Committees, conferences and working parties: House of Commons Select Committee on Nationalised Industries; report on LTB; observations by Minister of Transport, 1965-1966.

Piece number 42 = Transport Co-Ordinating Council for London (TCCL) - Development with Transport implications: relocation of Covent Garden Market to Nine Elms; action arising from Government's decision with diagrams and maps, 1964-1965.

Piece number 43 = Transport Co-Ordinating Council for London (TCCL) - Access to airports: Heathrow; link between Gloucester Road station and West London Air Terminal with plans, 1966-1970.

Piece number 45 = Transport Co-Ordinating Council for London (TCCL) - Access to airports: London transportation study; methods of improving access to Heathrow; Piccadilly Line extension with plans, 1966.

ORDNANCE SURVEY:

OS1 = Ordnance Survey, Correspondence and Plans:

Piece number 135 = London Underground Railways*: depiction of details on plans of the London area, 1928-1955. * For plans of London Underground Railways, see OS7.

OS3 = Ordnance Survey, Miscellanea:

Piece number 21 = Omnibus routes in the Metropolitan Area of London: horse omnibus routes 1 sheet, Dec 1907.

Piece number 22 = Omnibus routes in the Metropolitan Area of London: motor omnibus routes 1 sheet, Dec 1907.

OS5 = Ordnance Survey, Maps and Plans:

Piece numbers 133-171 = London Passenger Transport Maps: One Inch Series, 1933.

Piece numbers 172-183 = London Passenger Transport Maps: two inch to mile series: London Passenger Transport Road Boundary, 1936.

OS7 = Ordnance Survey, London Underground Railways Plans (1948):

Piece number 1 = Bakerloo Line, various sheet numbers plus index sheet.

Piece number 2 = Central Line, various sheet numbers.

Piece number 3 = Central Line, various sheet numbers (index sheet missing).

Piece number 4 = Metropolitan and District Lines, various sheet numbers.

Piece number 5 = Metropolitan and District Lines, various sheet numbers.

Piece number 6 = Metropolitan and District Lines, various sheet numbers.

Piece number 7 = Metropolitan and District Lines, various sheet numbers plus index sheet.

Piece number 8 = Northern Line, various sheet numbers.

Piece number 9 = Northern Line, various sheet numbers plus index sheet.

Piece number 10 = Piccadilly Line, various sheet numbers.

Piece number 11 = Piccadilly Line, various sheet numbers plus index sheet.

Piece number 12 = Kingsway Subway (Tramway Tunnel), various sheet numbers plus index sheet.

Piece number 13 = Post Office (London) Railway, various sheet numbers plus index sheet.

Piece number 14 = Waterloo and City Railway (British Railways, Southern Region), various sheet numbers (index sheet wanting).

Piece number 15 = Colour key to all lines.

Government Department Records etc:

PUBLIC RECORD OFFICE:

PRO 1 = Correspondence, Etc: General Correspondence:

Piece number 648 = Provision of new repository space including proposed use of tube shelters, 1944-1945.

Piece number 752 = Goodge Street underground shelter: arrangements with Ministry of Works for record storage, 1946.

Piece number 795 = Goodge St. repository: Correspondence, plans of tunnels and storage of records, Jan 1947-Dec 1947.

Piece number 812 = Correspondence: schedules of documents for removal from Portslade to Belsize Park, Feb 1947-Jan 1948.

Piece number 816 = Correspondence and general notes on meetings on proposed storage of the Board of Trade records in Clapham North Shelter (now housed at Ponders End), Apr 1947-Dec 1947.

Piece number 844 = Storage of records at Yeading and Camden Town deep shelters, Aug 1947-Dec 1947.

Piece number 859 = Goodge Street repository, 1948.

Piece number 860 = Clapham North repository, 1948.

Piece number 861 = Camden Town repository, 1948.

Piece number 1048 = Deep level shelters for use as repositories, 1950-1951.

Piece number 1154 = Storage of records in deep shelters, 1950.

Piece number 1173 = Removal of records from deep shelters to Hayes, 1951.

Piece number 1318 = Clearance of deep shelters, 1952.

PRO 10 = Specimens of Scheduled Documents (See also MT1):

Piece number 1000 = Ministry of Transport. London Passenger Transport Arbitration Tribunal. Class 1, 1933-1935 and Class 2, 1934-1936.

Piece number 1001 = Ministry of Transport. London Passenger Transport Arbitration Tribunal. Class 3, Thomas Tilling Ltd. Schedule of documents, award (<u>copies</u>) and exhibits T1-8, 10-15, 17 and 20, 1924-1935.

Piece number 1002 = Ministry of Transport. London Passenger Transport Arbitration Tribunal. Class 3, Thomas Tilling Ltd. Exhibits T.21-30, 35, 36, 40, 48, and 52-55, 1915-1934.

Piece number 1003 = Ministry of Transport. London Passenger Transport Arbitration Tribunal. Class 3, Thomas Tilling Ltd. Exhibits T.56-61, 1934.

Piece number 1004 = Ministry of Transport. London Passenger Transport Arbitration Tribunal. Class 3, Thomas Tilling Ltd. Exhibits various etc, 1924-1934.

Piece number 1005 = Ministry of Transport. London Passenger Transport Arbitration Tribunal. Class 4, Firms, A-C, 1933-1936.

Piece number 1006 = Ministry of Transport. London Passenger Transport Arbitration Tribunal. Class 4, Firms, E-Pa, 1933-1936.

Piece number 1007 = Ministry of Transport. London Passenger Transport Arbitration Tribunal. Class 4, Firms, Pe-Re, 1933-1936.

Piece number 1008 = Ministry of Transport. London Passenger Transport Arbitration Tribunal. Class 4, Firms, Ro-W, 1933-1936.

Piece number 1009 = Ministry of Transport. London Passenger Transport Arbitration Tribunal. Class 4, City of London corporation and suburban borough and district councils, 1922-1936 and Ditto, 1934-1936.

LIST OF PHOTOGRAPHS NOTED IN PART D:

AN31/12 - Photograph of Aylesbury station (undated), among others.

AN31/14 - Photograph of Edgware station (undated), among others.

MEPO 2/2255 = Photographic record of 'B' type omnibus driving tests carried out at New Scotland Yard, 1923.

MT114/320 - Underground railway accidents: electrical fire between Shepherds Bush and Holland Park stations (Central Line tube): damaged components, fire damage to train interiors, 17 photographs, 1958.

MT114/322 - London Transport Executive: fusing test on car no 3647, purpose of test to produce fusing as it occurred on Central Line tube train between Gants Hill and Redbridge, Essex on 11 Aug 1960: view of damaged equipment chamber bulkhead in Redbridge incident and test car 3647, 4 photographs, 1960 (See also MT114/323).

MT114/323 - Railway accidents: fire on tube train between Gants Hill and Redbridge, Essex; damage to outside of train, cab bulkhead and power receptacle box, 7 photographs, 1960 (See also MT114/322).

MT114/624 - London Transport: rolling stock programme policy; replacement of tube stock, single manning, braking circuits, emergency lighting and other issues, photographs, 1960-1971.

PRO8/64 - One photograph of Public Record Office: Furnival Street, deep shelter (undated). This was probably taken in the deep tube shelter constructed by London Transport during World War Two, underneath Chancery Lane station.

		# APPENDIX 1		
	Class Ref: MT6.	**BOARD OF TRADE/MINISTRY OF TRANSPORT: RAILWAYS: CORRESPONDENCE AND PAPERS.**		
Piece number:	**Original file ref:**	**Description**	**First date:**	**Last date:**
2/44	1299	Tottenham and Farringdon Street Railway: plan of line and traffic tables	1845	1845
23/7	118	South Kensington Museum: proposed railway	1861	1861
27/38	757	Hammersmith and City Railway: appointment of umpires	1863	1863
31/15	1249R	Hammersmith and City Railway	1864	1864
33/3	305R	Railways Construction Facilities Act, 1864 - Eastern Metropolitan Underground Railway	1864	1865
33/9	558R	Hammersmith and City Railway	1864	1865
34/7	1235R	Hammersmith and City Railway: land acquisition	1865	1865
36/10	2548R	Metropolitan Railway: Finsbury extension	1865	1865
50/7	R193	Metropolitan Railway: Kings Cross and Farringdon Street	1867	1868
51/2	R617	Metropolitan District Railways and Metropolitan Board of Works: Arbitrator's award	1867	1868
51/6	R819	Metropolitan and St. John's Wood Railway: working agreement	1868	1868
52/13	R1497	Metropolitan Railway: Kings Cross; junction railway	1868	1868
53/8	R2350	Metropolitan Railway: Notting Hill and Brompton extension	1868	1868
53/13	R2449	Aylesbury and Buckingham Railway: engine turning at Verney Junction	1868	1868
54/2	R2701	Watford and Rickmansworth Railway: opening	1862	1868
55/2	R3107	Metropolitan Railway: Gloucester Road to South Kensington	1868	1868
55/4	R3125	Metropolitan District Railway: South Kensington to Westminster Bridge	1868	1868
58/5	R1320	North Metropolitan Railway: extension of time	1869	1869
66/15	R1348	Metropolitan District Railway: Westminster to Blackfriars	1870	1870
67/12	R1869	Tower Subway	1870	1870
69/10	R3247	North Metropolitan Tramways: High Street, Stratford	1870	1870
73/4	R1019	London Tramways: Deptford Bridge to East Greenwich	1871	1871
73/5	R1026	East London and London, Brighton and South Coast Railways	1869	1871
74/1	R1233	London Tramways Company: Stockwell to Clapham	1871	1871
75/1	R1705	Metropolitan District Railway: South Kensington station	1871	1871
75/13	R2236	Metropolitan District Railway: Blackfriars to Mansion House	1871	1871
76/10	R2519	Metropolitan District Railway: West London Railway and Earls Court	1869	1871
76/13	R2611	Metropolitan Railway: Smithfield Junction Curve	1871	1871
78/6	R3522	North Metropolitan Railway: abandonment	1871	1871
80/4	R158	London Street Tramways: Kentish Town to Hampstead Road	1871	1872
81/10	R1651	Metropolitan Railway: Chalton Street: signalling	1872	1872
82/6	R2127	London Street Tramways: Camden Road to Kings Cross	1872	1872
89/3	R5469	London Street Tramways: Brecknock Arms to Holloway Road	1872	1872
89/9	R5865	North Metropolitan Tramways: Commercial Road lines	1872	1872
90/16	R6560	North Metropolitan Tramways: Essex Road, Balls Pond Road to City Road	1872	1872
91/13	R7004	London Tramways Company: purchase of Metropolitan Street Tramways Company and Pimlico, Peckham and Greenwich Street Tramways Company	1871	1872
94/5	R7861	North Metropolitan Tramways: Goswell Road lines	1872	1872
96/12	R546	London Street Tramways; Bye-laws	1872	1873
98/4	R1769	Uxbridge and Rickmansworth Railway: abandonment	1870	1873
101/5	R2536	North Metropolitan Tramway: Burdett Road	1873	1873
104/11	R3795	Kensington Station and North and South London Joint Railway: abandonment	1872	1873
104/17	R3839	North Metropolitan Tramways	1873	1873
105/21	R4418	Hammersmith Extension Railway: deviation	1873	1873
105/25	R4489	North Metropolitan Tramways: Clapton Pond to Lea Bridge Road	1873	1873
107/5	R5417	Metropolitan Railway: St. John's Wood and Baker Street Stations	1873	1873
109/11	R7248	East London Railway: gradient	1873	1873
109/18	R7594	Metropolitan Railway: Farringdon Street	1873	1873
109/20	R7664	Metropolitan and Metropolitan District Railways: South Kensington Joint Station	1873	1873
114/5	R2479	Metropolitan District Railway: Earls Court Junction	1874	1874
119/5	R5561	London Tramways Company	1872	1874
126/5	R8677	Metropolitan Railway: Bye-Laws	1874	1874
127/1	R8852	Metropolitan and St John's Wood Railway: Bye-laws	1874	1874
127/16	R9029	Metropolitan Tramways: Bye-laws	1873	1874

Piece no:	Original file ref:	Description	First date:	Last date:
130/4	R596	Metropolitan Railway: Moorgate Street to Liverpool Street	1874	1875
130/7	R647	Hammersmith and City Railway: Bye-laws	1874	1875
130/9	R678	London Tramways: Kennington to Old Kent Road	1874	1875
135/3	R2522	North Metropolitan Tramways: Lower Clapton to Stamford Hill	1874	1875
136/14	R3295	East London Railway: Bye-laws	1875	1875
137/10	R3946	London Street Tramways: Junction Road Extension	1874	1875
138/19	R4700	Hammersmith Extension and Metropolitan District Railways	1874	1875
139/12	R5081	Metropolitan Railway: Bishopsgate Station	1875	1875
141/9	R5935	Watford and Rickmansworth Railway: Bye-laws	1875	1875
151/3	R722	Metropolitan District Railway: Hammersmith North End	1876	1876
154/6	R2410	Metropolitan District Railway: Bye-laws	1876	1876
166/12	R8126	Metropolitan Railway: Bishopsgate Street Station to Aldgate	1876	1876
167/18	R8504	Metropolitan District Railway: Earls Court	1876	1876
181/1	R4706	Metropolitan District Railway: Richmond Extension	1877	1877
194/7	R11084	Metropolitan District Railway: Warwick Road and West Kensington; signals	1877	1877
194/15	R10406	Metropolitan Railway: Aldersgate to Moorgate Stations	1877	1877
198/6	R810	Shepherds Bush and Priory Road Acton Tramway	1877	1878
205/17	R3934	Metropolitan District Railway: Earl's Court	1877	1878
212/6	R6712	North Metropolitan Tramways: Ropemaker Street to Islington Green	1871	1878
214/7	R7824	London Street Tramways: Caledonian Road	1878	1878
223/2	R2725	Metropolitan and Metropolitan District Joint Railway: High Street, Kensington	1879	1879
237/3	R7689	North Metropolitan Tramways	1878	1879
238/6	R8257	Metropolitan District Railway: Ealing extension	1879	1879
241/12	R10472	Croydon Tramways: Bye-laws	1879	1879
245/10	R1889	Metropolitan District Railway: Fulham extension	1879	1880
246/8	R2450	Metropolitan District Railway: Elizabeth Street signals	1880	1880
249/1	R3924	London Street Tramways	1880	1880
249/6	R4338	London Tramways: Bye-laws	1873	1880
254/9	R6332	Metropolitan and St John's Wood Railway: Harrow extension	1879	1880
265/3	R10783	South London Tramways	1880	1880
269/10	R2540	South London Tramways: Bye-laws	1880	1881
279/9	R6555	North London Tramways: Tottenham Local Board; arbitration	1880	1881
281/16	R7747	North London Suburban Tramways: extension of time	1881	1881
282/11	R8192	London Tramways	1881	1881
285/4	R8877	London Central Railway	1881	1881
285/5	R8916	Southwark and Deptford Tramways	1879	1881
285/6	R8937	North London Suburban Tramways: Bye-laws	1881	1881
286/2	R9189	Woolwich and South East London Tramways: Bye-laws	1881	1881
286/4	R9258	Woolwich and South East London Tramways	1880	1881
303/8	R2914	Croydon Tramways	1880	1882
305/13	R3666	Uxbridge & Rickmansworth Railway	1882	1882
318/7	R9222	Metropolitan Railway: Aldgate to Tower of London	1882	1882
321/3	R9890	Metropolitan & District Railway: arbitrations	1882	1882
326/6	R93	North London Suburban Tramways	1879	1883
329/5	R2250	London Tramways	1881	1883
330/11	R3035	Metropolitan District Railway: Ealing Junction	1883	1883
334/3	R4900	Hounslow & Metropolitan Railway: Byelaws	1883	1883
335/11	R5508	West Metropolitan Tramways	1883	1883
340/1	R8063	Highgate Hill Tramways: extension of time	1883	1883
341/9	R8633	London Street Tramways	1883	1883
344/1	R9580	West Metropolitan Tramways	1882	1883
349/1	R10302	North Metropolitan Tramways: extension	1883	1883
349/6	R10838	South London Tramways	1881	1883
351/9	R11004	Woolwich & South East London Tramways: return of deposit	1883	1883
354/11	R12240	East London Railway: Cheap Trains	1883	1883
354/18	R12430	Metropolitan District Railway: Cheap Trains	1883	1883
358/3	R1523	North London Tramways: Byelaws	1883	1884
358/11	R1700	Metropolitan District Railway: Mill Hill Park Station	1884	1884
359/6	R1890	East London Railway: Whitechapel Extension	1883	1884
361/1	R2751	Metropolitan Railway: cheap trains	1883	1884
365/9	R4284	London Tramways: workmen's fares	1872	1884
368/7	R5240	Hounslow & Metropolitan Railway: Lampton Junction to Hounslow Barracks	1882	1884
369/14	R5957	Metropolitan District Railway: Whitechapel Terminus Railway	1884	1884

Piece no:	Original file ref:	Description	First date:	Last date:
370/3	R6105	Metropolitan District Railway: Mansion House Station	1884	1884
370/5	R6146	London Southern Tramways: Byelaws	1884	1884
370/6	R6149	Metropolitan Railway: South Kensington	1884	1884
385/7	R2874	Croydon & Norwood Tramways: Byelaws	1885	1885
385/8	R2894	London Southern Tramways	1883	1885
386/7	R2986	Metropolitan Railway: Harrow to Pinner	1885	1885
394/14	R4529	North Metropolitan Tramways	1885	1885
402/3	R172	East London Railway: Shoreditch	1885	1886
402/9	R412	Metropolitan District Railway: cheap trains	1886	1886
402/16	R797	North Metropolitan Tramways	1881	1886
403/13	R1707	Metropolitan District Railway: Hounslow Barracks Branch; Lampton Road	1886	1886
403/14	R1708	Metropolitan District Railway: Acton Green	1886	1886
416/2	R4623	North Metropolitan Tramways	1884	1886
423/1	R5941	London Street Tramways	1886	1886
429/3	R1221	London, Hendon & Harrow Railway: abandonment	1887	1887
439/2	R3614	London Southern Tramways	1886	1887
452/15	R337	Metropolitan Railway: Pinner to Rickmansworth	1887	1888
455/4	R1146	Uxbridge & Rickmansworth Railway: abandonment	1888	1888
457/9	R2142	London Street Tramways: Mekarski Automatic Car	1882	1888
463/8	R3614	Metropolitan Railway: Neasden	1888	1888
463/9	R3620	Metropolitan Railway: West Hampstead	1888	1888
469/2	R4997	North Metropolitan Tramways	1887	1888
472/13	R6162	Harrow Road and Paddington Tramways: Bye-laws	1888	1888
482/7	R2873	Metropolitan Railway: Rickmansworth	1889	1889
486/4	R4400	London Street Tramways	1887	1889
488/4	R8403	Croydon & Norwood Tramways	1887	1889
488/17	R8689	Metropolitan District and London & South Western Railways: Putney Bridge Junction	1889	1889
492/11	R10522	Tower Subway: Byelaws	1869	1889
495/7	R11607	Metropolitan Railway: Harrow	1889	1889
522/2	R8231	South Eastern Metropolitan Tramways: Lewisham	1890	1890
522/9	R8411	North Metropolitan Tramways Co: Byelaws	1873	1890
524/11	R8961	East London Railway Joint Committee: orders under Regulation of Railways Act 1889	1890	1890
527/5	R9679	Metropolitan District Railway: fares	1890	1890
532/6	R11328	London Tramways Co. Ltd. Totterdown extension	1889	1890
532/13	R11407	North Metropolitan Tramways Co: Whitechapel	1889	1890
534/1	R11519	West Metropolitan Tramways: Shepherds Bush & Hammersmith	1881	1890
537/8	R224	South Eastern Metropolitan Tramways: Byelaws	1890	1891
537/11	R310	Highgate Hill Cable Tramways: accident	1883	1890
538/12	R1076	Peckham & East Dulwich Tramways	1884	1891
543/6	R2974	Croydon and Norwood Tramways: Bye laws	1883	1891
554/2	R7128	Metropolitan District Railway: Blackfriars; failure of block system	1878	1891
571/7	R2023	City & South London Railway: signalling	1892	1892
581/11	R6129	Metropolitan Railway: Workmen's trains	1891	1892
583/9	R6646	Harrow Road & Paddington Tramways	1892	1892
602/2	R11003	Metropolitan District Railway: Cromwell Road & Gloucester Road	1871	1892
626/3	R9125	City & South London Railway: Oval to Stockwell; additional signal	1893	1893
629/10	R10852	Woolwich & South East London Tramways	1881	1893
632/12	R11785	Croydon & Norwood Tramways	1883	1893
633/14	R12249	Metropolitan Railway: extension of time	1890	1893
637	R13409	North London Suburban Tramways	1885	1893
648/16	R1742	City & South London Railway: signalling	1893	1894
657/10	R5425	London, Deptford & Greenwich Tramways: Electric traction regulations	1894	1894
659/2	R5936	Charing Cross, Euston & Hampstead Railway: electric traction regulations	1894	1894
666/1	R8419	Great Western & Metropolitan Joint Railway: Aylesbury	1893	1894
673/11	R11495	Croydon Tramways: Gas Motor Car	1893	1894
686/2	R2135	Metropolitan Outer Circle Railway: Abandonment	1893	1895
690/6	R11346	Metropolitan District Railway: fares	1893	1895
691/2	R11491	City & South London Railway: Motor Car Train	1895	1895
692/4	R11663	Metropolitan Railway: land acquisition	1895	1895
694/11	R13102	County of London: Road Bridges over Railways	1894	1895
700/1	R15372	North Metropolitan Tramways	1892	1895

Piece no:	Original file ref:	Description	First date:	Last date:
705/1	R17394	London County Council = Lease of tramways to London Street Tramways Company	1894	1895
706/2	R17578	Croydon Tramways: Byelaws	1895	1895
710/14	R19525	Metropolitan Railway: Finchley Road & West Hampstead	1895	1895
713/7	R21024	Metropolitan Railway: Aldgate signalling	1894	1895
717/2	R23074	Central London Railway	1895	1895
727/2	R657	London United Tramways: Acton	1895	1896
728/1	R1116	London Street Tramways	1891	1896
730/4	R1359	City & South London Railway: King William Street Station	1895	1896
730/7	R1634	London County Tramways	1895	1896
732/6	R2459	Metropolitan Railway: Baker Street Station	1892	1896
736/1	R4350	Metropolitan Railway: Wembley Park Station	1893	1896
737/7	R5020	London Camberwell & Dulwich Tramways: Byelaws	1896	1896
743/7	R12541	Croydon Corporation Tramways	1895	1896
756/2	R14748	Metropolitan Railway: Rickmansworth	1896	1896
763/5	R17567	Metropolitan Railway	1896	1896
777/1	R3888	London Deptford & Greenwich Tramways: Connelly Motor and Ribbe's accumulator car	1892	1897
780/6	R7037	Croydon Tramways: lease	1896	1897
780/10	R7136	Metropolitan Railway: Verney Junction; signals	1894	1897
782/10	R7739	Croydon Tramways	1896	1897
788/3	R9197	London Tramways	1894	1897
789/14	R9548	Metropolitan Railway: West Hampstead Station	1897	1897
804/1	R12903	City & South London Railway	1888	1897
837/1	R8978	East London Railway: Whitechapel Station	1898	1898
844/7	R11066	London United Tramways: Kew Observatory	1898	1898
851/3	R12739	Metropolitan Railway: Neasden Station	1897	1898
853/8	R13620	Metropolitan Railway: St John's Wood Road	1895	1898
855/8	R14715	City & South London Railway	1898	1898
862/4	R790	City & South London Railway: Moorgate Street & Clapham Common	1899	1899
863/1	R978	North Metropolitan Tramways	1899	1899
873/3	R4318	Metropolitan Railway	1898	1899
873/6	R4405	Metropolitan Railway: Finchley Road to Wembley	1899	1899
877/12	R6388	Metropolitan Railway	1898	1899
885/5	R7851	Whitechapel & Bow Railway	1899	1899
886/6	R8287	Ealing & South Harrow Railway	1898	1899
894/2	R9958	North Metropolitan Tramways	1899	1899
898/5	R10907	South London Tramways: accounts	1899	1899
902/6	R11707	London Tramways: Capital Return	1899	1899
917/5	R14750	Croydon Tramways: extension of time	1895	1899
925/3	R423	London United Tramways (Light Railways Extensions)	1898	1900
928/6	R1191	Metropolitan Railway: Aylesbury Station	1900	1900
930/3	R1564	North Metropolitan Tramways: Accounts	1900	1900
930/12	R1713	Metropolitan Railway: Chesham	1889	1900
931/4	R1844	North Metropolitan Tramways	1900	1900
933/6	R2373	Latimer Road & Acton Railway: Abandonment	1900	1900
938/6	R3155	Surbiton Urban District Tramways	1900	1900
949/3	R6796	Latimer Road & Acton Railway	1882	1900
952/8	R7962	Metropolitan Railway: Preston Road & Harrow	1899	1900
959/7	R9781	South London Tramways: sale to London County Council	1900	1900
959/8	R9844	North Metropolitan Tramways	1900	1900
959/9	R9871	South London Tramways: Waterloo Road; conveyance	1900	1900
959/10	R9874	Barking Town Urban District Tramways	1899	1900
959/13	R9999	London Deptford & Greenwich Tramways	1900	1900
960/5	R10301	North Metropolitan Tramways	1897	1900
988/2	R727	Central London Railway: Cheap trains	1900	1901
1000/3	R4721	Metropolitan Railway: electrification	1896	1901
1002/1	R5177	Baker Street and Waterloo Railway	1900	1901
1004/1	R5680	Metropolitan Railway; Harrow	1900	1901
1012/1	R8917	Metropolitan District Railway: Mill Hill Park	1882	1901
1013/1	R9404	London United Tramways: Electrical Regulations	1898	1901
1019/3	R9950	Central London Railway: vibration	1900	1901
1020/3	R10259	Bexley Tramways Bill	1901	1901
1022/9	R11021	London County Council Tramways	1901	1901
1024/6	R11352	Great Northern & City Railway; Drayton Park	1901	1901

Piece no:	Original file ref:	Description	First date:	Last date:
1031/13	R13957	Metropolitan District Railway; Brompton & Piccadilly Railway; extensions	1901	1901
1040/7	R16605	City and South London Railway: Moorgate to Islington extension	1894	1901
1040/8	R16606	City and South London Railway: London Bridge: lifts and subway	1901	1901
1041/6	R17257	County of Middlesex Light Railway	1901	1901
1042/1	R17351	Metropolitan and District Railway: Electrical working	1901	1901
1050/3	R498	Locomotion in subways or shallow tunnels	1901	1902
1050/6	R583	Metropolitan Railway; Harrow	1901	1902
1058/7	R2801	Harrow Road and Paddington Tramways	1888	1902
1065/4	R4139	London County Council Tramways: Bermondsey	1902	1902
1069/3	R5562	South Eastern Metropolitan Tramways	1902	1902
1073/3	R6290	Metropolitan District Railway Bill: House of Commons Committee recommendation about reporting by the Board on electrical undertakings	1902	1902
1083/4	R8260	Underground Railways: Committee on "Tube" Railway Bills	1902	1902
1089/2	R9021	Edgware & Hampstead Railway: cheap trains	1902	1902
1096/1	R9822	London Underground: Cheap fares	1902	1902
1100/15	R10440	Croydon Corporation Tramways	1901	1902
1107/6	R11837	Great Northern & City Railway: Electric Motors	1902	1902
1111	R12406	County of Middlesex Light Railway	1899	1902
1113/2	R12726	Metropolitan Railway: Kilburn Viaduct Extension	1902	1902
1115/1	R13130	Electric Tube Railways: inspection of plans by office of works	1902	1902
1121/1	R14361	North Metropolitan Tramways: Middlesex lines: transfer to Metropolitan Electric Tramways	1902	1902
1121/7	R14566	South London Tramways: sale to London County Council	1901	1902
1125	R15199	London Tramways: Cable routes	1891	1902
1128/3	R15963	Metropolitan Railway: Croxley Green	1902	1902
1139/1	R1284	Metropolitan Railway: Farringdon Street	1901	1903
1140/9	R1716	London United Tramways: Bye laws	1883	1903
1142/1	R1964	Whitechapel & Bow Railway: signalling	1902	1903
1143/7	R2691	Metropolitan Railway: Northwood	1903	1903
1145/3	R2905	Underground Railways: Bills	1902	1903
1145/4	R2966	Royal Commission on Means of Locomotion and Transport in London	1903	1903
1149/1	R3345	London County Council Tramways & Subways	1902	1903
1149/5	R3435	London Tilbury & Southend Railway and Metropolitan District Railway	1903	1903
1159/1	R5386	City & South London Railway Bill, 1903	1903	1903
1159/4	R5503	London County Council Electric Tramways: opening	1903	1903
1162/5	R5903	Metropolitan Railway: tunnel cables	1903	1903
1165	R6160	London United Tramways	1900	1903
1207/1	R15207	Metropolitan Railway: Kingsbury to Neasden	1903	1903
1212/6	R62	Metropolitan District Railway: Mill Hill Park and Ealing Common	1903	1904
1212/8	R241	North Metropolitan Tramways: sale to Metropolitan Electric Tramways	1903	1904
1213	R350 (Part 1)	Middlesex Light Railway	1901	1904
1214	R350 (Part 2)	Middlesex Light Railway	1901	1904
1215	R350 (Part 3)	Middlesex Light Railway	1901	1904
1221/5	R1183	Metropolitan District Railway: generating station, Lots Road	1902	1904
1223/12	R2029	London County Council Tramways: Holborn Strand Subway	1903	1904
1227/1	R2677	Metropolitan District Railway: electrification	1902	1904
1231/9	R3649	East London Railway & others V The Conservators of the River Thames: Dredging: Wapping to Rotherhithe	1904	1904
1231/12	R3737	Paris Tube Railway; report of fire accident, August 1903	1903	1904
1235/5	R4008	Metropolitan Railway: Praed Street	1904	1904
1245/1	R5402	London United Tramways: extension of time	1901	1904
1254	R6153	Croydon Corporation: Tramways	1900	1904
1260/3	R7007	Metropolitan District Railway: Earls Court to West Kensington	1904	1904
1274/5	R8776	East Ham District Council Tramways: Byelaws	1904	1904
1285/2	R11007	East Ham Tramways	1904	1904
1289/15	R12039	Charing Cross, Euston & Hampstead Railway: Highgate	1904	1904
1298/6	R13276	Metropolitan Railway: West Hampstead	1904	1904
1302/13	R13873	London County Council Tramways	1904	1904
1306/4	R14930	West Ham Corporation Tramways; loan	1904	1904
1307	R15098	London United Tramways	1901	1904
1312/1	R167	Metropolitan Railway: Tower Street accident	1905	1905
1312/2	R281	Metropolitan Railway; Baker Street	1904	1905
1314/1	R696	Baker Street & Waterloo Railway	1905	1905
1315/6	R1069	Metropolitan Railway: Kenton Rd signals	1904	1905

Piece no:	Original file ref:	Description	First date:	Last date:
1322/2	R2363	London County Council Tramways: Westminster Bridge	1904	1905
1325/1	R2933	Great Northern & City Railway	1905	1905
1326/2	R3122	Great Northern Piccadilly & Brompton Railway: Kings Cross subway	1904	1905
1327/3	R3206	Metropolitan District Railway: Westminster	1905	1905
1328/1	R3343	Great Northern & City Railway	1902	1905
1334/3	R3599	Great Northern Piccadilly & Brompton Railway	1905	1905
1340/2	R4736	Edgware & Hampstead Railway	1904	1905
1340/11	R4865	Metropolitan District Railway: Hammersmith	1905	1905
1346	R5100	Great Northern Piccadilly & Brompton Railway: Down Street	1902	1905
1350/6	R5476	Metropolitan District Railway: Parsons Green: signals	1905	1905
1354/3	R5886	Central London Railway: Fire; Notting Hill Gate	1904	1905
1354/6	R5908	Metropolitan Railway; Praed Street	1891	1905
1363/1	R6412	Metropolitan District Railway: fires in National Telephone Coy. premises	1905	1905
1368/3	R7134	Metropolitan Electric Tramways; Byelaws	1905	1905
1375/2	R8022	Metropolitan Railway: Quainton Road Junction	1905	1905
1375/8	R8060	Baker Street & Waterloo Railway	1905	1905
1377/2	R8141	Metropolitan District Railway: South Kensington	1905	1905
1378/1	R8318	Edgware & Hampstead Railway	1904	1905
1380/5	R8568	Metropolitan Railway; South Kensington	1905	1905
1385/1	R9382	North Metropolitan Tramways Co accounts	1905	1905
1393/12	R10007	Metropolitan District Railway; West Kensington East & Hammersmith, signals	1905	1905
1397/3	R10111	London United Tramways: extension of time	1901	1905
1398/6	R10132	Baker Street & Waterloo Railway; signals	1903	1905
1403/8	R10737	Metropolitan District Railway; electrification and signalling	1904	1905
1403/9	R10740	Metropolitan District Railway: Gloucester Road to Earls Court	1905	1905
1411/9	R12040	Baker Street & Waterloo Railway: Piccadilly Circus	1905	1905
1415/14	R12852	Great Northern & City Railway: Byelaws	1905	1905
1416/2	R12947	Metropolitan District Railway: Barons Court	1905	1905
1417/6	R13189	Charing Cross Euston & Hampstead Railway: Mornington Crescent & Tufnell Park	1905	1905
1418/5	R13208	Metropolitan District Railway: Ealing signals	1905	1905
1418/6	R13210	Metropolitan District Railway: Earls Court; signals	1905	1905
1418/16	R13447	London Tilbury & Southend and Metropolitan District Railways: Whitechapel & Bow Joint Committee; Byelaws	1905	1905
1421/1	R13777	Baker Street & Waterloo Railway: accounts	1905	1905
1423/11	R14181	Great Western & Metropolitan Railway: Byelaws	1905	1905
1426/7	R14585	Waterloo & City Railway: Byelaws	1905	1905
1429/2	R14788	Metropolitan & District Railway Automatic signals	1905	1905
1429/3	R14799	Metropolitan Railway: Ickenham Halt	1905	1905
1439/7	R902	Metropolitan Railway: Byelaws	1905	1906
1442/1	R1007	Metropolitan Railway: Willesden Green	1905	1906
1444/9	R1521	Middlesex County Council Tramways	1906	1906
1444/11	R1625	East London Railway; Byelaws	1905	1906
1445/2	R1652	Hammersmith City and North East London Tube Railway	1903	1906
1447/11	R2327	Baker Street and Waterloo Railway: Byelaws	1906	1906
1448/4	R2385	Croydon Corporation Tramways: regulations	1906	1906
1450/1	R2616	Metropolitan District Railway; Mark Lane; fire	1906	1906
1453	R3239	London, Camberwell and Dulwich Tramways	1890	1906
1456/2	R3384	Metropolitan Railway	1904	1906
1457/13	R3807	Baker Street & Waterloo Railway; cheap trains	1906	1906
1472/9	R5706	Metropolitan and Great Central Joint Committee: Bye-laws	1906	1906
1477/1	R6444	East London Railway Joint Committee: East London Junction and New Cross	1906	1906
1484/6	R7613	Metropolitan Railway: Moorgate Street	1906	1906
1486/2	R7753	Metropolitan Railway: Kings Cross	1906	1906
1495/1	R8777	Metropolitan District Railway: Aldgate East & Minories Junction; signals	1906	1906
1495/5	R8925	Metropolitan District Railway: memorandum of meeting with Board of Trade on safety precautions	1906	1906
1500/8	R9811	Charing Cross Euston & Hampstead Railway: Charing Cross Station	1905	1906
1500/9	R9812	Great Northern Piccadilly & Brompton Railway: signals	1905	1906
1513/4	R11917	Metropolitan District Railway: automatic signals	1905	1906
1518/3	R13220	Metropolitan Railway: Eastcote Road Halt	1906	1906
1518/5	R13356	Metropolitan Railway: Aldersgate Street	1906	1906

Piece no:	Original file ref:	Description	First date:	Last date:
1519/1	R13538	Metropolitan Electric Tramways: County of Middlesex Light Railway Regulations	1906	1906
1528/12	R14301	Great Northern, Piccadilly & Brompton Railway: Byelaws	1906	1906
1534/8	R15339	London Southern Tramways: Sale	1906	1906
1537	R15729	West Ham Corporation Tramways	1904	1906
1539	R15978 (Part 1)	Croydon & District Electric Tramways: Mitcham Light Railways: British Electric Traction Co.	1905	1906
1540	R15978 (Part 2)	Croydon & District Electric Tramways: Mitcham Light Railways: British Electric Traction Co.	1905	1906
1548/3	R261	Metropolitan District Railway: Ealing and South Harrow Extension; automatic signals	1901	1907
1551/13	R841	Gt. Northern Piccadilly & Brompton Railway: cheap trains	1907	1907
1552/6	R1079	Great Western Railway: Bishops Road - Hammersmith, electric working	1906	1907
1556/2	R1413	Hammersmith City & N.E. London Railway Bill 1906-1907	1906	1907
1558/9	R1828	London United Electric Tramways: Street accident at Shepherds Bush	1907	1907
1559/10	R2101	Metropolitan Railway: High Street Kensington	1906	1907
1560/1	R2102	Metropolitan District Railway: High Street Kensington	1907	1907
1561/1	R2292	Croydon Corporation Tramways: Regulations	1907	1907
1561/4	R2405	Whitechapel & Bow Railway: Whitechapel to Bow Road	1906	1907
1564/9	R3254	Walthamstow Light Railways: extension of time	1905	1907
1568/8	R3636	London Tilbury & Southend and Metropolitan District Railways: cheap trains	1902	1907
1570	R4042	Walthamstow UDC, Light Railways	1903	1907
1575/3	R4518	Harrow Road & Paddington Tramways: Regulations	1906	1907
1577/4	R4814	Charing Cross, Euston & Hampstead Railway: Bye Laws	1907	1907
1578/4	R5151	Metropolitan Railway: accident at Neasden	1905	1907
1581/1	R5570	Middlesex Light Railway: Extension of Lands	1905	1907
1585	R6108	City & South London Railway: Euston Extension	1902	1907
1599/5	R7938	Baker Street & Waterloo Railway: Edgware Road Station	1907	1907
1600/5	R8000	Whitechapel & Bow Railway: Whitechapel	1907	1907
1609/1	R8817	Metropolitan Railway; Praed Street Junction to Aldgate; signals	1907	1907
1613	R9170 (Part 1)	London United Tramways	1900	1907
1614	R9170 (Part 2)	London United Tramways	1900	1907
1615	R9170 (Part 3)	London United Tramways	1900	1907
1616/4	R9333	East Ham Corporation Tramways; Bye-laws	1901	1907
1616/8	R9441	Charing Cross, Euston & Hampstead Railway; Cheap trains	1907	1907
1625/12	R10700	Barking Town UDC Light Railways: Bye laws	1903	1907
1628/5	R11014	Barking Town UDC Light Railways; Regulations	1907	1907
1634/6	R12341	London United Tramways & Light Railways: Regulations	1907	1907
1649/9	R13650	Metropolitan Railway: Baker Street	1907	1907
1656/1	R14075	London County Council Tramways: Bye laws	1906	1907
1658/2	R14292	Metropolitan District Railway: cheap trains	1906	1907
1660/4	R14829	Ilford UDC Tramways: Station to Valentines Park	1907	1907
1666/7	R16076	Charing Cross, Euston & Hampstead Railway; Villiers Street	1903	1907
1667/1	R16080	Harrow Road Paddington Tramways	1907	1907
1667/2	R16135	Metropolitan Railway: Chalfont Road; fatal accident	1906	1907
1667/4	R16224	Metropolitan Railway: West Hampstead collision	1907	1907
1682/1	R1117	County of Middlesex Light Railways: arbitration	1908	1908
1685	R2222	Highgate Hill Tramways	1891	1908
1693/10	R4073	London United Tramways: extension of time	1907	1908
1698/5	R4609	London County Council Tramways: Subway; Strand to Victoria Embankment	1908	1908
1698/8	R4719	London County Council Tramways: Blackfriars Bridge Accident; 28/11/07	1907	1908
1701/13	R5636	Walthamstow UDC, Light Railways: application for refund of tramcar licence fees	1908	1908
1702/7	R5816	Central London Railway: Shepherds Bush extension	1908	1908
1703/10	R6326	Tottenham and Walthamstow Light Railways: deposit before exercise of powers	1907	1908
1703/16	R6457	Trolley pole connection with roof: observations by Metropolitan Police	1908	1908
1704/3	R6478	North Metropolitan Tramways and East Ham Corporation: conveyance	1905	1908
1704/5	R6501	Metropolitan Railway: electric working	1908	1908
1710/10	R6592	Metropolitan District Railway: West Kensington	1908	1908
1713/2	R7136	Metropolitan Railway: Gloucester Road	1908	1908
1713/3	R7138	Metropolitan Railway: Preston Road	1908	1908

Piece no:	Original file ref:	Description	First date:	Last date:
1715/5	R7676	Metropolitan District Railway: Northfield Lane	1908	1908
1718/1	R7927	Croydon & District Tramways: Regulations	1906	1908
1718/7	R7964	Metropolitan District Railway: Mill Hill Park and Cromwell Road	1908	1908
1734/6	R10149	London County Council and Westminster Electric Supply Corporation: Arbitrations	1908	1908
1735/11	R10609	Great Central, Great Western and Metropolitan Railways: Aylesbury Station	1908	1908
1740/2	R11460	Metropolitan District Railway: Mansion House	1908	1908
1741/4	R12027	Metropolitan District Railway: Hammersmith signals	1906	1908
1742/9	R12146	County of Middlesex Light Railways: extension of time	1905	1908
1743/5	R12288	Metropolitan Railway: Kings Cross and Farringdon Street; signals	1908	1908
1750/2	R12852	Metropolitan Railway: Harrow	1908	1908
1751/1	R12853	Harrow Road & Paddington Tramways	1905	1908
1758/5	R13585	Metropolitan Railway: Moorgate; signals	1908	1908
1760/7	R13811	London County Council Tramways	1908	1908
1760/11	R13906	Charing Cross Euston & Hampstead Railway: Charing Cross; signals	1908	1908
1760/12	R13907	Great Northern Piccadilly & Brompton Railway: Finsbury Park; signals	1908	1908
1771/2	R740	Highgate Hill Tramways: transfer	1889	1909
1772/1	R745	Metropolitan Electric Tramways: Friern Barnet Road bridge	1909	1909
1773	R1021 (Part 1)	Middlesex Light Railway	1902	1909
1774	R1021 (Part 2)	Middlesex Light Railway	1902	1909
1775	R1021 (Part 3)	Middlesex Light Railway	1902	1909
1779/2	R1545	City & South London Railway: Cheap trains	1892	1909
1783/10	R2350	Metropolitan District Railway: Mansion House & Whitechapel	1909	1909
1786/1	R2518	Baker Street & Waterloo Railway: signals	1909	1909
1786/2	R2521	Great Northern Piccadilly & Brompton Railway: signals	1909	1909
1795/3	R4052 (Part 1)	East Ham Urban District Council Tramways	1902	1909
1796	R4052 (Part 2)	East Ham Urban District Council Tramways	1902	1909
1798/2	R4400	Metropolitan District Railway: Earls Court	1909	1909
1805/7	R5432	West Ham Corporation Tramways: extension of time	1908	1909
1806/1	R5460	London County Council Tramways: Streatham Hill	1909	1909
1815/4	R6702	Great Northern Piccadilly and Brompton Railway: Finsbury Park	1909	1909
1818/8	R7481	Metropolitan Railway: Baker Street	1908	1909
1818/9	R7483	Metropolitan Railway: Smithfield market	1908	1909
1824/9	R8431	Metropolitan Railway: Farringdon Street	1908	1909
1824/10	R8451	West Ham Corporation Tramways: Clarke V the Corporation: electric shock	1909	1909
1828/2	R9146	County of Middlesex Light Railways: Extension of time	1908	1909
1833/2	R9773	Corporation of London: Blackfriars Bridge tramway	1909	1909
1835/9	R10148	Metropolitan District Railway: Hounslow Town	1909	1909
1835/11	R10229	Ilford U.D.C., Tramways: new cars	1909	1909
1838/6	R10650	Charing Cross Euston and Hampstead Railway: Highgate; Signals	1909	1909
1841/1	R10990	Underground railways: fire precautions; proposed inspection of appliances by London Fire Brigade	1908	1909
1841/3	R11019	Metropolitan Railway: Dollis Hill	1909	1909
1842/1	R11132	Metropolitan Railways: Automatic signals	1906	1909
1842/2	R11133	Metropolitan Railway: Aldersgate	1909	1909
1844/1	R11150	Metropolitan Railway: Fire Extinguishers	1908	1909
1844/2	R11153	Metropolitan Railway: St John's Wood Extension	1909	1909
1844/6	R11258	London United Tramways: Uxbridge Road points	1909	1909
1848/5	R12097	Metropolitan District Railway: Mansion House	1909	1909
1854/9	R12823	Whitechapel & Bow Railway: Bye-laws	1909	1909
1859/1	R13521	Corporation of London Tramways: regulations	1909	1909
1868/1	R467	London County Council Tramways	1910	1910
1868/5	R635	London United Tramways	1910	1910
1869/7	R798	Metropolitan Association of Electric Tramway Managers: through running, leasing and bookings	1910	1910
1870/6	R1024	North East London Railway	1905	1910
1870/10	R1227	London Electric Railway Amalgamation	1910	1910
1874/9	R1832	County of Middlesex Light Railway: extension of time	1910	1910
1875/4	R1895	West Ham Corporation Tramways	1909	1910
1875/7	R2018	Metropolitan Railway: Harrow and Uxbridge extension	1903	1910
1878/8	R2581	County of Middlesex Light Railway	1908	1910
1880/2	R2782	Baker Street and Waterloo Railway	1908	1910
1880/4	R2798	Metropolitan Railway: Liverpool Street	1910	1910
1881/5	R2934	Metropolitan Railway: Aldgate; signals	1909	1910

Piece no:	Original file ref:	Description	First date:	Last date:
1882/3	R3036	Metropolitan Railway: Baker Street signals	1909	1910
1887/4	R3685	Metropolitan Railway: Wembley Park	1910	1910
1887/8	R3793	County of Middlesex Light Railway: extension of time	1906	1910
1895/5	R4792	Whitechapel & Bow Railway: Whitechapel	1910	1910
1895/6	R4805	London Electric Railway Amalgamation Bill	1910	1910
1896/1	R4844	Charing Cross Euston & Hampstead Railway: Golders Green	1910	1910
1896/3	R4873	Metropolitan District Railway: South Harrow	1910	1910
1901/4	R5714	Metropolitan Railway: Sandy Lodge	1910	1910
1901/7	R5722	Metropolitan District Railway: Heston & Hounslow	1910	1910
1902/5	R5889	London Underground Electric Railways: signal alterations	1910	1910
1904/6	R6270	Metropolitan District Railway Bill	1910	1910
1909/5	R6916	East Ham Corporation Tramways: regulations	1908	1910
1911/2	R6994	Metropolitan District Railway: Hammersmith	1910	1910
1913/4	R7293	Metropolitan District Railway: Acton Town	1909	1910
1925/5	R9001	Metropolitan Railway: South Harrow	1910	1910
1925/10	R9153	Walthamstow Urban District Council Light Railway	1910	1910
1926/4	R9254	Metropolitan District Railway: Gloucester Road signals	1910	1910
1926/5	R9361	Metropolitan Railway: Willesden Green	1910	1910
1930/5	R10334	Metropolitan Railway: Edgware Road	1910	1910
1930/6	R10335	Metropolitan Railway: Aldgate	1910	1910
1933/1	R10668	London County Council Tramways: speed limit on Victoria Embankment	1908	1910
1933/5	R10802	Tramway Undertakings within London County boundary; financial tables	1910	1910
1935/8	R11106	Metropolitan Electric Tramways: Warwick Crescent to Harrow Road	1909	1910
1937/3	R11542	Metropolitan Railway: communication cord in passenger trains	1910	1910
1946/1	R195	London County Council Tramways	1911	1911
1946/3	R199	Metropolitan Electric Tramways	1911	1911
1946/5	R207	Metropolitan Electric Tramways	1909	1911
1947/2	R451	Metropolitan District Railway: Mansion House	1911	1911
1948/3	R575	Croydon Corporation Tramways: doubling in Addiscombe Road	1910	1911
1952/5	R1129	Metropolitan Electric Tramways: Harrow Road	1910	1911
1953/8	R1333	Metropolitan Railway: Baker Street signals	1910	1911
1954/5	R1363	County of Middlesex Light Railway	1909	1911
1970	R3052 (Part 1)	Middlesex County Council Light Railway	1909	1911
1971	R3052 (Part 2)	Middlesex County Council Light Railway	1909	1911
1972	R3052 (Part 3)	Middlesex County Council Light Railway	1909	1911
1973	R3052 (Part 4)	Middlesex County Council Light Railway	1909	1911
1974/2	R3094	Leyton Urban District Tramways	1905	1911
1976/2	R3371	Metropolitan District Railway: Minories junctions; speed limit	1909	1911
1976/3	R3373	Metropolitan Railway: Finchley Road & Neasden; signals	1910	1911
1976/5	R3416	Croydon & District Tramways	1911	1911
1981/2	R4085	County of Middlesex Light Railways	1907	1911
1984/1	R4471	London County Council: Blackfriars Bridge tramway shelter	1911	1911
1987/3	R5036	West Ham Corporation Tramways: through running with Barking and East Ham	1911	1911
1987/5	R5056	City & South London Railway: Elephant & Castle: signals	1911	1911
1987/6	R5058	London Electric Railway: Westminster Bridge Road: signals	1911	1911
1988/1	R5110	Metropolitan District Railway; Earls Court & Mansion House; signals	1911	1911
1988/3	R5174	Metropolitan Electric Tramways	1911	1911
1992/1	R5349	London County Council Tramways: coupled cars	1911	1911
1992/3	R5366	London Underground Railways: Conciliation Boards	1908	1911
1999/2	R6360	Great Central & Metropolitan Joint Railways: accident at Northwood	1911	1911
2002/2	R6551	Royal Commission on London Traffic and Royal Commission on Canals & Waterways: transfer of plans & documents to the Board of Trade	1906	1911
2003/3	R6411	Greater London Railway Bill	1911	1911
2004/13	R6814	Croydon Corporation Tramways	1906	1911
2005/1	R6833	Metropolitan Electric Tramways	1911	1911
2005/3	R6877	Metropolitan Railway: Neasden: signal box	1911	1911
2005/4	R6894	London County Council Tramways	1911	1911
2005/7	R6930	London County Council Tramways: Embankment & Blackfriars Bridge	1911	1911
2010/7	R7473	London County Council Tramways Bill	1911	1911
2011/8	R7593	London Electric Railway: lighting at Tunnel stations & emergency supplies for lifts	1911	1911
2013	R7673	London United Tramways	1904	1911

Piece no:	Original file ref:	Description	First date:	Last date:
2018/8	R8299	Walthamstow & District Light Railways: Byelaws	1905	1911
2024/3	R8990	Metropolitan District Railway: Studland Road & Acton Lane, Ravenscourt Park & Chiswick Park, signalling	1911	1911
2034/5	R10103	London Electric Railways: Piccadilly Circus Station	1911	1911
2034/9	R10177	East London Railway: automatic signalling	1911	1911
2038	R10498 (Part 1)	Metropolitan Electric Tramways	1905	1911
2039	R10498 (Part 2)	Metropolitan Electric Tramways	1905	1911
2042/2	R10749	London County Council Tramways: Balham	1911	1911
2042/3	R10777	London United Tramways: Brentford	1911	1911
2046/6	R11518	Metropolitan & Great Central Railway: Winslow Road	1911	1911
2049/5	R11737	London County Council Tramways: (Southern System)	1911	1911
2049/12	R11966	Metropolitan Railway: Rickmansworth	1911	1911
2050/5	R12066	Great Northern Piccadilly & Brompton Railway: Piccadilly Circus; lifts	1911	1911
2058/4	R56	Metropolitan Railway Bill 1912	1912	1912
2058/5	R57	Metropolitan District Railway Bill 1912	1903	1912
2058/11	R98	Metropolitan Railway: inner home signals	1911	1912
2058/12	R99	Metropolitan Railway: Moorgate Street	1911	1912
2059/2	R211	Central London Railway: payment of interest from capital	1912	1912
2060/4	R414	Metropolitan Railway Bill 1912	1912	1912
2061/4	R728	Edgware and Hampstead Railway Bill 1912	1912	1912
2061/9	R833	Central London Railway: Liverpool Street Extension	1912	1912
2063/1	R1075	Richmond to Kew Road Tramway: Sale to London United Tramways Co Ltd.	1894	1912
2063/4	R1164	Metropolitan District Railway: Earls Court East	1911	1912
2064/1	R1287	London United Tramways: Report by London Traffic Branch	1912	1912
2064/5	R1344	London Electric Railway: Oxford Circus	1912	1912
2064/6	R1345	London Electric Railway: Charing Cross	1912	1912
2066/4	R1818	London Electric Railway: Edgware and Hampstead Railway	1912	1912
2066/6	R1901	Disabled tram-cars: removal in Metropolitan area	1909	1912
2068/5	R2142	Barking U.D.C. Light Railways: Regulations; Disabled cars	1912	1912
2068/6	R2143	Bexley U.D.C. Tramways: Regulations; disabled cars	1912	1912
2068/7	R2144	Croydon Corporation Tramways: Regulations; disabled cars	1912	1912
2068/8	R2146	East Ham Corporation Tramways: Regulations; disabled cars	1912	1912
2068/9	R2147	Erith U.D.C. Tramways: Regulations; disabled cars	1912	1912
2068/10	R2148	Ilford U.D.C. Tramways: Regulations; disabled cars	1912	1912
2068/11	R2149	Leyton U.D.C., Tramways: Regulations disabled cars	1912	1912
2068/12	R2150	London United Tramways: Regulations disabled cars	1912	1912
2068/13	R2152	County of Middlesex and County of Hertford Light Railways, Metropolitan Electric, Harrow Road, Harrow Road and Paddington Tramways: Regulations; disabled cars	1912	1912
2068/14	R2155	Walthamstow U.D.C., Tramways: Regulations disabled cars	1912	1912
2069/1	R2205	Metropolitan and Great Central Joint Committee: Explosives Bye laws	1912	1912
2069/3	R2217	Southall Hounslow and Twickenham Railless Traction Bill, 1912	1912	1912
2071/4	R2416	Barking U.D.C. Light Railways	1900	1912
2072/3	R2446	Inspection of lifts	1900	1912
2074/4	R2695	Metropolitan Railway: wagon brakes	1912	1912
2076/1	R2839	Metropolitan District Railway: Earls Court to West Brompton; signals	1912	1912
2076/2	R2842	West Ham Corporation Tramways: Byelaws	1903	1912
2077/4	R3158	West Ham Corporation Tramways	1908	1912
2078/3	R3225	Ilford U.D.C., Tramways: Byelaws	1903	1912
2078/6	R3316	London Electric Railway: movable step on new rolling stock	1911	1912
2078/8	R3384	Croydon and District Tramways, - Mitcham Light Railways: Regulations	1912	1912
2081/1	R3456	West Ham Corporation Tramways: removal of disabled carriages	1912	1912
2085/3	R4042	County of Hertford Light Railways; Cheshunt Light Railways; lease to Metropolitan Electric Tramways	1909	1912
2085/4	R4109	West Ham Corporation Bill, 1912: Workmens fares	1912	1912
2085/7	R4161	County of Hertford Light Railway: Regulations	1912	1912
2089/2	R4824	Metropolitan Electric Tramways: increased speeds	1911	1912
2090/3	R4976	Harrow Road and Paddington Tramways: increased speeds	1912	1912
2091/4	R5205	County of Middlesex Light Railways: increased speeds	1912	1912
2092/11	R5342	Walthamstow and District Light Railway: doubling at junction of Chingford Road and Hoe Street	1912	1912
2093/6	R5481	London County Council Tramways: L.C.C., v Stoke Newington Boro' Council re Wood Paving	1911	1912
2098/4	R5741	Metropolitan District Railway: Earls Court West	1912	1912

Piece no:	Original file ref:	Description	First date:	Last date:
2098/5	R5742	Metropolitan District Railway: Hammersmith	1912	1912
2098/6	R5743	London Electric Railway: Barons Court	1911	1912
2099/4	R5981	East Ham Tramways: doubling in High Street	1912	1912
2099/6	R6088	West Ham Corporation Tramways: Regulations	1907	1912
2105/4	R6433	Metropolitan Railway: Gloucester Road	1912	1912
2105/6	R6469	Metropolitan District Railway Bill	1912	1912
2109/9	R6988	County of Middlesex Light Railways: Aldermans Hill	1912	1912
2114/3	R7323	London Electric Railway: Edgware Road Station	1912	1912
2115/2	R7405	London Electric Railway Bill, 1912	1911	1912
2119/6	R7738	London County Council Tramways: East India Dock Road	1912	1912
2120/1	R7758	London County Council (Tramways and Improvements) Bill, 1912	1912	1912
2121/5	R8000	Metropolitan Railway: South Kensington Station	1911	1912
2121/6	R8001	Metropolitan Railway: Kings Cross Station	1912	1912
2122/1	R8095	London County Council Tramways: Battersea Park Road	1912	1912
2125/5	R8508	London Electric Railways: electric current failures	1908	1912
2126/1	R8533	London Electric Railway: conciliation	1912	1912
2128/8	R8798	London County Council Tramways: Lordship Lane	1912	1912
2128/11	R8810	Metropolitan Railway: Rayner's Lane	1912	1912
2130/2	R9252	London County Council Tramways: Bye-law	1912	1912
2130/4	R9300	Ilford Urban District Tramways	1912	1912
2131/7	R9727	London County Council Tramways: trailer cars	1912	1912
2132/1	R9979	Metropolitan District Railway: Heston Hounslow	1912	1912
2132/2	R9987	London Electric Railway: rolling stock	1912	1912
2133/3	R10220	Royal Commission on London Traffic: proposed London Traffic Board	1906	1912
2136/1	R10514	London Electric Railway: Edgware Road; signals	1912	1912
2137/7	R10923	Metropolitan District Railway: third rail protection planking	1912	1912
2138/1	R11314	Metropolitan Railway: Baker Street Station	1912	1912
2140/6	R11530	Metropolitan District Railway: Conciliation Boards	1912	1912
2141/3	R11688	London County Council Tramways: working regulations	1912	1912
2160/6	R542	Great Northern and City Railway: conciliation	1913	1913
2160/7	R553	Walthamstow and District Light Railways	1912	1913
2160/8	R565	Metropolitan Railway: conciliation	1913	1913
2161/5	R675	London United Tramways: accident	1912	1913
2165/1	R1812	Metropolitan Railway: Baker Street	1911	1913
2166/3	R2087	Central London Railway: Liverpool Street; Broad Street	1910	1913
2166/5	R2220	London Electric Railway: Caledonian Road; accident; sight testing of motormen	1912	1913
2167/5	R2296	Metropolitan Railway: Eastcote	1912	1913
2169/5	R2735	London Electric Railway: removal of locking bars from facing points	1913	1913
2169/6	R2737	Metropolitan District Railway	1913	1913
2170/2	R2886	London Underground Railways: fires	1907	1913
2170/10	R2919	Metropolitan Railway: Praed Street to Aldgate; signals	1913	1913
2171/4	R3002	City and South London Railway: signals	1913	1913
2174/10	R3532	East Ham Corporation Bill	1913	1913
2175/7	R3673	Hertfordshire County Light Railway	1907	1913
2177/8	R4063	London transport amalgamations	1911	1913
2179/2	R4211	Post Office (London) Railway Bill	1913	1913
2179/5	R4262	Metropolitan District Railway Bill	1913	1913
2181/3	R4492	Metropolitan Electric Tramways	1908	1913
2182/3	R4592	Metropolitan District Railway: Ealing Broadway	1912	1913
2182/4	R4593	Metropolitan District Railway: Earls Court East	1912	1913
2182/5	R4594	Metropolitan District Railway: Turnham Green Station	1913	1913
2182/6	R4596	Metropolitan District Railway: Whitechapel	1912	1913
2183/1	R4597	Metropolitan District Railway: Hammersmith	1913	1913
2183/2	R4598	Metropolitan District Railway: Parsons Green	1912	1913
2183/7	R4693	London Electric Railway Bill, 1913	1913	1913
2184/8	R4857	Metropolitan Electric Tramways: Barber radial truck	1911	1913
2185/7	R4964	"Tramway and Railway World": Greater London Traffic	1913	1913
2186/2	R5015	London Electric Railway: working of 6 car trains	1913	1913
2188/12	R5499	Middlesex County Council Tramways: Bye-laws	1904	1913
2188/13	R5500	Hertfordshire County Council Tramways: Bye-laws	1909	1913
2190/6	R5754	Metropolitan Electric Tramways: warning systems	1910	1913
2195/1	R6145	Metropolitan Railway Bill as amended	1913	1913
2198/3	R6569	Metropolitan Railway: Aldgate to Edgware Road; signals	1913	1913
2199/6	R6697	Croydon Corporation Tramways: Bye-laws	1901	1913
2206/2	R7458	Metropolitan District Railway: Heston, Hounslow & Hounslow Barracks	1912	1913

Piece no:	Original file ref:	Description	First date:	Last date:
2206/3	R7496	London County Council Tramways: Byelaws	1911	1913
2208/3	R7898	London United Tramways: Hammersmith	1908	1913
2209/1	R7936	Metropolitan Electric Tramways: Tottenham Urban District Council	1910	1913
2209/8	R8144	London County Council Tramways: Improvements Bill	1913	1913
2210/12	R8458	Metropolitan Railway: Aldgate Station	1913	1913
2211/5	R8659	City & South London Railway: Byelaws	1890	1913
2211/6	R8660	Central London Railway: Byelaws	1900	1913
2226/8	R11266	London United Tramways: Wimbledon	1909	1913
2226/9	R11267	London County Council Tramways: electrical regulations and Byelaws	1913	1913
2228/4	R11977	London Electric Railway: conciliation agreements	1912	1913
2233/6	R13121	Metropolitan Railway: Baker Street	1913	1913
2233/7	R13122	Metropolitan Railway: Aldgate	1913	1913
2234/6	R13276	Metropolitan District Railway: Conciliation Boards	1913	1913
2237/4	R13905	Metropolitan Railway: Liverpool St. & Moorgate St. Stations	1913	1913
2237/5	R13906	Metropolitan Railway: Aldgate Station; signalling	1913	1913
2237/6	R13907	Metropolitan Railway: West Harrow & Rayners Lane	1913	1913
2237/7	R13908	Metropolitan Railway: Eastcote & Ickenham	1913	1913
2238/6	R14109	Metropolitan District Railway: Byelaws	1905	1913
2246/2	R34	North Metropolitan Electric Power Supply Bill, 1914	1914	1914
2248/7	R484	Central London Railway: staff; conditions of service	1913	1914
2251/3	R591	Metropolitan District Railway: Aldgate East; signalling	1913	1914
2251/10	R723	Metropolitan Railway: Conciliation Boards	1909	1914
2252/2	R835	Great Northern & City Railway: Conciliation Board	1911	1914
2252/3	R890	Bexley Urban District Tramways: speed limit and brakes	1911	1914
2254/5	R1341	London Electric Railway: fire precautions	1914	1914
2255/2	R1682	County of Hertford Light Railway: Watford and Bushey abandonment	1913	1914
2258/9	R2070	Motor buses: proposed control of routes	1914	1914
2258/11	R2163	Central London Railway: Conciliation Board	1913	1914
2259/11	R2441	Electric Railways: removal of persons from "live rail"; award of Albert Medal to H F Ewington	1913	1914
2260/4	R2550	Willesden Urban District Council: private tramway at Waxlow Road	1914	1914
2264/6	R3079	Metropolitan District Railway: Putney Bridge Station	1910	1914
2267/2	R3630	London United Tramways Bill	1914	1914
2268/1	R3704	Metropolitan Electric Tramways: Wood Green	1914	1914
2268/8	R3813	Metropolitan Railway: Goldhawk Road and Shepherds Bush	1914	1914
2269/6	R4018	L.C.C. Tramways: stopping places	1914	1914
2270/1	R4308	Metropolitan Electric Tramways: Byelaws	1904	1914
2271/5	R4513	Central London Railway: vibration	1900	1914
2275/2	R5169	L.C.C. Tramways: carriage of excess passengers	1913	1914
2278/4	R5460	West Ham Corporation Tramways	1913	1914
2283/6	R6367	London County Council Tramways: Forest Gate: collision	1914	1914
2285/5	R6716	Central London Railway: automatic signalling	1912	1914
2287/11	R6956	Metropolitan & Great Northern Railway: rates and charges	1914	1914
2287/13	R7051	Metropolitan Electric Tramways: Byelaws & regulations	1914	1914
2290/5	R7620	London Electric Railway: Charing Cross extension	1913	1914
2296/3	R8655	Metropolitan Railway: Hammersmith & City Line; signalling	1914	1914
2296/6	R8710	Bexley Urban District Tramways: Wickham Lane Railway Bridge	1913	1914
2300/3	R9048	London County Council Tramways	1914	1914
2300/6	R9153	Baker Street & Waterloo Railway: Oxford Circus Station; escalators	1914	1914
2302	R9156	London County Council Tramways: Byelaws and Regulations	1913	1914
2304/5	R9283	Bexley Urban District Tramways: loans	1905	1914
2304/7	R9369	London Electric Railways: Camden Town extension	1914	1914
2310/1	R10053	Metropolitan District Railway: Earls Court East; signalling	1914	1914
2317/5	R10640	County of Hertfordshire Light Railways: Byelaws and regulations	1914	1914
2317/7	R10726	Metropolitan Railway: Rayners Lane, Ruislip; signalling	1914	1914
2317/8	R10727	Metropolitan & Great Central Joint Railway: Northwood	1914	1914
2317/12	R10784	London United Tramways: Hanwell to Ealing	1913	1914
2320/1	R10923	Metropolitan Electric Tramways: Highgate	1914	1914
2328/11	R11981	Metropolitan District and Whitechapel & Bow Railway: Whitechapel Station	1914	1914
2329/1	R11982	Metropolitan District Railway: West Kensington to Earls Court; signalling	1914	1914
2333/8	R12567	Ilford Urban District Tramways	1912	1914
2344/2	R45	London County Council (Tramways & Improvements) Bill, 1915	1915	1915
2345/5	R522	London Electric Railway: operation of lifts	1913	1915
2365/3	R3515	Metropolitan and Great Central Joint Railways: North Harrow	1915	1915

Piece no:	Original file ref:	Description	First date:	Last date:
2365/4	R3516	Metropolitan Railway: Kings Cross to Farringdon Street	1913	1915
2365/5	R3517	Metropolitan Railway: Ruislip Manor	1912	1915
2365/6	R3518	Metropolitan Railway: Drayton Park	1914	1915
2365/11	R3701	London County Council Tramways	1915	1915
2365/12	R3702	London Electric Railway: Baker Street	1914	1915
2366/8	R3942	Ilford UDC., Tramways: discontinuance of certain services	1915	1915
2366/9	R4008	Bakerloo Railway: Position of Positive Rail	1906	1915
2367/3	R4061	Leyton UDC., Tramways: Loans	1906	1915
2367/5	R4072	East London Railway: Sale of Superfluous Lands	1914	1915
2369/6	R4641	Walthamstow UDC, Tramways: Loan	1910	1915
2379/5	R5927	London Electric Railway: Drummond Street and Seymour Street	1914	1915
2379/6	R5932	Leyton UDC, Tramways: Brakes	1915	1915
2381/1	R6455	Metropolitan Railway: Kilburn to West Hampstead	1913	1915
2382/9	R6698	London Electric Railways: Maida Vale	1913	1915
2383/10	R6847	Baker Street and Waterloo Railway: Maida Vale	1915	1915
2391/2	R7986	West Ham Corporation Tramways: Agreement with Leyton UDC	1909	1915
2392/1	R8060	London United Tramways: Experimental Air Brakes	1914	1915
2392/2	R8085	London Electric Railways: Piccadilly Circus	1915	1915
2392/5	R8173	East Ham Corporation Tramways: Regulations	1915	1915
2392/8	R8371	London County Council Tramways: removal of disabled carriages	1912	1915
2394/6	R8575	Metropolitan Railways: Pinner	1915	1915
2394/7	R8584	London County Council Tramways: Cessation of Powers	1915	1915
2394/9	R8591	Gravesend and Northfleet Electric Tramways: Regulations	1915	1915
2399/7	R10130	Metropolitan District Railway: Earls Court	1913	1915
2400/7	R10485	London Electric Railway: Westminster Bridge Road Station to London Road Depot	1914	1915
2404/5	R10961	London United Tramways: Haydon's Road Wimbledon	1915	1915
2409/9	R12405	London County Council Tramways: Regulations	1914	1915
2416/8	R13365	London United Tramways: Claremont Road Surbiton	1915	1915
2423/1	R7	Metropolitan Railways: Failure of Automatic signals Liverpool Street and Neasden	1915	1916
2423/2	R16	London United Tramways: Connecting line with Metropolitan Electric Tramways in King Street, Acton	1915	1916
2433/8	R1946	West Ham Corporation Tramways: Woodgrange Road doubling	1916	1916
2433/10	R1953	Metropolitan Railway: Farringdon Street	1915	1916
2433/11	R1954	Great Northern and City Railway: Finsbury Park and Moorgate Street	1915	1916
2434/14	R2128	Walthamstow District Tramways: Ferry Lane Bridge	1916	1916
2436/27	R2801	Metropolitan Railway: Cheap Trains Act 1883; certification of urban districts	1886	1916
2436/28	R2824	Metropolitan Railway: Whitecross Street	1916	1916
2438/12	R3179	London Traffic Branch: Report of Colonel Hellard	1916	1916
2441/7	R3482	Metropolitan Railway: Aldgate	1916	1916
2442/5	R3565	Metropolitan Railway: Midland Junction, Kings Cross	1916	1916
2442/6	R3605	Metropolitan Railway: Ruislip and Uxbridge	1915	1916
2443/24	R3907	Metropolitan Railway: Pinner to Harrow North	1915	1916
2443/25	R3908	Metropolitan Railway: Rayners' Lane	1914	1916
2444/5	R4039	Electric trains: one man in motor cab: trip cock and "Dead Man's Handle"	1905	1916
2453/3	R701	Metropolitan Railway: Westbourne Park	1917	1917
2453/11	R769	East London Railway Joint Committee: New Cross	1913	1917
2454/11	R1090	London United Tramways: modification of car	1917	1917
2455/7	R1324	City and South London Railway: footways in tunnels	1905	1917
2457/6	R1647	London Electric Railway: Watford Service	1916	1917
2459/25	R2120	Metropolitan Railway: Northwood	1915	1917
2460/2	R2168	South Metropolitan Electric Tramways: Byelaws	1906	1917
2460/3	R2179	Metropolitan Railway: Praed Street to South Kensington; signals	1917	1917
2460/15	R2334	Metropolitan Railway: Watford Road; signals	1916	1917
2461/1	R2346	London Electric Railway: Oxford Circus; traffic barriers	1917	1917
2461/6	R2366	London County Council Tramways: Purchase of London United Tramways	1909	1917
2462/15	R2883	London County Council Tramways: Woolwich and Plumstead	1915	1917
2464/7	R3286	Metropolitan Railway: Harrow; signals	1917	1917
2466/4	R3654	Railways under Thames; danger in air raids	1917	1917
2466/11	R3756	Metropolitan Electric Tramways: The Hyde, Hendon	1917	1917
2466/24	R3949	London Electric Railway: Holborn Station	1907	1917
2467/1	R4019	London United Tramways: Byelaws	1917	1917

Piece no:	Original file ref:	Description	First date:	Last date:
2471/3	R33	Metropolitan Railway: Farringdon Street fatal accident	1917	1918
2473/1	R326	Treasury: cabs plying for hire at London Railway Stations	1895	1918
2474/5	R513	City & South London Railway: extension of time	1917	1918
2478	R818 (Part 1)	West Ham Corporation Tramways: including Arbitrations between North Metropolitan Tramways, London County Council, West Ham Corporation and Leyton District Council	1898	1918
2479	R818 (Part 2)	West Ham Corporation Tramways: including Arbitrations between North Metropolitan Tramways, London County Council, West Ham Corporation and Leyton District Council	1898	1918
2481/2	R877	Metropolitan Electric Tramways: trailer cars	1916	1918
2481/7	R933A	London United Tramways Bill	1918	1918
2487/1	R1273	London Electric Railway: Byelaws	1912	1918
2489/11	R1400	Home Office: railway raid shelters	1917	1918
2494/5	R1581	City and South London Railway: extension of time	1918	1918
2499/15	R2223	London Electric Railway: Maida Vale; accident	1918	1918
2502/1	R2409	Tramways: women drivers	1915	1918
2504/2	R2507	London Electric Railway: removal of hydrants	1918	1918
2518/11	R4077	Metropolitan Railway: Farringdon Street; signals	1918	1918
2525/5	R109	Baker Street and Waterloo Railway: fire appliances	1916	1919
2535/5	R938	London Electric Railway: strike	1919	1919
2540/6	R1280	London County Council Tramways: extension of time	1916	1919
2541/5	R1459	Central London Railway: high tension cables, metal covers, removal	1912	1919
2556	R2699	East Ham Corporation Tramways: loans	1899	1919
2565/3	R3825	London Electric Railway: use of fog repeaters	1917	1919
2565/9	R4014	London County Council Tramways and Improvement Bill	1919	1919
2569/11	R4412	Dartford and District Tramways: extension of time	1913	1919
2572	R4564	Croydon Corporation Tramways: loans	1899	1919
2579/2	R4892	London Traffic Problem: railway passenger statistics	1919	1919
2582	R5146	London County Council Tramways: Bye laws	1898	1919
2588/3	R5466	Metropolitan District Railway: Northfields Station	1919	1919
2601/1	R58	London County Council Tramways: Woolwich to Eltham	1902	1910
2601/2	R8469	London County Council Tramways: electrification	1903	1904
2601/3	R533	London County Council Tramways: trailer cars	1906	1910
2601/4	R14557	London County Council Tramways: speed	1906	1906
2601/5	R5877	London County Council Tramways: paving	1907	1907
2601/6	R3300	London County Council Tramways: Aldgate to Bow; reconstruction	1909	1909
2602/1	R8177	London County Council Tramways: trailer cars	1910	1915
2602/2	R5388	London County Council Tramways: petrol electric car	1912	1913
2602/3	R8340	London County Council Tramways: coupled cars	1910	1911
2606	ZR.1/1/4	Government Control (London Passenger Transport Board)	1938	1939
2716	ZR.4/3/13	Evacuation - London schoolchildren (Railway Executive Committee)	1940	1940
2726	ZR.5/6	London Passenger Transport Board Underground Railways: ventilation	1931	1940
2727	ZR.5/6/3	Flooding: Underground Railways	1938	1939
2728	ZR.5/6/47	Deep level shelters: London Underground Railways	1940	1949
2759	ZR.5/79/5	Bomb damage - Underground Railway tunnelling	1940	1941
2760	ZR.5/79/5/1	Bomb Damage (London Passenger Transport Board)	1940	1941
2766	ZR.5/79/5/7	Bomb damage - Underground Railway stations	1941	1942
2767	ZR.5/79/6	Bomb damage - Daily Reports (London Passenger Transport Board)	1940	1942
2771	ZR.5/145/2	London (Post-War Reconstruction)	1942	1942
2772	ZR.5/145/2/1	London - Suggestions - F. Samuely (Post-War Reconstruction)	1946	1946
2773	ZR.5/145/3	County of London Plan - London County Council and Railway Companies	1942	1943
2774	ZR.5/145/4	Main Line Railways and London Transport (Post-War Reconstruction)	1942	1944
2780	ZR.5/145/7	Tramways & Trolley Vehicles: Supply - Post War Reconstruction (includes correspondence from LPTB re South London Tramways conversion to Trolleybuses)	1943	1945
2781	ZR.5/145/21	Appointment and Terms of Reference - Post-War Reconstruction (Railways (London Plan) Committee)	1943	1946
2782	ZR.5/145/21/1	Agenda and Minutes of Meetings (Railways (London Plan) Committee)	1944	1948
2783	ZR.5/145/21/2	Evidence and memoranda submitted (Railways (London Plan) Committee)	1944	1946
2784	ZR.5/145/21/3	First Interim Report (Railways (London Plan) Committee)	1943	1945
2785	ZR.5/145/21/4	Sub-Committee on Traffic Facilities (Railways (London Plan) Committee)	1944	1945
2786	ZR.5/145/21/5	Report (Railways (London Plan) Committee)	1945	1946
2787	ZR.5/145/21/6	Report - Printing and Publication (Railways (London Plan) Committee)	1946	1946

Piece no:	Original file ref:	Description	First date:	Last date:
2788	ZR.5/145/21/7	Report - Consideration by Railway Companies and London County Council (Railways (London Plan) Committee)	1944	1947
2789	ZR.5/145/21/8	Northern Terminals (Railways (London Plan) Committee)	1945	1947
2790	ZR.5.145/21/10	Inner and Outer Goods Rings (Railways (London Plan) Committee)	1946	1948
2791	ZR.5/145/21/11	Final Report - Northern Terminals and Goods Rings (Railways (London Plan) Committee)	1943	1948
2793	ZR.5/145/29	Charing Cross Bridge - Railways (London Plan) Committee	1943	1945
2795	ZR.5/145/32	City of London Plan	1944	1947
2796	ZR.5/145/43	Greater London Plan 1944	1942	1945
2798	ZR.5/145/61	Greater London Plan - Satellite and Enlarged Towns	1945	1948
2799	ZR.5/145/61/1	Greater London Plan - Interdepartmental Committee	1947	1949
2800	ZR.5/145/65	Heath Row Airport - Development	1945	1952
2803	ZR.5/145/77	Railway Works Programme - London Area - 1946	1946	1947
2804	ZR.5/145/89	Recommendations for Production Committee (Railway (London Plan) Committee)	1947	1949
2882	SRD.36	Metropolitan Railway - Extension of platforms	1929	1936
2927	SR.99	Extension of Tube System north of Finsbury Park	1921	1925
2935	SR.222	London Electric Railways - Removal of pressure in emergency	1920	1923
2945	SR.366	London Electric Railway Bill, 1923	1923	1923
2987	PUR.840	Underground Works and Rolling Stock - Approval Policy	1930	1939
3023	PUR.1223	Aldgate - Metropolitan and District Lines New cabin (Signals)	1946	1960
3024	PUR.1224	Breakdowns - Arrangements for warning public	1946	1947
3033	PUR.1337	Greater London Replanning - British Transport Commission Working Party Report	1946	1949
3041	PUR.1544	Public Works (Festival of Britain) Bill, 1949. (Siting and Transport Problems)	1948	1951
3047	PUR.1695	Railways (London Plan) Committee - British Transport Commission - Report	1943	1949
3062	D.1811	L.C.C. Tramways Improvements Bill, 1920	1919	1921
3091	TO.2322	London railways: grouping	1920	1920
3094	SR.2422	Hammersmith Extension: London Electric Railways Act 1913	1923	1929
3111	ST.2692	Coupled cars - Metropolitan Electric Tramways Company	1921	1928
3176	SR.1933	London Underground - Development (Unemployment Relief)	1921	1931
3185	SR.2384	Escalators - London Underground Railways	1911	1924
3210	ST.4041	London and Home Counties Traffic Advisory Committee - Report	1927	1928
3224	SR.5841	Golders Green - London Electric Railway (Signals)	1923	1929
3228	ST.5943	London United Tramways - Approval of Trolley Vehicles	1930	1933
3232	SR.6100	London County Council area (Electrification)	1925	1925
3242	SR.6620	London Underground Goods Railway	1925	1941
3243	SR.6631	Metropolitan Railway - Rickmansworth Watford extension - Opening	1924	1927
3244	SR.6691	Tottenham Court Road Station - Central London Railway, Escalators	1925	1926
3248	ST.6980	Glasgow District Subway (Part Two of this file contains a copy of the Report into the Vibration Produced by the Working of the traffic on the Central London Railway, 1902 and a number of CSLR/LER drawings).	1933	1944
3250	ST.7008	Licensing - Metropolitan Traffic Area (Tramways and Trolley Vehicles)	1931	1936
3253	ST.7074	London Passenger Transport Board (Lost Property) Regulations	1933	1946
3255	ST.7124	London Passenger Transport Board, Bill, 1934	1933	1934
3257	SR.7408	London Electric Railways - Exemption from block working	1925	1925
3259	SR.7613	Kings Cross Junction - London Electric Railway (Signals)	1926	1929
3271	SR.8217	Trafalgar Square Station - London Electric Railway, Escalators	1926	1927
3272	ST.8373	London Passenger Transport Board, Act, 1937 - Trolley vehicle approvals	1937	1942
3274	ST.8440	London Passenger Transport Act 1937, S.69 - Queue bye-laws	1937	1938
3277	SR.8661	Bond Street Station - Central London Railway Escalators	1923	1926
3279	SR.8848	Morden Extension - City and South London Railway Act, 1923	1926	1927
3283	SR.10022	Travelling - North and East London - Public Enquiries	1924	1937
3289	SR.11211	Waterloo Station - London Electric Railway - Escalators	1927	1927
3294	SR.12915	London Traffic Advisory Committee report	1928	1928
3300	SR.13805	Oxford Circus Station - London Electric Railway Escalators	1925	1929
3303	SR.14101	New Station - Piccadilly Circus - London Electric Railway	1925	1938
3314	SR.15339	London Railways - Paper by H J Leaning	1915	1934
3318	SR.15970	Explosives: Metropolitan Railway Byelaws	1929	1939
3324	SR.16290	London Electric, Metropolitan District, Central London, and City and South London Railway Companies Bill 1930	1930	1930
3329	SR.17252	Western Extension - Piccadilly Railway	1930	1931

Piece no:	Original file ref:	Description	First date:	Last date:
3331	SR.17694	Experimental train - Hammersmith and Cockfosters Extensions - Piccadilly Railway	1930	1931
3333	SR.17942	London Electric, Metropolitan District, and Central London Railway Companies (Works) Bill 1931	1931	1931
3337	SR.18164	Southgate Extension - Turnpike Lane Station - London Electric Railway	1931	1933
3338	SR.18259	Park Royal and Osterley Stations - Piccadilly Railway Extension (West)	1931	1934
3339	SR.18285	Southgate Extension - Manor House Station - London Electric Railway	1931	1936
3340	SR.18363	Stanmore - Metropolitan Railway (Signals)	1931	1931
3343	SR.18548	Knightsbridge Station - London Electric Railway - Escalators	1931	1934
3347	SR.18964	Boston Manor - Western Extension, London Electric Railway	1932	1932
3349	SR.19028	Southgate Extensions (Finsbury Park to Arnos Grove) - London Electric Railway	1932	1934
3350	SR.19029	Western Extension - London Electric Railway	1932	1932
3353	SR.19163	New Station and escalators - Chancery Lane - London Electric Railway	1932	1934
3354	SR.19225	West Kensington - Boston Manor Extension - Piccadilly Railway (Signals)	1932	1933
3364	SR.19854	Earls Court Station - London Electric Railway - Automatic lifts	1932	1933
3368	SR.20099	Southgate Extension - Arnos Grove to Enfield West - London Electric Railway	1933	1933
3371	SR.20188	Leicester Square Station - London Electric Railway - Reconstruction	1933	1936
3372	SR.20214	Holborn, Chancery Lane, Bank, Monument, Leicester Square and Tottenham Court Road Stations - London Electric Railway - Ventilation	1933	1933
3373	SR.20251	Tottenham Court Road Station - London Electric Railway - Escalators	1933	1933
3374	SR.20329	Holborn Station - London Electric Railway - Reconstruction	1933	1933
3377	SR.20616	Subway - Cockfosters - Application for Order	1933	1934
3378	SR.20683	Green Park Station - London Electric Railway Escalators	1933	1933
3379	SR.20977	London Passenger Transport Board Bill 1934	1934	1934
3380	SR.21083	Wood Green and Manor House Stations - Installation of variable speed escalators	1933	1935
3381	SR.21104	Subway - Cockfosters Road (Southgate Extension)	1934	1934
3383	SR.21306	West Kensington - London Passenger Transport Board - Remote control (Signals)	1934	1936
3384	SR.21339	London and North Eastern Railway: suburban lines: North London suburban area: Highgate Tube extension: petition by Finchley B.C. and others	1924	1938
3389	SR.21736	Moorgate Station - Escalators	1934	1938
3391	SR.21738	Piccadilly Circus Station - Connection - Subway No. 3 and Criterion Restaurant	1934	1935
3394	SR.21816	Experimental "Metadyne" train	1934	1935
3395	SR.21967	Queensbury - Metropolitan Railway, Construction of new station	1934	1934
3402	SR.22455	Piccadilly Circus Station - Connection - Subway No.2 and Swan and Edgar's	1935	1944
3404	SR.22630	Rayners Lane - London Passenger Transport Board - Resignalling	1935	1939
3405	SR.22646	London and North Eastern Railway, Great Western Railway and London Passenger Transport Board. Suburban line and Tube extension electrification - Government financial guarantee	1935	1939
3412	SR.23123	Standardisation of signalling equipment - London Passenger Transport Board	1935	1939
3415	SR.23656	Experimental stream-lined coach - Approval (London Passenger Transport Board)	1936	1937
3416	SR.23713	Kings Cross Station (Piccadilly Line) Reconstruction	1936	1939
3417	SR.23722	Aldgate East Station - Reconstruction	1936	1939
3418	SR.23809	Metropolitan Line Improvements	1936	1950
3419	SR.24178	Uxbridge Line Extension - London Passenger Transport Board	1936	1939
3420	SR.24432	Sloane Square Station - Improvements	1936	1940
3423	SR.24534	Uxbridge, Stanmore and Aldgate: Metropolitan Line (Signals)	1936	1939
3424	SR.24682	Goodge St. Station - Automatic High Speed Lifts	1937	1940
3425	SR.24706	Highgate Station - Escalators	1937	1941
3426	SR.25018	Tottenham Court Road Station - Subway and staircases to platforms	1937	1938
3429	SR.25273	New Tube rolling stock - Approval	1937	1939
3431	SR.25573	Kings Cross Station - Reconstruction	1937	1941
3541	ST.2591	West Ham Corporation Tramways: loan for reconstruction of track	1926	1927